A Collection of Poems in Six Volumes, Volume 4

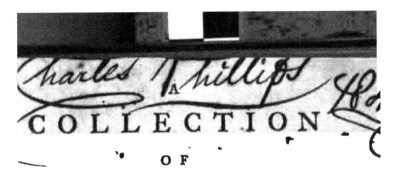

A COLLECTION

OF

POEMS

IN SIX VOLUMES.

BY

SEVERAL HANDS.

LONDON: Printed by J. Hughs,

For J. DODSLEY, in PALL-MALL.

MDCCLXV.

An E L E G Y

WRITTEN IN A

COUNTRY CHURCH YARD.

By Mr. GRAY.

THE curfew tolls the knell of parting day,
   The lowing herd wind flowly o'er the lea,
The plowman homewards plods his weary way,
And leaves the world to darknefs and to me.

A 3   Now

Now fades the glimmering landfcape on the fight,
And all the air a folemn ftillnefs holds,
Save where the beetle wheels his drony flight;
And drowfy tinklings lull the diftant folds ;

Save that from yonder ivy-mantled tow'r
The mopeing owl does to the moon complain
Of fuch, as wand'ring near her fecret bow'r,
Moleft her ancient, folitary reign.

Beneath thofe rugged elms, that yew-tree's fhade,
Where heaves the turf in many a mould'ring heap,
Each in his narrow cell for ever laid,
The rude Forefathers of the hamlet fleep.

The breezy call of incenfe-breathing Morn,
The fwallow twittering from the ftraw-built fhed,
The cock's fhrill clarion, or the echoing horn
No more fhall roufe them from their lowly bed.

For them no more the blazing hearth fhall burn,
Or bufy houfwife ply her evening care :
No children run to lifp their fire's return,
Or climb his knees the envied kifs to fhare.

Oft

Oft did the harveſt to their ſickle yield,
Their furrow oft the ſtubborn glebe has broke ;
How jocund did they drive their team afield !
How bow'd the woods beneath their ſturdy ſtroke !

Let not Ambition mock their uſeful toil,
Their homely joys, and deſtiny obſcure ;
Nor Grandeur hear, with a diſdainful ſmile,
The ſhort and ſimple annals of the poor.

The boaſt of heraldry, the pomp of pow'r,
And all that beauty, all that wealth e'er gave,
Await alike th' inevitable hour.
The paths of glory lead but to the grave.

Nor you, ye Proud, impute to Theſe the fault,
If Mem'ry o'er their Tomb no Trophies raiſe,
Where through the long-drawn iſle and fretted vault
The pealing anthem ſwells the note of praiſe.

Can ſtoried urn or animated buſt
Back to its manſion call the fleeting breath ?
Can Honour's voice provoke the ſilent duſt,
Or Flatt'ry ſooth the dull cold ear of Death ?

A 4   Perhaps

Perhaps in this neglected fpot is laid
Some heart once pregnant with celeftial fire;
Hands, that the rod of empire might have fway'd,
Or wak'd to extafy the living lyre.

But Knowledge to their eyes her ample page
Rich with the fpoils of Time did ne'er unroll;
Chill Penury reprefs'd their noble rage,
And froze the genial current of the foul.

Full many a gem of pureft ray ferene,
The dark unfathom'd caves of ocean bear;
Full many a flower is born to blufh unfeen,
And wafte its fweetnefs on the defart air.

Some village-Hampden, that with dauntlefs breaft.
The little Tyrant of his fields withftood;
Some mute inglorious Milton here may reft,
Some Cromwell guiltlefs of his country's blood.

Th' applaufe of lift'ning fenates to command,
The threats of pain and ruin to defpife,
To fcatter plenty o'er a fmiling land,
And read their hift'ry in a nation's eyes

Their

Their lot forbad : nor circumfcrib'd alone
Their growing virtues, but their crimes confin'd ;
Forbad to wade through flaughter to a throne,
And fhut the gates of mercy on mankind,

The ftruggling pangs of confcious truth to hide,
To quench the blufhes of ingenuous fhame,
Or heap the fhrine of Luxury and Pride
With incenfe kindled at the Mufe's flame.

Far from the madding crowd's ignoble ftrife,
Their fober wifhes never learn'd to ftray ;
Along the cool fequefter'd vale of life
They kept the noifelefs tenor of their way.

Yet ev'n thefe bones from infult to protect
Some frail memorial ftill erected nigh,
With uncouth rhimes and fhapelefs fculpture deck'd,
Implores the paffing tribute of a figh.

Their name, their years, fpelt by th' unletter'd Mufe,
The place of fame and elegy fupply :
And many a holy text around fhe ftrews,
That teach the ruftic moralift to dye.

For

For who to dumb Forgetfulnefs a prey,
This pleafing anxious being e'er refign'd,
Left the warm precincts of the chearful day,
Nor caft one longing ling'ring look behind?

On fome fond breaft the parting foul relies,
Some pious drops the clofing eye requires;
'Ev'n from the tomb the voice of Nature cries,
Ev'n in our Afhes live their wonted Fires.

For thee, who mindful of th' unhonour'd Dead
Doft in thefe lines their artlefs tale relate;
If chance, by lonely Contemplation led,
Some kindred Spirit fhall inquire thy fate,

Haply fome hoary-headed fwain may fay,
' Oft have we feen him at the peep of dawn
' Brufhing with hafty fteps the dews away
' To meet the fun upon the upland lawn.

' There at the foot of yonder nodding beech
' That rears its old fantaftic roots fo high,
' His liftlefs length at noon-tide would he ftretch,
' And pore upon the brook that babbles by.

' Hard

' Hard by yon wood, now fmiling as in fcorn,

' Mutt'ring his wayward fancies he would rove;

' Now drooping, woeful wan, like one forlorn,

' Or craz'd with care, or crofs'd in hopelefs love.

' One morn I mifs'd him on the cuftom'd hill,

' Along the heath and near his fav'rite tree:

' Another came; nor yet befide the rill,

' Nor up the lawn, nor at the wood was he;

' The next with dirges due in fad array,

' Slow through the church-way path we faw him born,

' Approach and read (for thou canft read) the lay,

' Grav'd on the ftone beneath yon aged thorn.

The E P I T A P H.

*H*E R E *refts his head upon the lap of Earth,*
    A Youth to Fortune and to Fame unknown,
Fair Science frown'd not on his humble birth,
And Melancholy mark'd him for her own.

Large

Large was his bounty, and his soul sincere,
Heav'n did a recompence as largely send:
He gave to Mis'ry all he had, a tear,
He gain'd from Heav'n ('twas all he wish'd) a friend.

No farther seek his merits to disclose,
Or draw his frailties from their dread abode,
(There they alike in trembling hope repose)
The bosom of his Father and his God.

HYMN to ADVERSITY.

By the Same.

DAUGHTER of Jove, relentless Pow'r,
  Thou Tamer of the human breast,
Whose iron scourge and tort'ring hour
  The Bad affright, afflict the Best!
Bound in thy adamantine chain
The Proud are taught to taste of pain,
And purple tyrants vainly groan
With pangs unfelt before, unpitied and alone.

When

When firft thy Sire to fend on earth
   Virtue, his darling Child, defign'd,
To thee he gave the heav'nly Birth,
   And bade to form her infant mind.
Stern rugged nurfe ! thy rigid lore
With patience many a year fhe bore :
What forrow was, thou bad'ft her know,
And from her own fhe learn'd to melt at others' woe.

Scared at thy frown terrific, fly
   Self-pleafing Folly's idle brood,
    Wild Laughter, Noife, and thoughtlefs Joy,
   And leave us leifure to be good.
Light they difperfe, and with them go
The fummer Friend, the flattering Foe ;
By vain Profperity received,
To her they vow their truth, and are again believed.

Wifdom in fable garb array'd,
   Immers'd in rapt'rous thought profound,
And Melancholy, filent maid
   With leaden eye, that loves the ground,
Still on thy folemn fteps attend :
Warm Charity, the gen'ral friend,

                   With

With Juſtice to herſelf ſevere,
And Pity, dropping ſoft the ſadly-pleaſing tear.

Oh! gently on thy Suppliant's head,
  Dread Goddeſs, lay thy chaſt'ning hand!
Not in thy Gorgon terrors clad,
  Nor circled with the vengeful Band
(As by the Impious thou art ſeen)
With thund'ring voice, and threat'ning mien,
With ſcreaming Horror's funeral cry,
Depair, and fell Diſeaſe, and ghaſtly Poverty.

Thy form benign, oh Goddeſs, wear,
  Thy milder influence impart,
Tl y philoſophic Train be there
  To ſoften, not to wound my heart,
The gen'rous ſpark extinct revive,
Teach me to love, and to forgive,
Exact my own defects to ſcan,
What others are to feel, and know myſelf a man.

XXXXXXXXXXXXXXXXXXXXXXXXXXXXXXXX

EDUCATION.

A POEM:

IN TWO CANTOS.

Written in Imitation of the Style and Manner of

SPENSER's FAIRY QUEEN.

Infcribed to Lady LANGHAM, Widow of Sir JOHN LANGHAM, Bart.

By GILBERT WEST, Efq;

*Unum ftudium vere liberale eft, quod liberum facit. Hoc
fapientiæ ftudium eft, fublime, forte, magnanimum:
cætera pufilla & puerilia funt.—Plus fcire velle quàm
fit fatis intemperantiæ genus eft. Quid, quòd ifta libera-
lium artium confeBatio moleftos, verbofos, intempeftivos,
fibi placentes facit, & ideo non dicentes neceffaria, quia
fupervacua didicerunt.* SEN. Ep. 88.

O Goodly DISCIPLINE! from heav'n y-fprong!
    Parent of Science, queen of Arts refin'd!
To whom the *Graces*, and the *Nine* belong:
O! bid thofe *Graces*, in fair chorus join'd

I   With

With each bright *Virtue* that adorns the mind !
O bid the *Mufes*, thine harmonious train,
Who by thy aid erſt humaniz'd mankind,
Inſpire, direct, and moralize the ſtrain,
That doth eſſay to teach thy treaſures how to gain !

And THOU, whoſe pious and maternal care,
The ſubſtitute of heavenly Providence,
With tendereſt love my orphan life did rear,
And train me up to manly ſtrength and ſenſe ;
With mildeſt awe, and virtuous influence,
Directing my unpractis'd wayward feet
To the ſmooth walks of Truth and Innocence ;
Where Happineſs heart-felt, Contentment ſweet,
Philoſophy divine aye hold their bleſt retreat.

THOU, moſt belov'd, moſt honour'd, moſt rever'd!
Accept this verſe, to thy large merit due !
And blame me not, if by each tye endear'd,
Of nature, gratitude, and friendſhip true,
The whiles this *moral theſis* I purſue,
And trace the *plan* of goodly * *Nurture* o'er,
I bring thy *modeſt virtues* into view ;
And proudly boaſt that from *thy* precious ſtore,
Which erſt enrich'd my heart, I drew this ſacred lore.

* Nurture, Education.   And

And thus, I ween, thus fhall I beft repay
The valued gifts, thy careful love beftow'd;
If imitating THEE, well as I may,
I labour to diffufe th' important good,
'Till this great truth by all be underftood;
" That all the pious duties which we owe,
" Our parents, friends, our country and our God;
" The feeds of every virtue here below,
" From *Difcipline* alone, and early *Culture* grow."

C A N T O I.

A R G U M E N T.

The Knight, as to [b] *PÆDÌA's houfe*
He his young Son conveys,
Is ftaid by CUSTOM; *with him fights,*
And his vain pride difmays.

A Gentle KNIGHT there was, whofe noble deeds
O'er *Fairy Land* by Fame were blazon'd round:
For warlike enterprize, and fage [c] areeds
Emong the chief alike was he renown'd;

[b] Pædìa is a Greek word, fignifying Education.
[c] Areeds, counfels.

Whence with the marks of higheſt honours crown'd
By GLORIANA, in domeſtic peace,
That port, to which the wiſe are ever bound,
He anchor'd was, and chang'd the toſſing ſeas
Of buſtling buſy life, for calm ſequeſter'd eaſe.

II.

There in domeſtic virtue rich and great
As erſt in public, 'mid his wide domain,
Long in primæval patriarchal ſtate,
The lord, the judge, the father of the plain,
He dwelt; and with him, in the golden chain
Of wedded faith y-link'd, a *matron* ſage
Aye dwelt; ſweet partner of his joy and pain,
Sweet charmer of his youth, friend of his age,
Skill'd to improve his bliſs, his ſorrows to aſſuage.

III.

From this fair union, not of ſordid gain,
But merit ſimilar and mutual love,
True ſource of lineal virtue, ſprung a train
Of youths and virgins; like the beauteous grove,
Which round the temple of *Olympic Jove*,
Begirt with youthful bloom the *parent tree*,
The *ſacred olive*; whence old *Elis* wove

Her

Parent tree, the ſacred olive.] This tree grew in the Altis, or
ſacred grove of Olympic Jupiter at Olympia, having, as the Eleans
pretended,

Her verdant crowns of peaceful victory,
The * guerdons of bold ftrength, and fwift activity.

IV.

So round their noble parents goodly rofe
Thefe generous fcyons: they with watchful care
Still, as the fwelling paffions 'gan difclofe
The buds of future virtues; did prepare
With prudent culture the young fhoots to rear :
And aye in this endearing pious toil
They by a ' Palmer fage inftructed were,
Who from deep thought and ftudious fearch erewhile
Had learnt to mend the heart, and till the human foil.

V.

For by cœleftial Wifdom whilom led
Through all th' apartments of th' immortal mind,
He view'd the fecret ftores, and mark'd the * fted
To judgment, wit, and memory affign'd ;
And how fenfation and reflection join'd
To fill with images her darkfome grotto,
Where varioufly disjointed or combin'd,

pretended, been originally planted there by Hercules. It was
efteemed facred, and from that were taken the Olympic crowns.
See Paufanias. Eliac. and the Differtation on the Olympic games.
 * Guerdons, rewards.
 f Palmer, pilgrim. The perfon here fignified is Mr. Locke,
characteriz'd by his works.
 * Sted, place, ftation.

As

As reafon, fancy, or opinion wrought,   [thought.
Their various mafks they play'd, and fed her penfive

VI.

^h Alfe through the fields of *Science* had he ftray'd
With eager fearch, and fent his piercing eye
Through each learn'd *fchool*, each *philofophic fhade*,
Where *Truth* and *Virtue* erft were deem'd to lie ;
If haply the fair vagrants he ⁱ mote fpy,
Or hear the mufic of their charming lore :
But all unable there to fatisfy
His curious foul, he turn'd him to explore
The *facred writ of Faith* ; to learn, believe, adore.

VII.

Thence foe profefs'd of *Falfhood* and *Deceit*,
Thofe fly artificers of tyranny,
^k Aye holding up before uncertain feet
His faithful light, to *Knowledge*, *Liberty*,
Mankind he led, to *Civil Policy*,
And mild *Religion*'s charitable law ;
That fram'd by *Mercy* and *Benignity*
The perfecuting fword forbids to draw,
And free-created fouls with penal terrours awe.

VIII.

^l Ne with thefe glorious gifts elate and vain
Lock'd he his wifdom up in churlifh pride ;

^h Alfe, alfo, further. ⁱ Mote, might. ^k Aye, ever. ^l Ne, nor.

But, ſtooping from his height, would even deign
The feeble ſteps of *Infancy* to guide.
Eternal glory Him therefore betide !
Let every generous youth *his* praiſe proclaim !
Who, wand'ring through the world's rude foreſt wide,
By him hath been y-taught his courſe to frame
To *Virtue's* ſweet abodes, and heav'n-aſpiring *Fame!*

IX.

For this the FAIRY KNIGHT with anxious thought,
And fond paternal care his counſel pray'd ;
And him of gentleſt courteſy beſought
His guidance to vouchſafe and friendly aid ;
The while his tender offspring he convey'd,
Through devious paths to that ſecure retreat ;
Where ſage PÆDIA, with each tuneful maid,
On a wide mount had fix'd her rural ſeat,
'Mid flow'ry gardens plac'd, untrod by vulgar feet.

X.

And now forth-pacing with his blooming heir,
And that ſame virtuous *Palmer* them to guide ;
Arm'd all to point, and on a courſer fair
Y-mounted high, in military pride,
His little train before he ſlow did ride.
Him eke behind a gentle *ſquire* ᵐ enſues,

* Enſues, follows.

With

With his young *lord* aye marching fide by fide,

His counfellour and guard, in goodly ᵑ thews,

Who well had been brought up, and nurs'd by every Mufe.

XI.

Thus as their pleafing journey they purfued,

With chearful argument beguiling pain ;

Ere long defcending from an hill they view'd

Beneath their eyes out-ftretch'd a fpacious plain,

That fruitful fhew'd, and apt for every grain,

For paftures, vines and flow'rs ; while Nature fair

Sweet-fmiling all around with count'nance ° fain

Seem'd to demand the tiller's aye and care,

Her wildnefs to correct, her lavifh wafte repair.

XII.

Right good, I ween, and bounteous was the foil,

Aye wont in happy feafon to repay

With tenfold ufury the peafant's toil.

But now 'twas ruin all, and wild decay ;

Untill'd the garden and the fallow lay,

The fheep-fhorne down with barren ᵖ brakes o'ergrown,

The whiles the merry peafants fport and play,

All as the public evil were unknown,

Or every public care from every breaft was flown.

ⁿ Thews, manners. ° Fain, earneft, eager. ᵖ Brakes, briars.

XIII. Afto-

XIII.

Aftonifh'd at a fcene at once fo fair
And fo deform'd; with wonder and delight
At man's neglect, and Nature's bounty rare,
In ftudious thought awhile the Fairy Knight,
Bent on that goodly ⁴ lond his eager fight:
Then forward rufh'd, impatient to defcry
What towns and caftles therein were ʳ empight;
For towns him feem'd, and caftles he did fpy,
As to th' horizon round he ftretch'd his roaming eye.

XIV.

Nor long way had they travell'd, ere they came
To a wide ftream, that with tumultuous roar
Emongft rude rocks its winding courfe did frame.
Black was the wave and fordid, cover'd o'er
With angry foam, and ftain'd with infants' gore.
Thereto along th' unlovely margin ftood,
A birchen grove that waving from the fhore,
Aye caft upon the tide its falling bud,
And with its bitter juice empoifon'd all the flood.

XV.

Right in the centre of the vale empight,
Not diftant far a *forked mountain* rofe;

⁴ Lond, land.   ʳ Empight, placed.

In

In outward form prefenting to the fight
That fam'd *Parnoffian* hill, on whofe fair brows
The *Nine Aonian Sifters* wont repofe;
Lift'ning to fweet *Caftalia*'s founding ftream,
Which through the plains of *Cirrba* murm'ring flows.
But This to That compar'd mote juftly feem
Ne fitting haunt for gods, ne worthy man's efteem.

XVI.

For this nor founded deep, nor fpredden wide,
Nor high up-rais'd above the level plain,
By toiling art through tedious years applied,
From various parts compil'd with ftudious pain,
Was ' erft up-thrown; if fo it mote attain,
Like that *poetic mountain*, to be ' hight
The noble feat of *Learning*'s goodly train.
Thereto, the more to captivate the fight,
It like a garden fair moft curioufly was " dight.

XVII.

In figur'd plots with leafy walls inclos'd,
By meafure and by rule it was out-lay'd;
With fymmetry fo regular difpos'd,
That plot to plot ftill anfwer'd, fhade to fhade;
Each correfpondent twain alike array'd

' Erft, formerly. ' Hight, called, named. " Dight, dreft.

With

With like embellifhments of plants and flow'rs,
Of ftatues, vafes, fpouting founts, that play'd
Through fhells of Tritons their afcending fhow'rs,
And labyrinths involv'd and trelice-woven bow'rs.

XVIII.

There likewife mote be feen on every fide
The yew obedient to the planter's will,
And fhapely box of all their branching pride
Ungently fhorne, and with prepofterous fkill
To various beafts and birds of fundry quill
Transform'd, and human fhapes of monftrous fize;
Huge as that giant-race, who, hill on hill
High-heaping, fought with impious vain * emprize,
Defpite of thund'ring *Jove*, to fcale the fteepy fkies.

XIX.

Alfe other wonders of the fportive fhears
Fair Nature mif-adorning there were found;
Globes, fpiral columns, pyramids and piers
With fpouting urns and budding ftatues crown'd;
And horizontal dials on the ground
In living box by cunning artifts trac'd;
And gallies trim, on no long voyage bound,
But by their roots there ever anchor'd faft,
* All were their bellying fails out-fpread to every blaft.

---

* Emprize; enterprize, attempt.
* All, ufed frequently by the old Englifh poets for although.

XX.

O'er all appear'd the mountain's forked brows
With terraffes on terraffes up-thrown;
And all along arrang'd in order'd rows,
And vifto's broad, the velvet flopes adown
The ever-verdant trees of *Daphne* fhone.
But aliens to the clime, and brought of old
From *Latian* plains, and *Grecian Helicon*,
They fhrunk and languifh'd in a foreign mold,
By changeful fummers ftarv'd, and pinch'd by winter's
[cold.

XXI.

Amid this verdant grove with folemn ftate,
On golden thrones of antique form reclin'd,
In mimic majefty *Nine Virgins* fate,
In features various, as unlike in mind:
Alfe boafted they themfelves of heav'nly kind,
And to the fweet *Parnaffian Nymphs* allied;
Thence round their brows the *Delphic bay* they twin'd,
And matching with high names their apifh pride,
O'er every learned *fchool* aye claim'd they to prefide.

XXII.

In antique garbs, for modern they difdain'd,
By *Greek* and *Roman* artifts' whilom made,
Of various woofs, and varioufly diftain'd
With tints of every hue, were they array'd;

¹ Whilom, formerly.

And

And here and there ambitiously display'd
A purple shred of some rich robe, prepared
Erst by the *Muses* or th' *Aonian Maid*,
To deck great *Tullius* or the *Mantuan Bard*;
Which o'er each motley vest with uncouth splendor
[glared.

XXIII.

And well their outward vesture did express
The bent and habit of their inward mind,
Affecting Wisdom's antiquated dress,
And usages by Time cast far behind.
Thence, to the charms of younger Science blind,
The customs, laws, the learning, arts and phrase
Of their own countries they with scorn declin'd;
Ne *sacred Truth* herself would they embrace,
Unwarranted, unknown in their fore-fathers' days.

XXIV.

Thus ever backward casting their survey;
To *Rome*'s old ruins and the groves forlorn
Of elder *Athens*, which in prospect lay
Stretch'd out beneath the mountain, would they turn
Their busy search, and o'er the rubbish mourn.
Then gathering up with superstitious care,
Each little scrap, however foul or torn,
In grave harangues they boldly would declare,
This *Ennius*, *Varro*; This the *Stagyrite* did wear.

XXV. Yet,

XXV.

Yet, under names of venerable found,
While o'er the world they ftretch'd their aweful rod ;
Through all the provinces of *Learning* own'd
For *teachers* of whate'er is wife and good.
Alfe from each region to their * drad abode
Came youth unnumber'd, crowding all to tafte
The *ftreams* of *Science* ; which united flow'd
Adown the *mount*, from *nine* rich fources caft ;
And to the vale below in one rude torrent pafs'd.

XXVI.

O'er every fource, protectrefs of the ftream,
One of thofe *Virgin Sifters* did prefide ;
Who, dignifying with her noble *name*
Her proper flood, aye pour'd into the tide
The heady vapours of *fcholaftic pride*
Defpotical and abject, bold and blind,
Fierce in debate, and forward to decide ;
Vain love of praife, with adulation join'd,
And difingenuous fcorn, and impotence of mind.

XXVII.

Extending from the hill on every fide,
In circuit vaft a verdant valley fpread ;
Acrofs whofe uniform flat bofom glide
Ten thoufand ftreams, in winding mazes led,

_____
* Drad, dreadful.

By

By various fluices from one common head;
A turbid mafs of waters, vaft, profound,
Hight of *Philology* the lake; and fed
By that rude torrent, which with roaring found
Came tumbling from the hill, and flow'd the level round.

XXVIII.

And every where this fpacious valley o'er,
Faft by each ftream was feen a numerous throng
Of beardlefs ftriplings to the birch'd-crown'd fhore,
By nurfes, guardians, fathers dragg'd along:
Who helplefs, meek, and innocent of wrong,
Were torn reluctant from the tender fide
Of their fond mothers, and by ⁎ *faitours* ftrong,
By pow'r made infolent, and hard by pride,
Were driv'n with furious rage, and lafh'd into the tide.

XXIX.

On the rude bank with trembling feet they ftood,
And cafting round their oft-reverted eyes,
If haply they mote 'feape the hated flood,
Fill'd all the plain with lamentable cries;
But far away th' unheeding father flies,
Conftrain'd his ftrong compunctions to reprefs;
While clofe behind, affuming the difguife

⁎ Faitour, doer, from faire to do, and fait deed, commonly
ufed by Spenfer in a bad fenfe.

Of nurturing care, and smiling tenderness,
With secret scourges arm'd those griesly *faitours* press.

XXX.

As on the steepy margin of a brook,
When the young sun with flowery *Maia* rides,
With innocent dismay a bleating flock
Crowd back, affrighted at the rolling tides:
The shepherd-swain at first exhorting chides
Their [b] seely fear; at length impatient grown,
With his rude crook he wounds their tender sides;
And all regardless of their piteous moan,
Into the dashing wave compels them furious down.

XXXI.

Thus urg'd by mast'ring *Fear* and dol'rous [c] *Teen*
Into the current plung'd that infant crowd:
Right piteous was the spectacle, I ween,
Of tender striplings stain'd with tears and blood,
Perforce conflicting with the bitter flood;
And labouring to attain the distant shore,
Where holding forth the *gown* of *manhood* stood
The *siren Liberty*, and ever-more
Sollicited their hearts with her inchanting lore.

XXXII.

Irksome and long the passage was, perplex'd
With rugged rocks on which the raving tide

[b] Seely, simple.   [c] Teen, pain, grief.

By

By fudden burfts of angry tempefts vex'd
Oft dafh'd the youth, whofe ftrength mote ill abide
With head up-lifted o'er the waves to ride.
Whence many wearied ere they had o'er-paft
The middle ftream (for they in vain have tried)
Again return'd ^d aftounded and aghaft ;
Ne one regardful look would ever backward caft.

XXXIII.

Some, of a rugged, more enduring frame,
Their toilfome courfe with patient pain purfu'd;
And though with many a bruife and ^e muchel blame,
Eft hanging on the rocks, and eft embru'd
Deep in the muddy ftream, with hearts fubdu'd
And quail'd by labour, gain'd the fhore at laft,
But in life's practic ^f lear unfkill'd and rude,
Forth to that *forked bill* they filent pac'd ;   [wafte.
Where hid in ftudious fhades their fruitlefs hours they

XXXIV.

Others of rich and noble lineage bred,
Though with the crowd to pafs the flood conftrain'd,
Yet o'er the crags with fond indulgence led
By *bireling* guides and in all depths fuftain'd,
Skimm'd lightly o'er the tide, undipt, unftain'd,
Save with the fprinkling of the wat'ry fpray:

<hr>

^d Aftounded, aftonifhed.   ^e Muchel, much.   ^f Lear, learning.

And

And aye their proud prerogative maintain'd,

Of ignorance and eafe and wanton play,

Soft harbingers of vice, and præmature decay.

XXXV.

A few, alas, how few! by heav'n's high will

With fubtile fpirits endow'd and finews ftrong,

§ Albe fore ʰ mated by the tempefts fhrill,

That bellow'd fierce and rife the rocks among,

By their own *native vigour* borne along.

Cut brifkly through the waves; and forces new

Gathering from toil, and ardour from the throng

Of rival youths, outftript the labouring crew,

And to the true ˡ *Parnaffe*, and heav'n-thron'd glory flew.

XXXVI.

Dire was the tumult, and from every fhore

Difcordant echoes ftruck the deafen'd ear,

Heart-thrilling cries, with fobs and ᵏ fingults fore

Short-interrupted, the imploring tear,

And furious ftripes, and angry threats fevere,

Confus'dly mingled with the jarring found

Of all the various fpeeches that ˡ while-ere

On *Shinar's* wide-fpread champain did aftound

High *Babel's* builders vain, and their proud works con-
[found.

§ Albe, although.   ʰ Mated, amazed, fcared.
ˡ Parnaffe, Parnaffus.   ᵏ Singults, fighs.   ˡ While-ere, formerly.

XXXVII. Much

XXXVII.

Much was the KNIGHT empaffion'd at the fcene,
But more his blooming fon, whofe tender breaft
Empierced deep with fympathizing teen
On his pale cheek the figns of dread imprefs'd,
And fill'd his eyes with tears, which fore diftrefs'd
Up to his fire he rais'd in mournful wife;
Who with fweet fmiles paternal foon redrefs'd
His troublous thoughts, and clear'd each fad furmife;
Then turns his ready fteed, and on his journey hies.

XXXVIIL.

But far he had not march'd ere he was ftay'd
By a rude voice, that like th' united found
Of fhouting myriads, through the valley bray'd,
And fhook the groves, the floods, and folid ground:
The diftant hills rebellow'd all around.
" Arreft, *Sir Knight*, it cried, thy fond career,
" Nor with prefumptuous difobedience wound
" That aweful majefty which all revere!
" In my commands, *Sir Knight*, the voice of nations hear!"

XXXIX.

Quick turn'd the KNIGHT, and faw upon the plain
Advancing tow'rds him with impetuous gate,
And vifage all inflam'd with fierce difdain,
A monftrous GIANT, on whofe brow elate

'Shone the bright enfign of imperial ftate;
Albeit lawful kingdom he had none;
But laws and kingdoms wont he oft create,
And oft'times over both erect his throne,
.While fenates, priefts and kings his ᵐ fov'ran fceptre own.

XL.

Cᴜsᴛᴏᴍ he hight; and aye in every land
Ufurp'd dominion with defpotic fway
O'er all he holds; and to his high command
Conftrains ev'n ftubborn *Nature* to obey;
Whom difpoffeffing oft, he doth affay
To govern in her right: and with a pace
So foft and gentle doth he win his way,
That fhe unwares is caught in his embrace,
And though deflowr'd and thrall'd nought feels her foul
[difgrace.

XLI.

For nurt'ring, even from their tend'reft age,
The docile fons of men withouten pain,
By difciplines and rules to every ftage
Of life accommodate, he doth them train
Infenfibly to wear and hug his chain.
'Alfe his behefts or gentle or fevere,
Or good or noxious, rational or vain,
He craftily perfuades them to revere,
As inftitutions fage, and venerable lear.

ᵐ Sov'ran, for fovereign.

XLII. Pro-

XLII.

Protector therefore of that *forked hill*,
And mighty patron of thofe *Sifters Nine*,
Who there enthron'd, with many a copious rill
Feed the full ftreams, that through the valley fhine,
He deemed was; and aye with rites divine,
ᵃ Like thofe, which *Sparta*'s hardy race of yore
Were wont perform at fell *Diana*'s fhrine,
He doth conftrain his vaffals to adore
Perforce their facred names, and learn their facred lore.

XLIII.

And to the FAIRY KNIGHT now drawing near,
With voice terrific and imperious mien,
(All was he wont lefs dreadful to appear,
When known and practifed than at diftance feen)
And kingly ftretching forth his fceptre fheen,
Him he commandeth, upon threat'ned pain
Of his difpleafure high and vengeance keen,
From his rebellious purpofe to refrain,
And all due honours pay to *Learning*'s rev'rend train.

ᵃ The Lacedemonians in order to make their children hardy and endure pain with conftancy and courage, were accuftomed to caufe them to be fcourged very feverely. And I myfelf (fays Plutarch, in his life of Lycurgus) have feen feveral of them endure whipping to death, at the foot of the altar of Diana furnamed Orthia.

XLIV.

So ſaying and foreſtalling all reply,
His peremptory hand without delay,
As one who little cared to juſtify
His princely will, long us'd to boundleſs ſway,
Upon the *Fairy Youth* with great diſmay
In every quaking limb convuls'd, he lay'd:
And proudly ſtalking o'er the verdant [o] lay,
Him to thoſe *ſcientific ſtreams* convey'd,
With many his young compeers therein to be [p] embay'd.

XLV.

The KNIGHT his tender ſon's diſtreſsful [q] ſtour
Perceiving, ſwift to his aſſiſtance flew:
Ne vainly ſtay'd to deprecate that pow'r,
Which from ſubmiſſion aye more haughty grew.
For that proud GIANT's force he wiſely knew,
Not to be meanly dreaded, nor defy'd
With raſh preſumption; and with courage true,
Rather than ſtep from Virtue's path aſide,
Oft had he ſingly ſcorn'd his all-diſmaying pride.

XLVI.

And now, diſdaining parle, his courſer hot
He fiercely prick'd, and couch'd his vengeful ſpear;

[o] Lay, mead. [p] Embay'd, bathed, dipt.
[q] Stour, trouble, misfortune, &c.

Where-

Where-with the GIANT he fo rudely fmot,
That him perforce conftrain'd to ' wend arrear.
Who, much abafh'd at fuch rebuke fevere,
Yet his accuftom'd pride recov'ring foon,
Forth-with his maffy fceptre 'gan up-rear;
For other warlike weapon he had none,
Ne other him behoved to quell his boldeft ' fone.

XLVII.

With that enormous *mace* the FAIRY KNIGHT
So fore he ' bet, that all his armour ' bray'd,
To pieces well-nigh riven with the might
Of fo tempeftuous ftrokes; 'but He was ftay'd,
And ever with deliberate valour weigh'd
The fudden changes of the doubtful fray;
From cautious prudence oft deriving aid,
When force unequal did him hard affay:
So lightly from his fteed he leapt upon the lay.

XLVIII.

Then fwiftly drawing forth his " trenchant blade,
High o'er his head he held his'fenceful fhield;
And warily fore-cafting to evade
The GIANT's furious arm, about him wheel'd
With reftlefs fteps aye traverfing the field.

' Wend arrear, move backwards.   ' Fone, foes.
' Bet, beat; bray'd, refounded.   " Trenchant, cutting.

     And

And ever as his foe's intemperate pride,
Through rage defencelefs, mote advantage yield,
With his fharp fword fo oft he did him ᵂ gride,
That his gold-fandal'd feet in crimfon floods were dyèd.

XLIX.

His bafer parts he maim'd with many a wound,
But far above his utmoft reach were ˣ pight
The forts of life : ne ever to confound
With utter ruin, and abolifh quite
A power fo puiffant by his fingle might
Did he prefume to hope : Himfelf alone
From lawlefs force to free, in bloody fight
He ftood; content to bow to Cᴜsᴛoᴍ's throne,
So Rᴇᴀsoɴ mote not blufh his fov'ran rule to own.

L.

So well he warded, and fo fiercely prefs'd
His foe, that weary wex'd he of the fray;
Yet ʸ nould he algates lower his haughty creft;
But mafking in contempt his fore difmay,
Difdainfully releas'd the trembling prey,
As one unworthy of his princely care;
Then proudly cafting on the warlike ˣ *fay*
A fmile of fcorn and pity, through the air
'Gan blow his fhrilling horn; the blaft was heard afar.

ᵂ Gride, cut, hack.　　　ˣ Pight, placed.
ʸNould he algates, would not by any means.　　ˣ Fay,　fairy.

LI.

Eftfoons aftonifh'd at th' alarming found,
The fignal of diftrefs and hoftile wrong,
Confufedly trooping from all quarters round,
Came pouring o'er the plain a numerous throng
Of every fex and order, old and young;
The vaffals of great Custom's wide domain,
Who to his lore inur'd by ufage long,
His every fummons heard with pleafure fain,
And felt his every wound with fympathetic pain.

LII.

They, when their bleeding *king* they did behold,
And faw an armed Knight him ftanding near,
Attended by that *Palmer* fage and bold;
Whofe vent'rous fearch of devious Truth while-ere
Spread through the realms of *Learning* horrors drear,
Y-feized were at firft with terrors great;
And in their boding hearts began to fear,
Diffention factious, controverfial hate,
And innovations ftrange in Custom's peaceful ftate.

LIII.

But when they faw the Knight his fauchion fheathe,
And climbing to his fteed march thence away,
With all his hoftile train, they 'gan to breathe
With freer fpirit, and with afpect gay

C 4

Soon

Soon chaced the gathering clouds of black affray,
Alfe their great monarch, cheared with the view.
Of myriads, who confefs his fov'ran fway,
His ruffled pride began to plume anew ;
And on his bugle clear a ftrain of triumph blew.

LIV.

There-at the multitude, that ftood around,
Sent up at once a univerfal roar
Of boifterous joy : the fudden-burfting found
Like the explofion of a warlike ftore
Of nitrous grain, th' afflicted * welkin tore.
Then turning towards the KNIGHT, with fcoffings lewd,
Heart-piercing infults, and revilings fore,
Loud burfts of laughter vain, and hiffes rude,
As through the throng he pafs'd, his parting fteps pur-
[fued.

LV.

Alfe from that *forked bill* the boafted feat
Of ftudious *Peace* and mild *Philofophy*,
Indignant murmurs mote be heard to threat,
Muftering their rage ; eke baleful *Infamy*,
Rouz'd from her den of bafe obfcurity
By thofe fame *Maidens Nine*, began to found
Her brazen trump of black'ning obloquy :
While *Satire*, with dark clouds encompaft round,
Sharp, fecret arrows fhot, and aim'd his back to wound.

* Welkin, fky.

LVI. But

LVI.

But the brave FAIRY KNIGHT no whit difmay'd
Held on his peaceful journey o'er the plain;
With curious eye obferving, as he ftray'd
Through the wide provinces of CUSTOM's reign;
What mote afrefh admonifh him remain
Faft by his virtuous purpofe; all around
So many objects mov'd his juft difdain;
Him feem'd that nothing ferious, nothing found
In city, village, bow'r, or caftle mote be found.

LVII.

In village, city, caftle, bow'r and hall,
Each fex, each age, each order and degree,
To vice and idle fport abandon'd all,
Kept one perpetual general jubilee.
Ne fuffer'd aught difturb their merry glee;
Ne fenfe of private lofs, ne public woes,
Reftraint of law, Religion's drad decree,
Inteftine defolation, foreign foes,
Nor heav'n's tempeftuous threats, nor earth's convulfive
[throws.

LVIII.

But chiefly they whom Heav'n's difpofing hand
Had feated high on Fortune's upper ftage;
And plac'd within their call the facred band
That waits on Nurture and Inftruction fage,

If

Saluting the return of morning bright
With matin-revels, by the mid-day hours
Scarce ended; and again with dewy night,
In cover'd theatres, or leafy bow'rs
Offering her evening-vows to *Pleafure*'s joyous pow'rs.

LXIV.

And ever on the way mote he efpy
Men, women, children, a promifcuous throng
Of rich, poor, wife and fimple, low and high,
By land, by water, paffing aye along
With mummers, antics, mufic, dance and fong,
To *Pleafure*'s numerous temples, that befide
The gliftening ftreams, or tufted groves among,
To every idle foot ftood open wide,
And every gay defire with various joys fupplied.

LXV.

For there each heart with diverfe charms to move,
The fly inchantrefs fummoned all her train:
Alluring *Venus*, queen of vagrant love,
The boon companion *Bacchus* loud and vain,
And tricking *Hermes*, god of fraudful gain,
Who, when blind *Fortune* throws, directs the die,
And *Phœbus* tuning his foft *Lydian* ftrain
To wanton motions, and the lover's figh,
And thought-beguilling fhew, and mafking revelry.

LXVI. Un-

LXVI.

Unmeet affociates there for noble youth,
Who to true honour meaneth to afpire;
And for the works of virtue, faith, and truth
Would keep his manly faculties entire.
The which avizing well, the cautious fire
From that foft *firen land* of *Pleafaunce* vain,
With timely hafte was minded to retire,
' Or ere the fweet contagion mote attain
His fon's unpractis'd heart, yet free from vicious ftain.

LXVII.

So turning from that beaten road afide,
Through many a devious path at length he paced,
As that experienc'd *Palmer* did him guide,
'Till to a mountain hoare they come at laft;
Whofe high-rais'd brows with filvan honours graced,
Majeftically frown'd upon the plain,
And over all an aweful horror caft.
Seem'd as thofe villas gay it did difdain,
Which fpangled all the vale like *Flora's* painted train.

LXVIII.

The hill afcended ftrait, ere-while they came
To a tall grove, whofe thick-embow'ring fhade,
Impervious to the fun's meridian flame
Ev'n at mid-noon a dubious twilight made;

' Or ere, before.   Like

Like to that fober light, which difarray'd
Of all its gorgeous robe, with blunted beams,
Through windows dim with holy acts pourtray'd,
Along fome cloifter'd abby faintly gleams,
Abftracting the rapt thought from vain earth-mufing
LXIX. [themes.

Beneath this high o'er-arching canopy
Of cluft'ring oaks, a filvan colonnade,
Aye lift'ning to the native melody
Of birds fweet-echoing through the lonely fhade,
On to the centre of the grove they ftray'd ;
Which, in a fpacious circle opening round,
Within its fhelt'ring arms fecurely laid,
Difclos'd to fudden view a vale profound,
With Nature's artlefs fmiles and tranquil beauties crown'd.

LXX.

There, on the bafis of an ancient pile,
Whofe crofs furmounted fpire o'erlook'd the wood,
A venerable MATRON they ere-while
Difcover'd have, befide a murm'ring flood
Reclining in right fad and penfive mood.
Retir'd within her own abftracted breaft
She feem'd o'er various woes by turns to brood ;
The which her changing chear by turns expreft,
Now glowing with difdain, with grief now ' over-keft.

' Over-keft, for over-caft.   LXXI. Her

LXXI.

Her thus immers'd in anxious thought profound
When-as the *Knight* perceiv'd, he nearer drew ;
To weet what bitter bale did her aftound,
And whence th' occafion of her anguifh grew.
For that right noble MATRON well he knew;
And many perils huge, and labours fore
Had for her fake endured ; her vaffal true,
Train'd in her love, and practiced evermore
Her honour to refpect, and reverence her lore.

LXXII.

O deareft drad ! he cried, fair *ifland queen !*
Mother of heroes ! *emprefs* of the *main !*
What means that ftormy brow of troublous teen ?
* Sith heav'n-born *Peace*, with all her fmiling train
Of fciences and arts, adorns thy reign
With wealth and knowledge, fplendour and renown ?
Each port how throng'd ! how fruitful every plain !
How blithe the country ! and how gay the town !
While *Liberty* fecures and heightens every boon !

LXXIII.

Awaken'd from her trance of penfive woe
By thefe fair flattering words, fhe rais'd her head ;
And bending on the KNIGHT her frowning brow,
Mock'ft thou my forrows, *Fairy's Son ?* fhe faid.

* Sith, fince.

Or

* Or is thy judgment by thy heart mifled
  To deem that certain, which thy hopes fuggeft?
  To deem them full of life and ꝟ luftihead,
  Whofe cheeks in *Hebe*'s vivid tints are dreft,
And with *Joy*'s carelefs mien, and dimpled fmiles impreft?

LXXIV.

Thy unfufpecting heart how nobly good
  I know, how fanguine in thy country's caufe!
  And mark'd thy virtue, fingly how it ftood
  Th' affaults of mighty Custom, which o'er-awes
  The faint and timorous mind, and oft withdraws
  From *Reafon*'s lore th' ambitious and the vain
  By the fweet lure of popular applaufe,
  Againft their better knowledge, to maintain
The lawlefs throne of *Vice*, or *Folly*'s childifh reign.

LXXV.

How vaft his influence! how wide his fway!
  Thy felf ere-while by proof didft underftand:
  And faw'ft, as through his realms thou took'ft thy way,
  How *Vice* and *Folly* had o'er-fpread the land.
  And can'ft thou then, O *Fairy*'s *Son*, demand
  The reafon of my woe? or hope to eafe
  The throbbings of my heart with fpeeches bland,
  And words more apt my forrows to increafe,
The once-dear names of *Wealth*, and *Liberty*, and *Peace*?

ꝟ Luftihead, ftrong health, vigour.   LXXVI. *Peace*,

LXXVI.

Peace, *Wealth*, and *Liberty*, that nobleſt boon,
Are bleſſings only to the *wiſe* and *good*.
To weak and vicious minds their worth unknown,
And thence abuſed but ſerve to furniſh food
For riot and debauch, and fire the blood
With high-ſpiced luxury ; whence ſtrife, debate,
Ambition, envy, Faction's vip'rous brood,
Contempt of order, manners profligate ;
The ſymptoms of a foul, diſeaſed and bloated ſtate.

LXXVII.

Ev'n *Wit* and *Genius*, with their learned train
Of Arts and Muſes, though from heav'n above
Deſcended, when their talents they prophane
To varniſh folly, kindle wanton love,
And aid excentric ſceptic *Pride* to rove
Beyond *cæleſtial Truth's* attractive ſphere,
This *moral ſyſtem's central ſun*, aye prove
To their fond votaries a curſe ſevere,
And only make mankind more obſtinately err.

LXXVIII.

And ſtand my ſons herein from cenſure clear ?
Have They conſider'd well, and underſtood
The uſe and import of thoſe bleſſings dear,
Which the great *Lord of Nature* hath beſtow'd

As well to prove, as to reward the good ?
Whence are thefe torrents then, thefe billowy feas
Of vice, in which, as in his proper flood,
The fell *leviatban* licentious plays,
And upon fhip-wreck'd faith, and finking virtue preys ?

LXXIX.

To you, ye Noble, Opulent and Great !
With friendly voice I call, and honeft zeal !
Upon your vital influences wait
The health and ficknefs of the common-weal ;
The maladies you caufe, yourfelves muft heal.
In vain to the unthinking harden'd crowd
Will *Truth* and *Reafon* make their juft appeal ;
In vain will *facred Wifdom* cry aloud ;
And *Juftice* drench in vain her vengeful fword in blood.

LXXX.

With You muft reformation firft take place :
You are the head, the intellectual mind
Of this vaft body politic ; whofe bafe,
And vulgar limbs, to drudgery confign'd,
All the rich ftores of Science have refign'd
To You, that by the craftfman's various toil,
The fea-worn mariner, and fweating hind,
In peace and affluence maintain'd, the while
You, for yourfelves and them, may drefs the mental foil.

LXXXI. Be-

LXXXI.

Bethink you then, my children, of the truft
In you repos'd ; ne let your heav'n-born mind
Confume in pleafure, or unactive ruft ;
But nobly roufe you to the tafk affign'd,
The godlike tafk to teach and mend mankind :
Learn that ye may inftruct : to virtue lead
Yourfelves the way : the herd will crowd behind,
And gather precepts from each worthy deed :
" Example is a leffon, that all men can read."

LXXXII.

But if (to All or Moft I do not fpeak)
In vain and fenfual habits now grown old,
The ftrong *Circæan charm* you cannot break,
Nor re-affume at will your native [s] mould,
Yet envy not the ftate, you could not hold :
And take compaffion on the rifing age :
In them redeem your errours manifold ;
And, by due difcipline and nurture fage,
In Virtue's lore betimes your docile fons engage.

LXXXIII.

You chiefly, who like me in fecret mourn
The prevalence of Custom lewd and vain ;
And you, who, though by the rude torrent borne
Unwillingly along you yield with pain

[s] Mould, fhape, form.

To

To his behefts, and act what you difdain,

  Yet nourifh in your hearts the gen'rous love

  Of piety and truth, no more reftrain

  The manly zeal; but all your finews move

The prefent to reclaim, the future race improve!

LXXXIV.

Eftfoons by your joint efforts fhall be quell'd

  Yon haughty GIANT, who fo proudly fways

  A fceptre by repute alone upheld;

Who where he cannot dictate ftrait obeys.

Accuftom'd to conform his flattering phrafe

  To numbers and high-plac'd authority,

  Your party he will join, your maxims praife,

  And drawing after all his menial fry,

Soon teach the general voice your act to ratify.

LXXXV.

Ne for th' atchievement of this great emprize

  The want of means or counfel may ye dread;

  From my TWIN-DAUGHTERS' fruitful wombs fhall rife

A race of letter'd fages, deeply read

In *Learning*'s various writ: by whom y-led

  Thro' each well-cultur'd plot, each beauteous grove,

  Where *antique Wifdom* whilom wont to tread,

  With mingled glee and profit may ye rove, [prove.

And cull each virtuous plant, each tree of knowledge

                    LXXXVI. Your-

LXXXVI.

Yourfelves with virtue thus and knowledge fraught
Of what, in ancient days of good or great
Hiftorians, bards, philofophers have taught;
Join'd with whatever elfe of modern date
Maturer judgment, fearch more accurate
Difcover'd have of Nature, Man, and God,
May by new laws reform the time-worn ftate
Of cell-bred difcipline, and fmoothe the road
That leads thro' *Learning's* vale to *Wifdom's* bright abode.

LXXXVII.

By you invited to her fecret bow'rs,
Then fhall PÆDÍA reafcend her throne
With vivid laurels girt, and fragrant flow'rs;
While from their *forked mount* defcending down
Yon fupercilious *pedant train* fhall own
Her empire paramount, ere long by Her
Y-taught a leffon in their fchools unknown,
" To *Learning's* richeft treafures to prefer
" The *knowledge* of the *world, and man's great bufinefs*
[*there.*"

LXXXVIII.

On this prime fcience, as the final end
Of all her difcipline, and nurturing care,
Her eye PÆDÍA fixing aye fhall bend
Her every thought and effort to prepare

D 3

Her

Her tender pupils for the various war,
Which *Vice* and *Folly* fhall upon them wage,
As on the perilous march of life they fare,
With prudent lore fore-arming every age
'Gainft *Pleafure*'s treacherous joys, and *Pain*'s embattled [rage.

LXXXIX.

Then fhall my youthful fons, to Wifdom led
By fair example and ingenuous praife,
With willing feet the paths of *Duty* tread;
Through the world's intricate or rugged ways
Conducted by *Religion*'s facred rays;
Whofe foul-invigorating influence
Shall purge their minds from all impure allays
Of fordid felfifhnefs and brutal fenfe,
And fwell th' ennobled heart with bleft benevolence.

XC.

Then alfo fhall this *emblematic pile*,
By *magic* whilom fram'd to fympathize
With all the fortunes of this changeful ifle,
Still, as my fons in fame and virtue rife,
Grow with their growth, and to th' applauding fkies
Its radiant crofs up-lift; the while, to grace
The *multiplying niches*, frefh fupplies
Of *worthies* fhall fucceed, with equal pace
Aye following their *fires* in virtue's glorious race.

XCI. Fir'd

XCI.

Fir'd with th' idea of her future fame
She rofe majeftic from her lowly fted;
While from her vivid eyes a fparkling flame
Out-beaming, with unwonted light o'erfpread
That *monumental pile*; and as her head
To every *front* fhe turn'd, difcover'd round
The venerable *forms* of heroes dead;
Who for their various merit erft renown'd,
In this bright fane of glory fhrines of honour found.

XCII.

On *thefe* that *royal dame* her ravifh'd eyes
Would often feaft; and ever as fhe fpy'd
Forth from the ground the *length'ning ftructure* rife
With *new-plac'd ftatues* deck'd on every fide,
Her parent-breaft would fwell with gen'rous pride.
And now with her in that fequefter'd plain,
The *Knight* awhile conftraining to abide,
She to the *Fairy Youth* with pleafure fain
Thofe *fculptur'd chiefs* did fhew, and their great lives ex-
[plain [h].

---

[h] *Great lives explain.*] I cannot forbear taking occafion from
thefe words to make my acknowledgments to the writers of *Bio-
graphia Britannica*, for the pleafure and profit I have lately received from perufing the two firft volumes of that ufeful and en-
tertaining work, of which the *monumental ftructure* above-men-
tioned,

tioned, decorated with the statues of *great* and *good* men, is no improper emblem. This work, which contains the *lives of the most eminent persons, who have flourished in* Great Britain *and* Ireland, *from the earliest ages, down to the present time,* appears to me, as far as it has hitherto gone, to be executed with great *spirit, accuracy,* and *judgment*; and deserves, in my opinion, to be encouraged by all, who have at heart the honour of their country, and that of their particular families and friends ; and who can any ways assist the ingenious and laborious authors, to render as perfect as possible, a design so apparently calculated to serve the public, by setting in the truest and fullest light the characters of persons already generally, though perhaps too indistinctly known ; and retrieving from obscurity and oblivion, examples of private and retired merit, which, though less glaring and ostentatious than the former, are not, however, of a less extensive or less beneficial influence. To those, who may happen not to have seen this repository of *British* glory, I cannot give a better idea of it, than in the following lines of *Virgil :*

Hic manus *ob patriam pugnando* vulnera passi ;
Quique *sacerdotes* casti, dum vita manebat ;
Quique pii *vates* & *Phœbo digna* locuti ;
Inventas aut qui *vitam excoluere per artes* ;
Quique *sui memores* alios fecere *merendo.*

Virg. Æn. L. 6.

The End of the FIRST CANTO.

PEN.

████████████████████████████████████

PENSHURST.

INSCRIBED TO

WILLIAM PERRY, Efq;

AND

The Honourable Mrs. ELIZABETH PERRY.

By the late Mr. F. COVENTRY.

GENIUS of Penſhurſt old !
Who faw'ſt the birth of each immortal oak,
Here ſacred from the ſtroke ;
And all thy tenants of yon turrets bold,
Infpir'ſt to arts or arms ;
Where * Sidney his Arcadian landſcape drew,
Genuine from thy Doric view ;
And patriot * Algernon unſhaken roſe
Above infulting foes ;
And Sacchariſſa nurs'd her angel charms.

* Sir Philip Sidney.   * Algernon Sidney.

O ſuffer

O fuffer me with fober tread
To enter on thy holy fhade ;
Bid fmoothly-gliding Medway ftand,
And wave his fedgy treffes bland,
A ftranger let him kindly greet,
And pour his urn beneath my feet.
And fee where Perry opes his door
To land me on the focial floor ;
Nor does the heirefs of thefe fhades deny
To bend her bright majeftic eye,
Where Beauty fhines, and Friendfhip warm,
And Honour in a female form.
With them in aged groves to walk,
And lofe my thoughts in artlefs talk,
I fhun the voice of Party loud,
I fhun loofe Pleafure's idle crowd,
And monkifh academic cell,
Where Science only feigns to dwell,
And court, where fpeckled Vanity
Apes her tricks in tawdry die,
And fhifts each hour her tinfel hue,
Still furbelow'd in follies new.
Here Nature no diftortion wears,
Old Truth retains his filver hairs,

And

And Chaftity her matron ftep,
And purple Health her rofy lip.
Ah ! on the virgin's gentle brow
How Innocence delights to glow !
Unlike the town-dame's haughty air,
The fcornful eye and harlot's ftare ;
But bending mild the bafhful front,
As modeft Fear is ever wont :
Shepherdeffes fuch of old,
Doric bards enamour'd told,
While the pleas'd Arcadian vale
Echo'd the enchanting tale.

   But chief of Virtue's lovely train,
A penfive exile on the plain,
No longer active now to wield
Th' avenging fword, protecting fhield,
Here thoughtful-walking Liberty
Remembers Britons once were free.
With her would Nobles old converfe,
And learn her dictates to rehearfe,
Ere yet they grew refin'd to hate
The hofpitable rural feat,
The fpacious hall with tenants ftor'd,
Where Mirth and Plenty crown'd the board;

Ere

Ere yet their *Lares* they forſook,
And loſt the genuine Britiſh look,
The conſcious brow of inward merit,
The rough, unbending, martial ſpirit,
To clink the chain of Thraldom gay,
And court-idolatry to pay;
To live in city ſmoaks obſcure,
Where morn ne'er wakes her breezes pure,
Where darkeſt midnight reigns at noon,
And fogs eternal blot the ſun.

But come, the minutes flit away,
And eager Fancy longs to ſtray:
Come, friendly Genius! lead me round
Thy ſylvan haunts and magic ground;
Point every ſpot of hill or dale,
And tell me, as we tread the vale,
" Here mighty Dudly once would rove,
" To plan his triumphs in the grove:
" There looſer Waller, ever gay,
" With Saccharifs in dalliance lay;
" And Philip, ſide-long yonder ſpring,
" His laviſh carols wont to ſing."
Hark! I hear the echoes call,
Hark! the ruſhing waters fall;

Lead

Lead me to the green retreats,
Guide me to the Mufes' feats,
Where ancient bards retirement chofe,
Or ancient lovers wept their woes.
What Genius points to yonder ^c oak ?
What rapture does my foul provoke ?
There let me hang a garland high,
There let my Mufe her accents try ;
Be there my earlieft homage paid,
Be there my lateft vigils made :
For thou waft planted in the earth
The day that fhone on Sidney's birth.
That happy time, that glorious day
The Mufes came in concert gay ;
With harps in tune, and ready fong,
The jolly Chorus tript along ;
In honour of th' aufpicious morn,
To hail an infant genius born :
Next came the Fauns in order meet,
The Satyrs next with cloven feet,

c An oak in Penfhurft park, planted the day Sir Philip Sidney
was born, of which Ben Johnfon fpeaks in the following manner :

  That taller tree, which of a nut was fet,
  At his great birth, where all the Mufes met.

The

The Dryads fwift that roam the woods,
The Naiads green that fwim the floods;
Sylvanus left his filent cave,
Medway came dropping from the wave;
Vertumnus led his blufhing fpoufe,
And Ceres fhook her wheaten brows;
And Mars with milder look was there,
And laughing Venus grac'd the rear.
They join'd their hands in feftive dance,
And bade the fmiling babe advance;
Each gave a gift; Sylvanus laft
Ordain'd, when all the pomp was paft,
Memorial meet, a tree to grow
Which might to future ages fhew,
That on felect occafion rare,
A troop of Gods affembled there:
The Naiads water'd well the ground,
And Flora twin'd a wood-bine round:
The tree fprung faft in hallow'd earth,
Co-æval with th' illuftrious birth.

Thus let my feet unwearied ftray;
Nor fatisfied with one furvey,
When morn returns with doubtful light,
And Phebe pales her lamp of night,

Still

Still let me wander forth anew,
And print my footsteps on the dew,
What time the swain with ruddy cheek
Prepares to yoke his oxen meek,
And early dreft in neat array
The milk-maid chanting shrill her lay,
Comes abroad with milking pail;
And the found of diftant flail
Gives the ear a rough good-morrow,
And the lark from out his furrow
Soars upright on matin wings,
And at the gate of heaven fings.

But when the fun with fervid ray
Drives upwards to his noon of day,
And couching oxen lay them down
Beneath the beechen umbrage brown;
Then let me wander in the hall,
Round whofe antique-vifag'd wall
Hangs the armour Britons wore,
Rudely caft in days of yore.
Yon fword fome heroe's arm might wield,
Red in the ranks of *Chalgrove*'s field,
Where ever-glorious Hampden bled,
And Freedom tears of forrow fhed.

Or

Or in the gallery let me walk,
Where living pictures seem to talk,
Where Beauty smiles serenely fair,
And Courage frowns with martial air;
Though whiskers quaint the face disguise,
And habits odd to modern eyes.
Behold what kings in Britain reign'd,
Plantagenets with blood distain'd,
And valiant Tudor's haughty race,
And Stuarts, England's worst disgrace.
The Norman first, with cruel frown,
Proud of his new-usurped crown,
Begins the list; and many more,
Stern heroes form'd of roughest ore.
See victor Henry there advance,
Ev'n in his look he conquers France;
And murd'rer Richard, justly slain
By Richmond's steel on Bosworth plain;
See the tyrant of his wives,
Prodigal of fairest lives,
And laureat Edward nurs'd in arts,
Minerva school'd his kingly parts:
But ah! the melancholy Jane,
A soul too tender for a queen!

She

She finks beneath imperial fway,
The dear-bought fcepter of a day !
And muft fhe mount the fcaffold drear ?
Hard-hearted Mary, learn to fpare !
Eliza next falutes the eye ;
Exalt the fong to Liberty,
The Mufe repeats the facred name,
Eliza fills the voice of fame.

From thence a bafer age began,
The royal ore polluted ran,
'Till foreign Naffau's valiant hand
Chac'd holy tyrants from the land :
Downward from hence defcend apace
To Brunfwic's high, illuftrious race ;
And fee the canvafs fpeaks them brave,
An injur'd nation born to fave,
Active in Freedom's righteous caufe,
And confcious of a juft applaufe.

But chiefly pleas'd, the curious eye
With nice difcernment loves to try
The labour'd wonders, paffing thought,
Which warm Italian pencils wrought ;
Fables of love, and ftories old,
By Greek or Latian poets told ;

How Jove committed many a rape,
How young Acteon loft his fhape;
Or what celeftial pen-men writ,
Or what the painter's genuine wit
From Fancy's ftore-houfe could devife;
Where Raphael claims the higheft prize.
Madonas here decline the head,
With fond maternal pleafure fed,
Or lift their lucid eyes above,
Where more is feen than holy love.
There temples ftand difplay'd within,
And pillars in long order feen,
And roofs rufh forward to the fight,
And lamps affeft a living light.
Or landfcapes tire the trav'ling eye,
The clouds in azure volumes fly,
The diftant trees diftinguifh'd rife,
And hills look little in the fkies.

When day declines, and ev'ning cool
Begins her gentle, filent rule,
Again, as Fancy points the way,
Benignant leader, let me ftray:
And wilt thou, Genius, bring along
(So fhall my Mufe exalt her fong)

The

The Lord who rules this ample scene,
His Consort too with gracious mien,
Her little offspring prattling round,
While Echo lisps their infant sound.
And let Good-nature, born to please,
Wait on our steps, and graceful Ease;
Nor Mirth be wanting as we walk,
Nor Wit to season sober talk;
Let gay Description too attend,
And Fable told with moral end,
And Satire quick that comes by stealth,
And flowing Laughter, friend to Health.
Meanwhile Attention loves to mark
The deer that crop the shaven park,
The steep-brow'd hill, or forest wild,
The sloping lawns, and zephyrs mild,
The clouds that blush with ev'ning red,
Or meads with silver fountains fed,
The fragrance of the new-mown hay,
And black-bird chanting on the spray;
The calm farewel of parting light,
And Ev'ning sad'ning into Night.

Nor wearied yet my roving feet,
Though Night comes on amain, retreat;

But

XXXXXXXXXXXXXXXXXXXXXXXXXXXXX

TO THE

Hon. WILMOT VAUGHAN, Efq; in WALES.

By the Same.

YE diftant realms that hold my friend
 Beneath a cold ungenial fky,
Where lab'ring groves with weight of vapours bend,
Or raving winds o'er barren mountains fly;
Reftore him quick to London's focial clime,
Reftore him quick to friendfhip, love and joy;
 Be fwift, ye lazy fteeds of Time,
 Ye moments, all your fpeed employ.
 Behold November's glooms arife,
 Pale funs with fainter glory fhine,
Dark gathering tempefts blacken in the fkies,
And fhiv'ring woods their fickly leaves refign.
Is this a time on Cambrian hills to roam,
To court difeafe in Winter's baleful reign,
 To liften to th' Atlantic foam,
 While rocks repel the roaring main,

While horror fills the region vaft,

Rheumatic tortures Eurus brings,

Pregnant with agues flies the northern blaft,

And clouds drop quartans from their flagging wings.

Doft thou explore Sabrina's fountful fource,

Where huge Plinlimmon's hoary height afcends:

Then downward mark her vagrant courfe,

'Till mix'd with clouds the landfcape ends?

Doft thou revere the hallow'd foil

Where Druids old fepulchred lie;

Or up cold Snowden's craggy fummits toil,

And mufe on ancient favage liberty?

Ill fuit fuch walks with bleak autumnal air,

Say, can November yield the joys of May?

When Jove deforms the blafted year,

Can Wallia boaft a chearful day?

The town expects thee.——Hark, around,

Through every ftreet of gay refort,

New chariots rattle with awak'ning found,

And crowd the levees, and befiege the court.

The patriot, kindling as his wars enfue,

Now fires his foul with liberty and fame,

Marfhals his threat'ning tropes anew,

And gives his hoarded thunders aim.

Now

Now feats their abfent lords deplore,
  Neglected villas empty ftand,
Capacious Gro'venor gathers all its ftore,
And mighty London fwallows up the land.
See fportive Vanity her flights begin,
See new-blown Folly's plenteous harveft rife,
    See mimic beauties dye their fkin,
    And harlots roll their venal eyes.
    Fafhions are fet, and fops return,
    And young coquettes in arms appear;
Dreaming of conqueft, how their bofoms burn,
Trick'd in the new fantaftry of the year.
Fly then away, nor fcorn to bear a part
In this gay fcene of folly amply fpread:
    Follies well us'd refine the heart,
    And pleafures clear the ftudious head;
    By grateful interchange of mirth
    The toils of ftudy fweeter grow,
As varying feafons recommend the earth,
Nor does Apollo always bend his bow.

A N

E P I S T L E

ADDRESS'D TO

Sir THOMAS HANMER,

On his EDITION of

SHAKESPEAR's WORKS.

By Mr. WILLIAM COLLINS.

S I R,

WHILE born to bring the Muſe's happier days,
 A patriot's hand protects a poet's lays:
While nurs'd by you ſhe ſees her myrtles bloom,
Green and unwither'd o'er his honour'd tomb:
Excuſe her doubts, if yet ſhe fears to tell
What ſecret tranſports in her boſom ſwell:
With conſcious awe ſhe hears the critic's fame,
And bluſhing hides her wreath at Shakeſpear's name.

Hard

Hard was the lot thofe injur'd ftrains endur'd,
Unown'd by Science, and by years obfcur'd:
Fair Fancy wept; and echoing fighs confefs'd
A fixt defpair in every tuneful breaft.
Not with more grief th' afflicted fwains appear,
When wintry winds deform the plenteous year;
When ling'ring frofts the ruin'd feats invade
Where Peace reforted, and the Graces play'd.

Each rifing art by juft gradation moves,
Toil builds on toil, and age on age improves:
The Mufe alone unequal dealt her rage,
And grac'd with nobleft pomp her earlieft ftage.
Preferv'd through time, the fpeaking fcenes impart
Each changeful wifh of Phædra's tortur'd heart:
Or paint the curfe that mark'd the [d] Theban's reign,
A bed inceftuous, and a father flain.
With kind concern our pitying eyes o'erflow,
Trace the fad tale, and own another's woe.

To Rome remov'd, with wit fecure to pleafe,
The Comic fifters kept their native eafe.
With jealous fear declining Greece beheld
Her own Menander's art almoft excell'd!
But every Mufe effay'd to raife in vain
Some labour'd rival of her Tragic ftrain;

[d] The Œdipus of Sophocles.

I

Ilyffus'

Ilyſſus' laurels though transferr'd with toil,
Droop'd their fair leaves, nor knew th' unfriendly ſoil.

   As arts expir'd, reſiſtleſs Dulneſs roſe;
Goths, prieſts, or Vandals,—all were Learning's foes.
'Till *Julius firſt recall'd each exil'd maid,
And Coſmo own'd them in th' Etrurian ſhade:
Then deeply ſkill'd in love's engaging theme,
The ſoft Provencial paſs'd to Arno's ſtream:
With graceful eaſe the wanton lyre he ſtrung,
Sweet flow'd the lays — but love was all he ſung.
The gay deſcription could not fail to move;
For, led by nature, all are friends to love.

   But heav'n, ſtill various in its works, decreed
The perfect boaſt of time ſhould laſt ſucceed.
The beauteous union muſt appear at length,
Of Tuſcan fancy, and Athenian ſtrength:
One greater Muſe Eliza's reign adorn,
And ev'n a Shakeſpear to her fame be born!

   Yet ah! ſo bright her morning's opening ray,
In vain our Britain hop'd an equal day!
No ſecond growth the weſtern iſle could bear,
At once exhauſted with too rich a year.
Too nicely Johnſon knew the critic's part;
Nature in him was almoſt loſt in art.

    * Julius II. the immediate predeceſſor of Leo X.

Qſ

Of softer mold the gentle Fletcher came,
The next in order, as the next in name.
With pleas'd attention 'midst his scenes we find
Each glowing thought, that warms the female mind;
Each melting sigh, and every tender tear,
The lover's wishes and the virgin's fear.
His [f] every strain the Smiles and Graces own;
But stronger Shakespear felt for Man alone :
Drawn by his pen, our ruder passions stand
Th' unrival'd picture of his early hand.

[g] With gradual steps, and flow, exacter France
Saw Art's fair empire o'er her shores advance:
By length of toil a bright perfection knew,
Correctly bold, and just in all she drew.
'Till late Corneille, with [h] Lucan's spirit fir'd,
Breath'd the free strain, as Rome and He inspir'd:
And classic judgment gain'd to sweet Racine
The temp'rate strength of Maro's chaster line.

---

[f] Their characters are thus distinguished by Dryden.

[g] About the time of Shakespear, the poet Hardy was in great repute in France. He wrote, according to Fontenelle, six hundred plays. The French poets after him applied themselves in general to the correct improvement of the stage, which was almost totally disregarded by those of our own country, Johnson excepted.

[h] The favourite author of the elder Corneille.

But

But wilder far the British laurel spread,
And wreaths less artful crown our poet's head.
Yet He alone to every scene could give
Th' historian's truth, and bid the manners live.
Wak'd at his call I view, with glad surprize;
Majestic forms of mighty monarchs rise.
There Henry's trumpets spread their loud alarms,
And laurel'd Conquest waits her hero's arms.
Here gentler Edward claims a pitying sigh,
Scarce born to honours, and so soon to die !
Yet shall thy throne, unhappy infant, bring
No beam of comfort to the guilty king :
The time [1] shall come, when Glo'ster's heart shall bleed
In life's last hours, with horror of the deed :
When dreary visions shall at last present
Thy vengeful image in the midnight tent,
Thy hand unseen the secret death shall bear,
Blunt the weak sword, and break th' oppressive spear.

   Where-e'er we turn, by Fancy charm'd, we find
Some sweet illusion of the cheated mind.
Oft, wild of wing, she calls the soul to rove
With humbler nature, in the rural grove ;

---

[1] Tempus erit Turno, magno cum optaverit emptum
Intactum Pallanta, &c.

Where

Where fwains contented own the quiet fcene,
And twilight fairies tread the circled green :
Drefs'd by her hand the Woods and Vallies fmile,
And Spring diffufive decks th' *inchanted ifle.*

O more than all in pow'rful genius bleft,
Come, take thine empire o'er the willing breaft !
Whate'er the wounds this youthful heart fhall feel,
Thy fongs fupport me, and thy morals heal !
There every thought the poet's warmth may raife,
There native mufic dwells in all the lays.
O might fome verfe with happieft fkill perfuade
Expreffive Picture to adopt thine aid !
What wond'rous draughts might rife from ev'ry page !
What other Raphaels charm a diftant age !

Methinks ev'n now I view fome free defign,
Where breathing Nature lives in every line :
Chafte and fubdu'd the modeft lights decay,
Steal into fhades, and mildly melt away.
— And fee, where* Anthony in tears approv'd,
Guards the pale relics of the chief he lov'd :
O'er the cold corfe the warrior feems to bend,
Deep funk in grief, and mourns his murder'd friend !
Still as they prefs, he calls on all around,
Lifts the torn robe, and points the bleeding wound.

* See the tragedy of Julius Cæfar.

But

But [1] who is he, whofe brows exalted bear
A wrath impatient, and a fiercer air?
Awake to all that injur'd worth can feel,
On his own Rome he turns th'avenging fteel.
Yet fhall not War's infatiate fury fall,
(So heav'n ordains it) on the deftin'd wall.
See the fond mother 'midft the plaintive train
Hung on his knees, and proftrate on the plain!
Touch'd to the foul, in vain he ftrives to hide
The fon's affection, in the Roman's pride:
O'er all the man conflicting paffions rife,
Rage grafps the fword, while *Pity* melts the eyes.

Thus, gen'rous Critic, as thy Bard infpires,
The fifter Arts fhall nurfe their drooping fires;
Each from his fcenes her ftores alternate bring,
Blend the fair tints, or wake the vocal ftring:
Thofe Sibyl-leaves, the fport of every wind,
(For poets ever were a carelefs kind)
By thee difpos'd, no farther toil demand,
But, juft to Nature, own thy forming hand.

So fpread o'er Greece, th'harmonious whole unknown,
Ev'n Homer's numbers charm'd by parts alone.

---

[1] Coriolanus. See Mr. Spence's dialogue on the Odyffey.

Their own Ulyſſes ſcarce had wander'd more,
By winds and water caſt on every ſhore:
When rais'd by Fate, ſome former HANMER join'd
Each beauteous image of the boundleſs mind:
And bade, like thee, his Athens ever claim
A fond alliance with the Poet's name.

A SONG

FROM

SHAKESPEAR's CYMBELINE.

Sung by GUIDERUS and ARVIRAGUS over FIDELE,
ſuppoſed to be dead.

By the Same.

I.

TO fair Fidele's graſſy tomb
 Soft maids and village hinds ſhall bring
Each op'ning ſweet, of earlieſt bloom,
 And rifle all the breathing Spring.

II. No

II.

No wailing ghoft fhall dare appear
    To vex with fhrieks this quiet grove:
But fhepherd lads affemble here,
    And melting virgins own their love.

III.

No wither'd witch fhall here be feen,
    No goblins lead their nightly crew;
The female fays fhall haunt the green,
    And drefs thy grave with pearly dew!

IV.

The red-breaft oft at ev'ning hours
    Shall kindly lend his little aid:
With hoary mofs, and gather'd flow'rs,
    To deck the ground where thou art laid.

V.

When howling winds, and beating rain,
    In tempefts fhake the fylvan cell,
Or 'midft the chace on every plain,
    The tender thought on thee fhall dwell,

VI.

Each lonely fcene fhall thee reftore,
    For thee the tear be duly fhed:
Belov'd, 'till life could charm no more,
    And mourn'd, 'till Pity's felf be dead.

XXXXXXXXXXXXXXXXXXXXXXXXXXXXXXXXXX

E L E G Y

To Mifs D———w———D.

In the Manner of OVID.

By the late Mr. HAMMOND.

O Say, thou dear poffeffor of my breaft,
   Where now's my boafted liberty and reft!
Where the gay moments which I once have known,
O where that heart I fondly thought my own!
From place to place I folitary roam,
Abroad uneafy, nor content at home,
I fcorn the beauties common eyes adore,
The more I view them, feel thy worth the more ;
Unmov'd I hear them fpeak, or fee them fair,
And only think on thee — who art not there.

In vain would books their formal fuccour lend,
Nor wit, nor wifdom can relieve their friend ;
Wit can't deceive the pain I now endure,
And wifdom fhews the ill without the cure.
When from thy fight I wafte the tedious day,
A thoufand fchemes I form, and things to fay ;
But when thy prefence gives the time I feek,
My heart's fo full, I wifh, but cannot fpeak.

   And could I fpeak with eloquence and eafe,
'Till now not ftudious of the art to pleafe,
Could I, at woman who fo oft exclaim,
Expofe (nor blufh) thy triumph and my fhame,
Abjure thofe maxims I fo lately priz'd,
And court that fex I foolifhly defpis'd,
Own thou haft foften'd my obdurate mind,
And thou reveng'd the wrongs of womankind :
Loft were my words, and fruitlefs all my pain,
In vain to tell thee all I write in vain ;
My humble fighs fhall only reach thy ears,
And all my eloquence fhall be my tears.

   And now (for more I never muft pretend)
Hear me not as thy lover, but thy friend ;
Thoufands will fain thy little heart enfnare,
For without danger none like thee are fair ;

But

But wifely chufe who beft deferves thy flame,
So fhall the choice itfelf become thy fame;
Nor yet defpife, though void of winning art,
The plain and honeft courtfhip of the heart:
The fkilful tongue in love's perfuafive lore,
Though lefs it feels, will pleafe and flatter more,
And meanly learned in that guilty trade
Can long abufe a fond, unthinking maid.
And fince their lips, fo knowing to deceive,
Thy unexperienc'd youth might foon believe,
And fince their tears in falfe fubmiffion dreft
Might thaw the icy coldnefs of thy breaft,
O! fhut thine eyes to fuch deceitful woe;
Caught by the beauty of thy outward fhow,
Like me they do not love, whate'er they feem,
Like me — with paffion founded on efteem.

Anfwer

Anſwer to the foregoing Lines.

By the late Lord HERVEY.

TOO well theſe lines that fatal truth declare,
    Which long I've known, yet now I bluſh to hear.
But ſay, what hopes thy fond ill-fated love,
What can it hope, though mutual it ſhould prove ?
This little form is fair in vain for you,
In vain for me thy honeſt heart is true ;
For would'ſt thou fix diſhonour on my name,
And give me up to penitence and ſhame ;
Or gild my ruin with the name of wife,
And make me a poor virtuous wretch for life :
Could'ſt thou ſubmit to wear the marriage chain,
(Too ſure a cure for all thy preſent pain)
No ſaffron robe for us the godhead wears,
His torch inverted, and his face in tears.
Though every ſofter wiſh were amply crown'd,
Love ſoon would ceaſe to ſmile where Fortune frown'd :

Then

Then would thy foul my fond confent deplore,
And blame what it follicited before ;
Thy own exhaufted would reproach my truth,
And fay I had undone thy blinded youth ;
That I had damp'd Ambition's nobler flame,
Eclips'd thy talents, and obfcur'd thy fame ;
To madrigals and odes that wit confin'd,
That would in fenates or in courts have fhin'd,
Glorioufly active in thy country's caufe,
Afferting freedom, and enacting laws.

  Or fay, at beft, that negatively kind
You only mourn'd, and filently repin'd ;
The jealous dæmons in my own fond breaft
Would all thefe thoughts inceffantly fuggeft,
And all that fenfe muft feel, tho' pity had fuppreft.
Yet added grief my apprehenfion fills
(If there can be addition to thofe ills)
When they fhall cry, whofe harfh reproof I dread,
" Twas thy own deed, thy folly on thy head !"
Age knows not to allow for thoughtlefs youth,
Nor pities tendernefs, nor honours truth ;
Holds it romantic to confefs a heart,
And fays thofe virgins act a wifer part
Who hofpitals and bedlams would explore
To find the rich, and only dread the poor ;

Who

Who legal proftitutes, for int'reft fake,
Clodios and Timons to their bofoms take,
And, if avenging heav'n permit increafe,
People the world with folly and difeafe.
Thofe titles, deeds, and rent-rolls only wed,
Whilft the beft bidder mounts the venal bed,
And the grave aunt and formal fire approve
This nuptial fale, this auction of their love.
But if regard to worth or fenfe be fhown,
That poor degenerate child her friends difown,
Who dares to deviate by a virtuous choice
From her great name's hereditary vice.
    Thefe fcenes my prudence ufhers to my mind,
Of all the ftorms and quickfands I muft find,
If I embark upon this fummer fea,
Where Flatt'ry fmooths, and Pleafure gilds the way.
Had our ill fate ne'er blown thy dang'rous flame
Beyond the limits of a friend's cold name,
I might upon that fcore thy heart receive,
And with that guiltlefs name my own deceive;
That commerce now in vain you recommend,
I dread the latent lover in the friend;
Of ignorance I want the poor excufe,
And know, I both muft take, or both refufe.

Hear

Hear then the safe, the firm resolve I make,
Ne'er to encourage one I must forsake.
Whilst other maids a shameless path pursue,
Neither to int'rest, nor to honour true,
And proud to swell the triumph of their eyes,
Exult in love from lovers they despise ;
Their maxims all revers'd I mean to prove,
And though I like the lover, quit the love.

EPISTLES in the Manner of OVID.

MONIMIA to PHILOCLES.

By the Same.

SINCE language never can describe my pain,
How can I hope to move when I complain ?
But such is woman's frenzy in distress,
We love to plead, though hopeless of redress.
    Perhaps, affecting ignorance, thou'lt say,
From whence these lines ? whose message to convey ?
Mock not my grief with that feign'd cold demand,
Too well you know the hapless writer's hand :

But

But if you force me to avow my fhame,
Behold it prefac'd with Monimia's name.

 Loft to the world, abandon'd and forlorn,
Expos'd to infamy, reproach, and fcorn,
To mirth and comfort loft, and all for you,
Yet loft, perhaps, to your remembrance too,
How hard my lot! what refuge can I try,
Weary of life, and yet afraid to die!
Of hope, the wretch's laft refort, bereft,
By friends, by kindred, by my lover, left.
Oh! frail dependence of confiding fools!
On lovers oaths, or friendfhip's facred rules,
How weak in modern hearts, too late I find,
Monimia's fall'n, and Philocles unkind!
To thefe reflections, each flow wearing day,
And each revolving night a conftant prey,
Think what I fuffer, nor ungentle hear
What madnefs dictates in my fond defpair;
Grudge not this fhort relief, (too faft it flies)
Nor chide that weaknefs I myfelf defpife.
One moment fure may be at leaft her due,
Who facrific'd her all of life for you.
Without a frown this farewel then receive,
For 'tis the laft my haplefs love fhall give;

Nor

Nor this I would, if reason could command,
But what restriction reins a lover's hand?
Nor prudence, shame, nor pride, nor int'rest sways,
The hand implicitly the heart obeys:
Too well this maxim has my conduct shews,
Too well that conduct to the world is known.

  Oft have I writ, and often to the flame
Condemn'd this after-witness of my shame;
Oft in my cooler recollected thought,
Thy beauties, and my fondness half forgot,
(How short those intervals for reason's aid!)
Thus to myself in anguish have I said.

  Thy vain remonstrance, foolish maid, give o'er,
Who act the wrong, can ne'er that wrong deplore.
Then sanguine hopes again delusive reign,
I form'd thee melting, as I tell my pain.
If not of rock thy flinty heart is made,
Nor tygers nurs'd thee in the desart shade,
Let me at least thy cold compassion prove,
That slender sustenance of greedy love:
Though no return my warmer wishes find,
Be to the wretch, though not the mistress, kind;
Nor whilst I court my melancholy state,
Forget 'twas love, and thee, that wrought my fate.

Without

Without reftraint habituate to range
The paths of pleafure ; can I bear this change ?
Doom'd from the world unwilling to retire,
In bloom of life, and warm with young defire,
In lieu of roofs with regal fplendor gay,
Condemn'd in diftant wilds to drag the day ;
Where beafts of prey maintain their favage court,
Or human brutes (the worft of brutes) refort.
Yes, yes, the change I could unfighing fee,
For none I mourn, but what I find in thee,
There center all my woes, thy heart eftrang'd,
I weep my lover, not my fortune, chang'd ;
Blefs'd with thy prefence, I could all forget,
Nor gilded palaces in huts regret,
But exil'd thence, fuperfluous is the reft,
Each place the fame, my hell is in my breaft ;
To pleafure dead, and living but to pain,
My only fenfe to fuffer, and complain.

As all my wrongs diftrefsful I repeat,
Say, can thy pulfe with equal cadence beat ?
Can'ft thou know peace ? is confcience mute within ?
That upright delegate for fecret fin ;
Is nature fo extinguifh'd in thy heart,
That not one fpark remains to take my part ?

Not one repentant throb, one grateful figh?
Thy breaft unruffled, and unwet thy eye?
Thou cool betrayer, temperate in ill!
Thou nor remorfe, nor thought humane can'ft feel:
Nature has form'd thee of the rougher kind,
And education more debas'd thy mind,
Born in an age when guilt and fraud prevail,
When Juftice fleeps, and Int'reft holds the fcale;
Thy loofe companions a licentious crew,
Moft to each other, all to us untrue,
Whom chance, or habit mix, but rarely choice,
Nor leagu'd in friendfhip, but in focial vice,
Who indigent of honour, or of fhame,
Glory in crimes which others blufh to name;
By right or wrong difdaining to be mov'd,
Unprincipled, unloving, and unlov'd.
The fair who trufts their proftituted vows,
If not their falfhood, ftill their boafts expofe;
Nor knows the wifeft to elude the harm,
Ev'n fhe whofe prudence fhuns the tinfel charm
They know to flander, though they fail to warm:
They make her languifh in fictitious flame,
Affix fome fpecious flander on her name,
And baffled by her virtue, triumph o'er her fame.

                                        Thefe

Thefe are the leaders of thy blinded youth,
Thefe vile feducers laugh'd thee out of truth;
Whofe fcurril jefts all folemn ties profane,
Or Friendfhip's band, or Hymen's facred chain;
Morality as weaknefs they upbraid,
Nor ev'n revere Religion's hallow'd head;
Alike they fpurn divine and human laws,
And treat the honeft like the chriftian caufe.
Curfe on that tongue whofe vile pernicious art
Delights the ear but to corrupt the heart,
That takes advantage of the chearful hour,
When weaken'd Virtue bends to Nature's pow'r,
And would the goodnefs of the foul efface,
To fubftitute difhonour in her place.

With fuch you lofe the day in falfe delights,
In lewd debauch you revel out the nights,
(O fatal commerce to Monimia's peace!)
Their arguments convince becaufe they pleafe;
Whilft fophiftry for reafon they admit,
And wander dazzled by the glare of wit,
Wit that on ill a fpecious luftre throws,
And in falfe colours every object fhows,
That gilds the wrong, depreciating the right,
And hurts the judgment, while it feafts the fight;

So in the prifm to the deluded eye
Each pictur'd trifle takes a rainbow dye,
With borrow'd charms the fhining profpect glows,
And truth revers'd the faithlefs mirror fhows,
Inverted fcenes in bright confufion lie,
The lawns impending o'er the nether fky;
No juft, no real images we meet,
But all the gaudy vifion is deceit.

Oft I revolve in this diftracted mind
Each word, each look, that fpoke my charmer kind;
But oh! how dear their memory I pay!
What pleafures paft can prefent cares allay?
Of all I love for ever difpoffefs'd:
Ah! what avails to think I once was blefs'd?
Hard difpofition of unequal fate!
Mix'd are our joys, and tranfient are their date;
Nor can reflection bring them back again,
Yet brings an after-fting to every pain.

Thy fatal letters, oh immoral youth,
Thofe perjur'd pledges of fictitious truth,
Dear as they were no fecond joy afford,
My cred'lous heart once leap'd at every word,
My glowing bofom throbb'd with thick-heav'd fighs,
And floods of rapture gufh'd into my eyes:

When

When now repeated (for thy theft was vain,
Each treasur'd syllable my thoughts retain)
Far other passions rule, and diff'rent care,
My joys and grief, my transports and despair.

Why dost thou mock the ties of constant love?
But half its joys the faithless ever prove,
They only taste the pleasures they receive,
When sure the noblest is in those we give.
Acceptance is the heav'n which mortals know,
But 'tis the bliss of angels to bestow.
Oh! emulate, my love, that task divine,
Be thou that angel, and that heav'n be mine.
Yet, yet relent, yet intercept my fate:
Alas! I rave, and sue for new deceit.
As soon the dead shall from the grave return,
As love extinguish'd with new ardor burn.
Oh! that I dar'd to act a Roman part,
And stab thy image in this faithful heart,
Where riveted for life secure you reign,
A cruel inmate, author of my pain:
But coward-like irresolute I wait
Time's tardy aid, nor dare to rush on fate;
Perhaps may linger on life's latest stage,
Survive thy cruelties, and fall by age:

No

No — grief fhall fwell my fails, and fpeed me o'er ⎤
(Defpair my pilot) to that quiet fhore   ⎬
Where I can truft, and thou betray no more. ⎦

Might I but once again behold thy charms,
Might I but breathe my laft in thofe dear arms,
On that lov'd face but fix my clofing eye,
Permitted where I might not live to die,
My foften'd fate I would accufe no more;
But fate has no fuch happinefs in ftore.
'Tis paft, 'tis done — what gleam of hope behind,
When I can ne'er be falfe, nor thou be kind?
Why then this care?—'tis weak—'tis vain—farewel—
At that laft word what agonies I feel!
I faint — I die — remember I was true —
'Tis all I afk — eternally — adieu! —

FLORA

✖✖✖✖✖✖✖✖✖✖✖✖✖✖✖*✖✖✖✖✖✖✖✖✖✖✖✖✖

FLORA to POMPEY.

By the Same.

Pompey, *when he was very young, fell in love with* Flora, *a* Roman *courtezan, who was so very beautiful that the* Romans *had her painted to adorn the temple of* Caſtor *and* Pollux. Geminius (Pompey's *friend) afterwards fell in love with her too; but ſhe, prepoſſeſſed with a paſſion for* Pompey, *would not liſten to* Geminius. Pompey, *in compaſſion to his friend, yielded him his miſtreſs, which* Flora *took ſo much to heart, that ſhe fell dangerouſly ill upon it; and in that ſickneſs is ſuppoſed to write the following letter to* Pompey.

E RE death theſe cloſing eyes for ever ſhade,
　(That death thy cruelties have welcome made)
Receive, thou yet lov'd man! this one adieu,
This laſt farewel to happineſs and you.
My eyes o'erflow with tears, my trembling hand
Can ſcarce the letters form, or pen command:
The dancing paper ſwims before my ſight,
And ſcarce myſelf can read the words I write.
　Think you behold me in this loſt eſtate,
And think yourſelf the author of my fate:

　　　　　How

How vaft the change! your Flora's now become
The gen'ral pity, not the boaft of Rome.
This form, a pattern to the fculptor's art,
This face, the idol once of Pompey's heart,
(Whofe pictur'd beauties Rome thought fit to place
The facred temples of her gods to grace)
Are charming now no more; the bloom is fled,
The lillies languid, and the rofes dead.
Soon fhall fome hand the glorious work deface,
Where Grecian pencils tell what Flora was:
No longer my refemblance they impart,
They loft their likenefs, when I loft thy heart.

   Oh! that thofe hours could take their turn again,
When Pompey, lab'ring with a jealous pain,
His Flora thus befpoke: " Say, my dear love!
" Shall all thefe rivals unfuccefsful prove?
" In vain, for ever, fhall the Roman youth
" Envy my happinefs, and tempt thy truth?
" Shall neither tears nor pray'rs thy pity move?
" Ah! give not pity, 'tis akin to love.
" Would Flora were not fair in fuch excefs,
" That I might fear, though not adore her lefs."

   Fool that I was, I fought to eafe that grief,
Nor knew indiff'rence follow'd the relief:

Experience

Experience taught the cruel truth too late,
I never dreaded, 'till I found my fate.
'Twas mine to afk if Pompey's felf could hear,
Unmov'd, his rival's unfuccefsful pray'r;
To make thee fwear he'd not thy pity move;
Alas! fuch pity is no kin to love.

'Twas thou thyfelf, (ungrateful as thou art)
Bade me unbend the rigour of my heart:
You chid my faith, reproach'd my being true,
(Unnat'ral thought!) and labour'd to fubdue
The conftancy my foul maintain'd for you;
To other arms your miftrefs you condemn'd,
Too cool a lover, and too warm a friend.

How could'ft thou thus my lavifh heart abufe,
To afk the only thing it could refufe?
Nor yet upbraid me, Pompey, what I fay,
For 'tis my merit that I can't obey;
Yet this alledg'd againft me as a fault,
Thy rage fomented, and my ruin wrought.
Juft gods! what tie, what conduct can prevail
O'er fickle man, when truth like mine can fail?

Urge not, to glofs thy crime, the name of friend,
We know how far thofe facred laws extend;
Since other heroes have not blufh'd to prove
How weak all paffions when oppos'd to love:

Nor

Nor boaft the virtuous conflict of thy heart
When gen'rous pity took Geminius' part;
'Tis all heroic fraud, and Roman art.
Such flights of honour might amufe the crowd,
But by a miftrefs ne'er can be allow'd;
Keep for the fenate, and the grave debate,
That infamous hypocrify of ftate,
There words are virtue, and your trade deceit.

   No riddle is thy change, nor hard t' explain,
Flora was fond, and Pompey was a man:
No longer then a fpecious tale pretend,
Nor plead fictitious merit to your friend:
By nature falfe, you follow'd her decree,
Nor gen'rous are to him, but falfe to me.

   You fay you melted at Geminius' tears,
You fay you felt his agonizing cares:
Grofs artifice! that this from him could move,
And not from Flora, whom you fay you love:
You could not bear to hear your rival figh,
Yet bear unmov'd to fee your miftrefs die.
Inhuman hypocrite! not thus can he
My wrongs, and my diftrefs, obdurate, fee.
He, who receiv'd, condemns the gift you made,
And joins with me the giver to upbraid,
Forgetting he's oblig'd, and mourning I'm betray'd.

He loves too well that cruel gift to ufe,
Which Pompey lov'd too little to refufe:
Fain would he call my vagrant lord again,
But I the kind ambaffador reftrain;
I fcorn to let another take my part,
And to myfelf will owe or lofe thy heart.
　Can nothing e'er rekindle love in thee?
Can nothing e'er extinguifh it in me?
That I could tear thee from this injur'd breaft!
And where you gave my perfon, give the reft,
At once to grant and punifh thy requeft.
That I could place thy worthy rival there!
No fecond infult need my fondnefs fear:
He views not Flora with her Pompey's eyes,
He loves like me, he doats, defpairs, and dies.
　Come to my arms, thou dear deferving youth!
Thou prodigy of man! thou man with truth!
For him, I will redouble every care,
To pleafe, for him, thefe faded charms repair;
To crown his vows, and fharpen thy defpair.
　Oh! 'tis illufion all! and idle rage!
No fecond paffion can this heart engage;
And fhortly, Pompey, fhall thy Flora prove,
Death may diffolve, but nothing change her love.

ARISBE

ARISBE to MARIUS Junior.

From FONTENELLE. By the Same.

When Marius *was expelled from* Rome *by* Sylla's *faction, and retired into* Africa, *his son (who accompanied him) fell into the hands of* Hiempfal *king of* Numidia, *who kept him prisoner.* One *of the mistresses of that king fell in love with* Marius *junior, and was so generous to contrive and give him his liberty, though by that means she sacrificed her love for ever. 'Twas after he had rejoin'd his father, that she writ him the following letter.*

I.

OF all I valued, all I lov'd, bereft,
    Say, has my heart this little comfort left?
That you the mem'ry of its truth retain,
And think with grateful pity on my pain?

II.

Though but with life my forrows can have end,
(For death alone can join me to my friend)
Yet think not I repent I fet you free,
I mourn your abfence, not your liberty.

III. Before

III.

Before my Marius left Numidia's coaft,
Each day I faw him ; fcarce an hour was loft:
Now months and years muft pafs, nay life fhall prove
But one long abfence from the man I love.

IV.

Painful reflection ! poyfon to my mind !
Was it but mortal too, it would be kind :
But mad with grief I fearch the palace round,
And in that madnefs dream you're to be found.

V.

Would'ft thou believe it ? to thofe walls I fly
Where thou wert captive held ; there frantic cry,
Thefe fetters fure my vagrant's flight reftrain'd ;
Alas ! thefe fetters I myfelf unchain'd.

VI.

The live-long day I mourn, I loath the light,
And wait impatient each returning night :
What, though the horrid gloom augment my grief?
'Tis grateful ftill, for I difclaim relief.

VII.

That coz'ner hope intrudes not on my woe ;
One only interval my forrows know ;
When dreams, the kind reverfers of my pain,
Bring back my charming fugitive again.

G 4   VIII. Yet

Yet there's a grief surpassing all the rest;
A jealous dæmon whispers in my breast,
Marius was false, for liberty alone
The show of love the hypocrite put on.

IX.

Then I reflect (ah! would I could forget!)
How much your thoughts on war and Rome were set.
How little passion did that conduct prove!
Too strong thy reason, but too weak thy love.

X.

Thy sword, 'tis true, a father's cause demands;
But 'twas a mistress gave it to thy hands:
To love, and duty just, give each their part,
His be the arm, and mine be all thy heart.

XI.

But what avail these thoughts? fond wretch, give o'er!
Marius, or false, or true, is thine no more:
Since Fate has cast the lot, and we must part,
Why should I wish to think I had his heart?

XII.

Yes: let me cherish that remembrance still;
That thought alone shall soften every ill;
To tell my soul, his love, his truth was such,
All was his due, nor have I done too much.

XIII. De-

XIII.

Deceitful comfort! let me not perfuade
My cred'lous heart its fondnefs was repaid;
It makes my foul with double anguifh mourn
Thofe joys, which never, never muft return.

XIV.

Perhaps ev'n you what moft I wifh oppofe,
And in the Roman all the lover lofe:
I'm a Numidian, and your foul difdains
To bear th' inglorious weight of foreign chains.

XV.

Can any climate then fo barb'rous prove,
To ftand excluded from the laws of Love?
His empire's univerfal, unconfin'd,
His proxy beauty, and his flaves mankind.

XVI.

Nor am I a Numidian but by name,
For I can int'reft for my love difclaim:
My virtue fhews what 'twas the gods defign'd,
By chance on Afric's clay they ftamp'd a Roman mind.

XVII.

Not all the heroes which your Rome can boaft,
So much for fame, as I for you have loft:
Yourfelf I loft: oh! grateful, then confefs,
My tryal greater, though my glory lefs.

XVIII. Yes,

Yes, partial gods! inflicters of my care!
Be witnefs what I felt, what grief, what fear!
When full of ftifled woes the night he fled,
No figh I dar'd to breathe, no tear to fhed.

XIX.

Whilft men of faith approv'd, a chofen crew,
Firm to their truft, and to their miftrefs true,
With care too punctual my commands obey,
And in one freight my life and thee convey.

XX.

The harder tafk was mine; condemn'd to bear
With brow ferene, my agonizing care;
To mix in idle talk, to force a fmile,
A king and jealous lover to beguile.

XXI.

Think in that dreadful interval of fate,
All I held dear, thy fafety in debate,
Think what I fuffer'd, whilft my heart afraid
Suggefts a thoufand times, that all's betray'd.

XXII.

A thoufand times revolving in my mind
The doubtful chance; oh! Love! faid I, be kind:
Propitious to my fcheme, thy vot'ry aid,
And be my fondnefs by fuccefs repaid.

XXIII. Now

XXIII.

Now bolder grown, with fanguine hopes elate,
My fancy reprefents thy fmiling fate;
The guards deceiv'd, and every danger o'er,
The winds already waft him from the fhore.

XXIV.

Thefe pleafing images anew impart
Life to my eyes, and gladnefs to my heart;
Difpel the gloomy fears that cloud my face,
And charm the little flutterer to peace.

XXV.

But now the king, or taftelefs to my charms,
Or weary of an abfent miftrefs' arms,
His own apartment feeks, and grateful reft;
That courted ftranger to the careful breaft.

XXVI.

Whilft I, by hopes and fears alternate fway'd,
Impatient afk the flaves if I'm obey'd.
'Tis done, they cry'd, and ftruck me with defpair;
For what I long'd to know, I dy'd to hear.

XXVII.

Fantaftic turn of a diftracted mind;
I blam'd the gods for having been too kind;
Curs'd the fuccefs they granted to my vows,
And this affiftant hand that fill'd my woes.

I

XXVIII. Such

XXVIII.

Such was my frenzy in that hour of care,
And fuch th' injuftice of my bold defpair;
That even thofe, ungrateful I upbraid,
Whofe fatal diligence my will obey'd.

XXIX.

Scarce, Marius, did thyfelf efcape my rage;
(Moft lov'd of men!) when fears of black prefage
Defcribe thy heart fo fond of liberty,
It never gave one parting throb for me.

XXX.

At every ftep you fhould have turn'd your eye,
Dropt a regretful tear, and heav'd a figh;
The nature of the grace I fhew'd was fuch,
You not deferv'd it, if it pleas'd too much.

XXXI.

A lover would have linger'd as he fled,
And oft in anguifh to himfelf have faid,
Farewel for ever! Ah! yet more he'd done,
A lover never would have fled alone.

XXXII.

To force me from a hated rival's bed,
Why comes not Marius at an army's head?
Oh! did thy heart but wifh to fee that day,
'Twould all my paft, and future woes o'erpay.

XXXIII. But

XXXIII.

But vain are all thefe hopes : preferve thy breaft
From falfhood only, I forgive the reft :
Too happy, if no envy'd rival boaft
Thofe joys Arifbe for her Marius loft.

R O X A N A to U S B E C K.

From LES LETTRES PERSANNES.

By the Same.

Roxana, one of Ufbeck's wives, was found (whilft be was in Europe) in bed with her lover, whom fhe had privately let into the feraglio. The guardian eunuch who difcovered them, had the man murdered on the fpot, and her clofe guarded 'till be received inftructions from bis mafter how to difpofe of her. During that interval fhe fwallowed poyfon, and is fuppofed to write the following letter whilft fhe is dying.

THINK not I write my innocence to prove,
    To fue for pity, or awake thy love :
No mean defence expect, or abject pray'rs ;
Thou know'ft no mercy, and I know no tears :
I laugh at all thy vengeance has decreed,
Avow the fact, and glory in the deed.

Yes,

Yes, tyrant! I deceiv'd thy fpies and thee:
Pleas'd in oppreffion, and in bondage free:
The rigid agents of thy cruel laws
By gold I won to aid my jufter caufe:
With dextrous fkill eluded all thy care,
And acted more than jealoufy could fear:
To wanton bow'rs this prifon-houfe I turn'd,
And blefs'd that abfence which you thought I mourn'd.
But fhort thofe joys allow'd by niggard Fate,
Yet fo refin'd, fo exquifitely great,
That their excefs compenfated their date.

I die: already in each burning vein
I feel the poys'nous draught, and blefs the pain:
For what is life unlefs its joys we prove?
And where is joy, depriv'd of what we love?

Yet, ere I die, this juftice I have paid
To my dear murder'd lover's injur'd fhade:
Thofe facrilegious inftruments of power,
Who wrought that ruin thefe fad eyes deplore,
Already with their blood their crimes atone,
And for his life have facrific'd their own.

Thee, though reftraint and abfence may defend
From my revenge, my curfes ftill attend:

Defpair

Despair like mine, barbarian! be thy part,
Remorse afflict, and sorrow sting thy heart.

　Nor think this hate commencing in my breast,
Though prudence long its latent force suppress'd;
I knew those wrongs that I was forc'd to bear,
And curs'd those chains Injustice made me wear.

　For could'st thou hope Roxana to deceive
With idle tales, which only fools believe?
Poor abject souls in superstition bred,
In ign'rance train'd, by prejudice misled;
Whom hireling dervises by proxy teach
From those whose false prerogative they preach.
Didst thou imagine me so weak of mind,
Because I murmur'd not, I ne'er repin'd,
But hugg'd my chain, and thought my jaylor kind?
That willingly those laws I e'er obey'd,
Which Pride invented, and Oppression made?
And whilst self-licens'd through the world you rove,
To quicken appetite by change in love;
Each passion sated, and each wish possess'd
That Lust can urge, or Fancy can suggest:
That I should mourn thy loss with fond regret,
Weep the misfortune, and the wrong forget?

　　　　　　　　　　　　　Could

Could I believe that heav'n this beauty gave,
(Thy tranfient pleafure, and thy lafting flave;)
Indu'd with reafon, only to fulfil
The harfh commands of thy capricious will?
No, Ufbeck, no, my foul difdain'd thofe laws;
And though I wanted pow'r t' affert my caufe,
My right I knew; and ftill thofe pleafures fought,
Which Juftice warranted, and Nature taught:
On Cuftom's fenfelefs precepts I refin'd,
I weigh'd what heav'n, I knew what man defign'd,
And form'd by her own rules my free-born mind.

  Thus whilft this wretched body own'd thy pow'r,
Doom'd, unredrefs'd, its hardfhips to deplore;
My foul fubfervient to herfelf alone,
And Reafon independent on her throne,
Contemn'd thy dictates, and obey'd their own.
Yet thus far to my conduct thanks are due,
At leaft I condefcended to feem true;
Endeavour'd ftill my fentiments to hide,
Indulg'd thy vanity, and footh'd thy pride.
Though this fubmiffion to a tyrant paid,
Whom not my duty, but my fears obey'd,
If rightly weigh'd, would more deferve thy blame,
Who call it Virtue, but prophane her name:

For

For to the world I fhould have own'd that love,
Which all impartial judges muft approve:
You urg'd a right to tyrannize my heart,
Which he folliciting, affail'd by art,
Whilft I, impatient of the name of flave,
To force refus'd, what I to merit gave.

   Oft, as thy flaves this wretched body led
To the detefted pleafures of thy bed;
In thofe foft moments, confecrate to joy,
Which extacy and tranfport fhould employ;
Clafp'd in your arms, you wonder'd ftill to find
So cold my kiffes, fo compos'd my mind:
But had thy cheated eyes difcern'd aright,
You'd found averfion, where you fought delight.

   Not that my foul incapable of love,
No charms could warm, no tendernefs could move;
For him, whofe love my every thought poffefs'd,
A fiercer paffion fill'd this conftant breaft,
Than truth e'er felt, or falfhood e'er poffefs'd.

   This ftile unufual to thy pride appears,
For truth's a ftranger to the tyrant's ears;
But what have I to manage or to dread?
Nor threats alarm, nor infults hurt the dead:
No wrongs they feel, no miferies they find;
Cares are the legacies we leave behind:

In the calm grave no Ufbecks we deplore,
No tyrant hufband, no oppreffive pow'r.
Alas! I faint — Death intercepts the reft.
The venom'd drug is bufy in my breaft:
Each nerve's unftrung: a mift obfcures the day:
My fenfes, ftrength, and ev'n my hate decay:
Though rage awhile the ebbing fpirits ftay'd,
'Tis paft — they fink beneath the tranfient aid.
Take then, inhuman wretch! my laft farewel;
Pain be thy portion here, hereafter, hell:
And when our prophet fhall my fate decree,
Be any curfe my punifhment, but thee.

EPILOGUE defign'd for SOPHONISBA,

And to have been fpoken by Mrs. OLDFIELD.

By the Same.

BEFORE you fign poor Sophonifba's doom,
In her behalf petitioner I come;
Not but our author knows, whate'er I fay,
That I could find objeftions to his play.

'This

This double marriage for her country's good,
I told him never would be underftood,
And that ye all would fay, 'twas flefh and blood.

Had Carthage only been in madam's head,
Her champion never had been in her — bed:
For could the ideot think a hufband's name
Would make him quit his intereft, friends and fame;
That he would rifque a kingdom for a wife,
And act dependent in a place for life?

Yet what ftern Cato fhall condemn the fair,
Whilft public good fhe thunder'd in your ear,
If private intereft had a *little* fhare?

You know, fhe acted not againft the laws
Of thofe old-fafhion'd times; that in her caufe
Old Syphax could no longer make a ftand,
And Maffiniffa woo'd her fword in hand.

But did fhe take the way to whet that fword?
Heroes fight coldly when wives give the word.
She fhould have kept him keen, employ'd her charms
Not as a bribe, but to reward his arms;
Have told him when Rome yielded fhe would yield,
And fent him frefh, not yawning, to the field.

She talk'd it well to roufe him to the fight,
But like Penelope, when out of fight,
All fhe had done by day, undid by night.

Is

Is this your wily Carthaginian kind?
No Englifh woman had been half fo kind.
What from a hufband's hand could fhe expect
But ratfbane, or that common fate, neglect?
Perhaps fome languifhing foft fair may fay,
Poyfon's fo fhocking—but confider pray,
She fear'd the Roman, he the marriage chain;
All other means to free them both were vain.
Let none then Maffiniffa's conduct blame,
He firft his love confulted, then his fame.
And if the fair one with too little art,
Whilft feemingly fhe play'd a patriot-part,
Was fecretly the dupe of her own heart;
Forgive a fault fhe ftrove fo well to hide,
Nor be compaffion to her fate deny'd,
Who liv'd unhappily, and greatly dy'd.

❀❀❀❀❀❀❀❀❀❀❀❀❀❀❀❀❀❀❀❀

An Imitation of the Eleventh Ode of the First
Book of HORACE.

By the Same.

FORBEAR, my dear Stephen, with a fruitlefs defire,
Into truths which are better conceal'd to enquire;
Perhaps many years are allow'd us by Fate,
Or next winter perhaps is the laft of their date:
Let the credulous fools whom aftrologers cheat,
Exult or defpond, as they vary deceit;
Who anticipate care, their own pleafure deftroy,
And invite difappointment who build upon joy;
All ills unforefeen we the eafieft endure,
What avails to forefee, unlefs forefight could cure?
And from ills by their art how can wretches be freed,
When that art muft be falfe, or thofe ills be decreed?
From reflection and hope little comfort we find,
To poffeffion alone let thy thoughts be confin'd;
To-day's all the treafure poor mortals can boaft,
For to-morrow's not gained, and yefterday's loft;

Even

Even now whilft I write, time fteals on our youth,
And a moment's cut off from thy friendfhip and truth.
Then feize the fwift blefling, enjoy the dear now,
And take, not expect, what hereafter 'll beftow.

A LOVE LETTER.

By the Same.

WHAT fhall I fay to fix thy wav'ring mind,
  To chafe thy doubts, and force thee to be kind?
What weight of argument can turn the fcale,
If interceffion from a lover fail?
By what fhall I conjure thee to obey
This tender fummons, nor prolong thy ftay?
If unabated in this conftant breaft
That paffion burns which once thy vows profefs'd;
If abfence has not chill'd the languid flame,
Its ardour and its purity the fame;
Indulge thofe tranfports, and no more controul
The dictates of thy fond confenting foul;
By no vain fcruple be thy purpofe fway'd,
And only Love implicitly obey'd:

Let

Let inclination this debate decide,
Nor be thy prudence, but thy heart thy guide:
But real prudence never can oppose
What Love suggests, and Gratitude avows:
The warm dear raptures which thy bosom move,
'Tis virtue to indulge, and wisdom to improve:
For think how few the joys allow'd by Fate,
How mix'd the cup, how short their longest date!
How onward still the stream of pleasure flows!
That no reflux the rapid current knows!
Not ev'n thy charms can bribe the ruthless hand
Of rigid Time, to stay his ebbing sand;
Fair as thou art, that beauty must decay;
The night of age succeeds the brightest day:
That cheek where Nature's sweetest garden blows,
Her whitest lily, and her warmest rose;
Those eyes, those meaning ministers of Love,
Who, what thy lips can only utter, prove;
These must resign their lustre, those their bloom,
And find with meaner charms one common doom:
Pass but a few short years, this change must be;
Nor one less dreadful shalt thou mourn in me:
For though no chance can alienate my flame,
While thine to feed the lamp, shall burn the same,

Yet

Yet ſhall the ſtream of years abate that fire,
And cold eſteem ſucceed to warm deſire:
Then on thy breaſt enraptur'd ſhall I dwell,
Nor feel a joy beyond what I can tell.
Or ſay, ſhould ſickneſs antedate that woe,
And intercept what Time would elſe allow;
If pain ſhould pall my taſte to all thy charms,
Or Death himſelf ſhould tear me from thy arms;
How would'ſt thou then regret with fruitleſs truth,
The precious ſquander'd hours of health and youth?
Come then, my love, nor truſt the future day,
Live whilſt we can, be happy whilſt we may:
For what is life unleſs its joys we prove?
And what is happineſs but mutual love?
Our time is wealth no frugal hand can ſtore,
All our poſſeſſion is the preſent hour,
And he who ſpares to uſe it, ever poor.
The golden *now* is all that we can boaſt;
And that (like ſnow) at once is graſp'd and loſt.
Haſte, wing thy paſſage then, no more delay,
But to theſe eyes their ſole delight convey.
Not thus I languiſh'd for thy virgin charms,
When firſt ſurrender'd to theſe eager arms,

When

When firſt admitted to that heav'n, thy breaſt,
To mine I ſtrain'd that charming foe to reſt;
How leaps my conſcious heart, whilſt I retrace
The dear idea of that ſtrict embrace?
When on thy boſom quite entranc'd I lay,
And lov'd unſated the ſhort night away;
Whilſt half reluctant you, and half reſign'd,
Amidſt fears, wiſhes, pain and pleaſure join'd,
Now holding off, now growing to my breaſt,
By turns reprov'd me, and by turns careſs'd.
Oh! how remembrance throbs in every vein!
I pant, I ſicken for that ſcene again;
My ſenſes ach, I can no word command,
And the pen totters in my trembling hand.
Farewel, thou only joy on earth I know,
And all that man can taſte of heav'n below.

VERSES

* VERSES to Dr. GEORGE ROGERS, on his taking the Degree of Doctor in Phyfic at Padua, in the Year 1664.

By Mr. WALLER.

WHEN as of old the earth's bold children ftrove,
 With hills on hills, to fcale the throne of Jove;
Pallas and Mars ftood by their fovereign's fide,
And their bright arms in his defence employ'd.
While the wife Phœbus, Hermes, and the reft,
Who joy in peace and love the Mufes beft,
Defcending from their fo diftemper'd feat,
Our groves and meadows chofe for their retreat.
There firft Apollo tried the various ufe
Of herbs, and learn'd the virtue of their juice,
And fram'd that art, to which who can pretend
A jufter title than our noble friend,

---

* This little poem was, among feveral others on the fame occafion, printed by Dr. Rogers, with his inaugural exercife at
Padua; and afterwards in the fame manner re-publifhed by him at
London, together with his Harveian oration before the college of
phyficians, in the year 1682; while Mr. Waller was yet living.

Whom

Whom the like tempeſt drives from his abode,
And like employment entertains abroad ?
This crowns him here ; and, in the bays ſo earn'd,
His country's honour is no leſs concern'd ;
Since it appears, not all the Engliſh rave,
To ruin bent : ſome ſtudy how to ſave.
And as Hippocrates did once extend
His ſacred art, whole cities to amend ;
So we, brave friend, ſuppoſe that thy great ſkill,
Thy gentle mind, and fair example, will,
At thy return, reclaim our frantic iſle,
Their ſpirits calm ; and peace again ſhall ſmile.

EDM. WALLER, Anglus.

Patavii, typis Pauli Frambotti.

VIRGIL's Tomb. NAPLES 1741.

———— *Tenues ignavo pollice chordas*
Pulſo ; Maroneique ſedens in margine templi
Sumo animum, & magni tumulis adcanto magiſtri. Stat.

I Came, great bard, to gaze upon thy ſhrine,
And o'er thy relicks wait th' inſpiring Nine :
For ſure, I ſaid, where Maro's aſhes ſleep,
The weeping Muſes muſt their vigils keep :

I   Still

Still o'er their fav'rite's monument they mourn,
And with poetic trophies grace his urn:
Have placed the fhield and martial trumpet here;
The fhepherd's pipe, and rural honours there:
Fancy had deck'd the confecrated ground,
And fcatter'd never-fading rofes round.
And now my bold romantic thought afpires
To hear the echo of celeftial lyres;
Then catch fome found to bear delighted home,
And boaft I learnt the verfe at Virgil's tomb;
Or ftretch'd beneath thy myrtle's fragrant fhade,
With dreams extatic hov'ring o'er my head,
See forms auguft, and laurel'd ghofts afcend,
And with thyfelf, perhaps, the long proceffion end.

I came — but foon the phantoms difappear'd;
Far other fcenes, than wanton Hope had rear'd;
No faery rites, no funeral pomp I found;
No trophied walls with wreaths of laurel round:
A mean unhonour'd ruin faintly fhow'd
The fpot where once thy maufoleum ftood:
Hardly the form remain'd; a nodding dome
O'ergrown with mofs is now all Virgil's tomb.
'Twas fuch a fcene as gave a kind relief
To memory, in fweetly-penfive grief:

Gloomy,

Gloomy, unpleafing images it wrought;
No mufing, foft complacency of thought:
For Time had canker'd all, and worn away
Ev'n the laft, mournful graces of decay:
Oblivion, hateful goddefs, fate before,
And cover'd with her dufky wings the door:
No filver harps I heard, no Mufe's voice,
But birds obfcene in horrid notes rejoice:
Fancy recoil'd, and with his tinfel train,
Forfook the chearlefs fcene; no more remain
The warm ambitious hopes of airy youth;
Severe Reflection came, and frowning Truth:
Away each glitt'ring gay idea fled,
And bade a melancholy train fucceed,
That form'd, or feem'd to form, a mournful call
In feeble echoes mutt'ring round the wall.

  Seek not the Mufes here! th' affrighted maids
Have fled Parthenope's polluted fhades:
Her happy fhores, the feats of joy and eafe,
Their fav'rite manfions once, no longer pleafe:
No longer, as of old, in tranfport loft,
The fifters rove along th' enchanted coaft;
They turn with horror from each much-lov'd ftream,
And loath the fields that were their darling theme:

The

The tuneful names themselves once fondly gave
To every swelling hill, and mossy cave,
So pleasing then, are only heard with sighs;
And each sad echo bids their sorrow rise.

Yet Nature smiles, as when their Virgil sung,
Nor 'midst a fairer scene his lyre was strung;
Still bloom the sweets of his elysium here,
And the same charms in every grove appear.
But ah! in vain indulgent suns prevail;
Health and delight in every balmy gale
Are wafted now in vain: small comfort bring
To weeping eyes the beauties of the spring.
To groaning slaves those fragrant meads belong,
Where Tully dictated, and Maro sung.
Long since, alas! those golden days are flown,
Where here each Science wore its proper crown;
Pale Tyranny had laid their altars low,
And rent the laurel from the Muse's brow:
What wonder then 'midst such a scene to see
The Arts expire with bleeding Liberty?
Pensive and sad, each fair angelic form
Droops, like the wearied dove beneath a storm:
Far other views the poet's thought engage,
Than the warm glories of th' Augustan age.

Can

Can mis'ry bid th' imagination glow ?
Or genius brighten 'midft domeftic woe ?
To fee defponding wretches round him pine,
Horace had wept beneath the Alban vine.
Sad fits the bard amidft his country's tears,
And fighs, regardlefs of the wreaths he wears.
Did ever Want and Famine fweetly fing ?
The fetter'd hand uncouthly ftrikes the ftring.
Lo ! ftern Oppreffion lifts her iron rod,
And Ruin waits th' imperious harpy's nod :
Black Defolation, and deftructive War,
Rife at the fignal, and attend her car.
From the dire pomp th' affrighted fhepherd flies,
And leaves his flock the rav'nous foldier's prize.
Where now are all the nymphs that bleft the plains ?
Where the full chorus of contented fwains ?
The fongs of love, of liberty and peace,
Are heard no more ; the dance and tabor ceafe :
To the foft oaten pipe, and paft'ral reed,
The din of arms, and clarion's blaft-fucceed :
Dire fhapes appear in every op'ning glade ;
And Furies howl where once the Mufes ftray'd ?

 Is this the queen of realms, for arts renown'd ?
This captive maid, that weeps upon the ground !

Alas !

Alas! how chang'd! — dejected and forlorn!
The miftrefs of the world become the fcorn!
Around ftand Rapine, Horror and Defpair;
And Ign'rance, dark ally of barb'rous War:
She, at th' ufurping Vandal's dread command,
Difplays her gloomy banner o'er the land:
Beneath its chilling fhade neglected lies
Each fifter Art; and unlamented dies.
Lo! Sculpture lets her ufelefs chiffel fall;
While on fome ruin'd temple's broken wall
Sad Architecture fits; and fees with fhame
Mif-fhapen piles ufurp her injur'd name:
Mufic and Verfe, unhappy twins! belong
To antique Mafque, and weak unmanly Song:
The gath'ring deluge fwells on every fide,
And monkifh Superftition fwells the tide.
By the refiftlefs torrent overborn
Floats every Virtue, from its bafis torn:
Fair Learning droops, the fick'ning Arts decay;
And every laurel fades, and every bay.
All is confus'd, no traces now are feen
To fhew what wretched Italy has been.

    Thus once Vefuvius, crown'd with circling wood,
Parthenope, thy beauteous neighbour ftood:

                                    Perpetual

Perpetual Spring cloath'd the fair mountain's fide;
And what is now thy terror, was thy pride.
Sudden th' imprifon'd flames burft forth; and laid
On fmoaky heaps each fhrieking Dryad's fhade:
Now deep in afhes finks the myrtle bow'r,
O'er beds of flow'rs fulphureous torrents roar;
And exil'd demi-gods their ruin'd feats deplore.

The LINK. A BALLAD.

YE ladies that live in the city or town,
    Fair Winton or Alresford fo fine and fo gay;
And ye neat country laffes in clean linen gown,
As neat and as blithe and as pretty as they:
Come away ftrait to Ovington, for you can't think
What a charming new walk there is made on the Link.

Look how lovely the profpect, the meadows how green,
The fields and the woods, in the vale or the hill:
The trees, and the cottage that peeps out between,
The clear ftream that runs bubbling in many a rill,
That will fhow your fair face as you ftand on the brink,
And murmurs moft fweetly all under the Link.

How pleafant the morning, how clear the blue fky,
How pure the frefh air, and how healthy the place!
Your heart goes a pit-a-pat light as a fly,
And the blood circles brifkly, and glows in your face:
Would you paint your fair cheeks with the rofe and the
Throw your wafhes away, take a walk on the Link. [pink?

After dinner the 'fquire ere the ladies retreat,
Marches off with fome friends that will ply the brifk glafs;
Gives us liquor enough, and a good pleafant feat,
And damns your fine tafte, and your finical lafs:
Al frefco, my lads, we'll caroufe and we'll drink,
Take your bottle each man, and away to the Link.

Not fo gentle Collin, whom love holds in thrall,
To Molly he fteals all in filence away;
And when nought can be heard but the rude water-fall,
And the woodbine breathes fweeteft at clofe of the day,
He takes her foft hand, and he tips her the wink,
Come, my dear, let us take a cool walk on the Link.

But, O ye fair maidens, be fure have a care,
Nor lay yourfelves open to love's cruel dart;
Of the hour and the place and the feafon beware,
And guard well each paffage that leads to your heart;

1   Sly

Sly Cupid will fteal in at fome little chink,
If you walk in the evening too late on the Link.

Ye poets fo lofty, who love to retire
From the noife of the town to the ftream and the wood ;
Who in epics and tragics, with marvellous fire,
Utter founds by mere mortals not well underftood :
Here mouthe your loud ftrain, and here ply pen and ink,
Quit Parnaffus and Pindus, and come to the Link.

And come you, who for thought are at little expence,
Who indite gentle paftoral, ballad, or fong ;
You fee with fmooth numbers, and not too much fenfe,
How the verfes run eafy and glibly along ;
And the rhime at the clofe how it falls with a clink,
So kind are the Mufes that fport on the Link !

THE

THE
SQUIRE of DAMES.
A POEM.
In SPENSER's STILE.

ADVERTISEMENT.

In the seventh Canto of the Legend of Chastity, *in* Spenser's Fairy Queen, *the Squire of* Dames *tells* Satyrane, *that by order of his mistress* Columbel *(after having served the ladies for a year) he was sent out a second time, not to return till he could find three hundred women incapable of yielding to any temptation. The bad success he met with in the course of three years, which is slightly touch'd upon by* Spenser, *is the foundation of the following poem.*

PROLOGUE.
I.

HARD is the heart that never knew to love,
  Ne felt the pleasing anguish of desire.
Ye British maids, more fair than Venus' dove,
For you alone I tune my humble lyre;
Adopt me, nymphs, receive me in your quire,
Make me your bard; for that is all my care:
Then shall I envy not that aged fire,
 Who doth for court his annual song prepare:
I lever myrtle wreath than Kefar's laurel wear.

II. Think

(133)

II.

Think not becaufe I write of Columbel
I thence would blaft the fex with impious tale;
Tranfactions vile of foreign ftronds I tell,
Ne 'gainft a Britifh female would I rail
For all the wealth that rolls on Indian grail.
Here, beauty, truth, and chaftity are found :
Eleonora here, with vifage pale,
Did fuck the poifon from her Edward's wound,
And Anna's nuptial faith fhall ftond for aye renown'd.

III.

See the fair fwans on Thamis' lovely tide,
The which do trim their pennons filver bright,
In fhining ranks they down the waters ride;
Oft have mine eyes devour'd the gallant fight.
Then caft thy looks with wonder and delight,
Where yon fweet nymphs enjoy the ev'ning air,
Some daunce along the green, like fairies light,
Some flow'rets cull to deck their flowing hair;
Then tell me, foothly, fwain, which fight thou deem'ft
[moft fair.

IV.

To you, bright ftars, that fparkle on our ifle,
I give my life, my fortune, and my fame;
For my whole guerdon grant me but a fmile,
A fmile from you is all I hope or claim;

I 3

Nor

Nor age's ice my ardent zeal fhall tame,
To my life's end I fhall your names adore,
Not hermits bofoms feel fo pure a flame,
Warm'd by approval I more high fhall foar:
Receive my humble lays, my heart was yours before.

V.

Should you confent, I'll quit my fhepherd's grey,
And don more graceful and more coftly gear,
My crook and fcrip I'll throw with fcorn away,
And in a famite garment ftreit appear.
Farewell, ye groves, which once I held fo dear;
Farewell, ye glens, I other joys purfue;
Then fhall the world your matchlefs pow'r revere,
And own what wonders your fweet fmiles can do,
That could a fimple clown into a bard tranfmew.

CANTO I.

ARGUMENT.

The Squire of Dames to Satyrane
His hiftory doth tell,
With all the toils he underwent
To gain his Columbel.

I. THE

I.

THE Squire of Dames his tale thus 'gan to tell;
    Sith you command my tongue, fir Satyrane,
I now will all declare that me befell,
The caufe of muchel fcath and dol'rous pain,
Ne fhall thy gentle eye from tears refrain.
Me Columbel commanded far to go
'Till I fhould full three hundred nymphs attain,
Whofe hearts fhould aye with Virtue's leffons glow,
And to all fwains but one cry out for ever, No.

II.

To find the fortilage that ne'er will yield
Is not an eafy matter, good fir Knight ;
Troy town, they fay, is now a grafs-mown field,
That long withftood the force of Grecian might ;
And caftles fall though deep in earth empight ;
Ne ought fo ftrong is found but what may fail,
The fun at laft fhall lofe his glorious light,
And vows or bribes o'er women may prevail ;
Their hearts are made of flefh, and mortal flefh is frail.

III.

With heavy heart, and full of cark I go
And take my congé of my blooming maid,
I kifs'd her hond, and louting very low,
To her beheft at length myfelf array'd :

I 4

The

The fair we love expects to be obey'd,
  Although she bid us with the kestrel fly;
  So forth I prick, though much by doubt dismay'd,
  The hard experiment resolv'd to try:
For she was wond'rous fair, and much in love was I.

IV.

A grove I reach'd, where tuneful throstles sung,
  The linnet here did ope his little throat,
  His twitting jests around the cuckoo flung,
  And the proud goldfinch show'd his painted coat,
  And hail'd us with no inharmonious note:
  The robin eke here tun'd his sonnet shrill,
  And told the soothing ditty all by rote,
  How he with leaves his pious beak did fill,
To shroud those pretty babes, whom Sib unkind would
                        [kill.

V.

And many a fair Narcissus deck'd the plain,
  That seem'd anew their passions to admire;
  Here Ajax told his dolors o'er again,
  And am'rous Clytie sicken'd with desire;
  Here the blown rose her odors sweet did spire;
  Through the dun grove a murm'ring river led
  His chrystal streams that wound in many a gyre;
  The baleful willow all the banks bespread,
And ever to the breeze ycurl'd his hoary head.

VI. Soon

VI.

Soon to the grove there came a lovely maid,
For maiden fure fhe did to me appear,
In plain check-laton was the nymph array'd,
Her fparkling eyes ftood full of many a tear,
And fhe bewept the abfence of her dear.
Alas! fhould beauty be to woe ally'd?
Beauty, methinks, fhould meet with better cheer,
Content fhould never wander from her fide;
Good luck, I pray to heav'n, the face that's fair betide.

VII.

" Ah! woe is mè, fhe cry'd, fince Colin's fled,
" Whofe gentle prefence did thefe plains adorn,
" Soon was he ravifh'd from the nuptial bed,
" Torn from thefe arms, from his dear leman torn!
" O grief! far fharper than the pointed thorn,
" I faw him ill-beftad by martial band.
" Alas the day that ever I was born!
" Where roves my Colin, on what foreign ftrand,
" Arraught from Laura's eyes, and his dear native land?

VIII.

" Alas! he only knew to prune the vine,
" Or through the earth to urge the biting fhare,
" To twift the bower with fragrant eglantine,
" Where free from heat we fhun'd the noon-tide air,

Or

" Or to the mart to lead his fleecy care.

" And is it fit in hacqueton and mail

· " The youth for war's grim terrors ſhould prepare !

" His voice outſung the love-lorn nightingale,

" And deftly could he daunce, or pipe along the dale.

IX.

" The gos-hawk fierce may pounce the trembling dove,

" The ſavage wolf may tear the bounding fawn,

" But ſparrows mild are form'd for feats of love,

" And kids dew not with blood the flow'ry lawn ;

" Then how ſhall he, in whom all graces dawn,

" In the red field the cruel paynim kill ?

" For ſcenes like theſe find men of helliſh ſpawn.

" 'Tis his with joy the virgin's heart to fill,

" And not on foreign ſhore his foemen's blood to ſpill.

X.

" No days of bliſs my ſorrows ſhall aſlake,

" For him I'll ever drop the dol'rous tear.

" Adieu the circled green, the buxom wake,

" Since Colin's gone I taſte of nought but drear.

" Stretch me, ye maidens, ſtretch me on the bier,

" And let my grave-ſtone theſe true words adorn :

" A wretched maiden lies intombed here,

" Who ſaw a ſhepherd brighter than the morn,

" Then pin'd her heart away, and dy'd of love forlorn."

XI. Much

XI.

Much was I grieved at her piteous plaint,
And greeted to myself, O happy Squire !
At length, though late, thou haft found out a faint,
Who, but for Colin, feels no warm defire.
Perdie, quoth Satyrane, I her admire;
No lozel loofe fhall here difcover'd be.
The other anfwer'd with his cheeks on fire,
Now by my hallidom you foon fhall fee
That words may with the heart full often ill agree.

XII.

I, nought accoy'd, came up unto the fair,
And fwore to love her all my length of life ;
Then offer'd her to gorgeous domes to bear,
Where haidegives are daunc'd to harp and fife.
She foon forgot fhe was another's wife,
And granted with me to defert the plain.
Are fuch enfamples emong women rife ?
If fo, my Columbel I ne'er fhall gain,
But hunt around the world, and find my labours vain.

XIII.

My lips I 'gan to royne in fell defpite,
And forth I rufhed from her falfe embrace,
Through the thick wood I wander'd day and night,
Ne met I living creature face to face:

At

At length a rifing city far I trace;
Thither in hopes my hafty fteps I bend,
Perchaunce, thought I, true Virtue may embrace
The courtly dome, and from the country wend.
Thus, where we leaft expect, we often find a friend.

XIV.

At e'en the town I reach'd, and eke a hall,
Which waxen tapers made as light as day;
Fair jovifaunce fat on the face of all,
And to the daunce the fprightly minftrels play,
Each feem'd as fportive as the wanton jay.
The dame, who own'd the houfe, was paffing old,
And had, it feems, that morning dealt away
To her kind grandfon many bags of gold,
Who took a bonnibel to haven and to hold.

XV.

The bride was named Viola the fair,
The loaded rofiere is not half fo fweet.
Aye, aye, quoth I, enfamples are but rare
To find fo many charms in one difcreet;
With you, fair lafs, I mean not now to treat.
The fpringal was in wholefome luftihed,
And him by name of Pamphilus they greet;
He was to doughty chevifance ybred,
Yet oft in courtly halls the active meafure led.

XVI. The

XVI.

The auncient dame they do Avara call,
And much fhe hobbled as fhe trod the ground;
Yet many angels in her crumenal,
If fair report fpeaks true, were always found.
Where riches flow there virtues too abound.
Her pannikel was as a badger grey,
And, as fhe walk'd the company around,
It nodded with fuch force, that, by my fay,
I thought it meant to fly from her old crag away.

XVII.

The lofty roof was fretted o'er with gold,
And all around, the walls depeinten were
With many hiftories of times of old,
Which brought not muchel credit to the fair.
There Leda held her fwan, with fhoulders bare,
And here the dame of Ephefus was found,
Lick other dames, whom my kind tongue fhall fpare,
And here ftood Helen for her charms renown'd,
Who foon her lord forfook, when fhe a leman found.

XVIII.

And many a beauteous dame and courtly knight
Came there the nuptials to celebrate:
Some vers'd to wing from bow the nimble flight,
Some the near foe with brondir'n to amate;

Me

Me too they welcome to the hall of ſtate;
With bel accoil they wiſhed me to take
A round or two, and chooſe me out a mate:
But my fond love which nothing could aſlake,
Caus'd me to ſlight them all, for Columbella's ſake.

XIX.

And now to artful ſteps the floor rebounds,
In graceful eaſe the ſhining beavys move,
The noice like thunder at a diſtance ſounds.
Mean time I ſat beneath a proud alcove,
And told Avara gentle tales of love.
Thought I, in eld the paſſions are more tame,
And here by craft I may ſuccefsful prove;
For ſhe perforce muſt now be void of blame
As wiſe Ulyſſes' wife, Penelopé by name.

XX.

Ne wants ſhe gelt, which oft the mind miſleads
To actions which it otherwiſe would ſhun.
The courtier lythe, if right report areeds,
Will unawhap'd to ſeize his vantage run;
And ſo will moſt men underneath the ſun,
Or be they patriot call'd, or bard, or knight;
But when they once the gilded prize have won,
They ſeek to clear their name, with ſhame bedight:
Befits to ſcour the ſteel, when ruſt offends the ſight.

XXI. At

XXI.

At every word I faid fhe look'd afkaunce,
Then faid, in unfoot whifpers, Fye! Sir, fye!
And turn'd as though fhe feem'd to mind the daunce,
Nathlefs on me fhe caft a languid eye:
Blift by thy form, my liefeft life, quoth I,
Caft your belgards upon an humble flave;
From love, alafs! in vain my heart would fly;
Then with a word thy quailing leman fave,
For if you frown, perdie, you doom me to the grave.

XXII.

It hap'd by chaunce fhe faw a golden heart
With flaming diamonds around befet;
This, the whole guerdon of my tedious fmart,
I, on a time, from Columbel did get.
As fimple birds are caught in fowler's net,
And 'caufe they fee no danger none they fear,
Ev'n fo Avara her eyen here did fet,
And turned round and whifper'd in mine ear,
Give me that di'mond heart, and be mine leman dear.

XXIII.

I ftarted from the couch where I was pight,
And thus I her befpake with muchel rage,
Avaunt, thou faytor falfe, thou imp of night!
I hate myfelf that I fhould thus engage,

On

On any terms to treat with wrizled age.

So, forth I flung, and left the frowy witch

To fhare her bed with coachman, groom or page;

The caftle too I quit, mine ire was fich,

And out I fet again, though night was dark as pitch.

XXIV.

But did I here relate, fir Satyrane,

The many weary miles I've travelled,

What dangers I've affoil'd, yet all in vain,

(For, by my truth, but ill my days I've fped)

Your hair would ftand upright upon your head.

Three hundred virtuous females, fide by fide,

By me to Columbella muft be led:

Can you direct me where for fuch to ride?

I cannot, in good footh, the courteous knight reply'd.

XXV.

The Squire purfu'd his tale; 'Tis now three years

Since curft Avara's vifage firft I faw;

Convents I've try'd, but there the lufcious freers

The fair-fac'd nuns to fornication draw;

Nor palaces are free from Cupid's law;

His darts are fiercer than the levin-brond;

Few, very few, there 'fcape his mighty paw;

And thofe in golden palls, who proudly ftond,

Had lever kifs their love's, than Kefar's royal hond.

XXVI. Fair

XXVI.

Fair Jenny of the mill I ſtrove to win,
And her benempt Paſtora of the dale ;
But they bilive agreed with me to ſin ;
One aſk'd an owch, and one a watchet veil.
Some wiſh o'er every female to prevail ;
My hope, my conqueſt is to be deny'd.
The ſtage I've try'd, but there my projects fail ;
For there is ſcarce a ſingle wedded bride
But doth her huſband's noul with horns of ront provide.

XXVII.

As couthful fiſhers at the benty brook,
By various arts aſſot the ſeely fry,
Now wriggling worms, now paſte conceals the hook,
And now they hide it with a colour'd fly ;
This takes the perch, and that the tench's eye :
So diff'rent nymphs a diff'rent charm invites,
Some yield for vantage, ſome for vanity,
A ſong this one, a daunce that maid delights :
Man throws the wimble bait, and greedy woman bites.

XXVIII.

With ſorrow overhent, the other day
I laid my weary limbs adown to reſt,
Where a tall beech o'erſpread the duſky way ;
My noyous thoughts a dream awhile ſuppreſs'd,

Oft weighty truths are in this garb ydrefs'd.

Grant that it fo may happen unto me;

Then joyance once again fhall footh this breaft,

My pining foul fhall be from anguifh free,

And I fhall tafte true blifs, dear Columbel, with thee.

XXIX.

Methought I faw a figure fair and tall,

And gentle fmiles fat dimpling on her face,

Yet feemed of a beauty nought at all,

'Till much beholding did improve each grace;

At length fhe feem'd too fair for human race.

Her kirtle white might vie with winter fnows,

Ne could you ought of her fair bofom trace,

Nought but her face would fhe to fight expofe,

So modeft maiden wends, the frannion muchel fhows.

XXX.

With vifage bland methought fhe hail'd me oft:

" Ne fear, quoth fhe, a female's mild requeft.

" The bark by tempefts that is whirl'd aloft,

" At length, the tempeft o'er, enjoyeth reft.

" My name is Chaftity, though out of queft

" With modern dames, yet thou fhalt ftill furvey

" A clime where beauty is with virtue bleft.

" Good fortune fpeed you on your happy way;

" Go, gentle Squire of Dames, and here no longer ftay.

XXXI. " To

XXXI.

" To Fairy lond your inftant journey bend,

" There Columbel may find her will obey'd;

" There Chaftity may boaft of many a friend,

" She vifits there each rofy-featur'd maid.

" Go on, nor be by former toils affray'd :

" Go where yon oaks difplay their verdant pride,

" 'Till, from the mountains torn and ftripp'd of fhade,

" On Neptune's billows they triumphant ride,

" Protect their happy lond, and conquer all befide.

XXXIL

" Hail happy lond ! for arms and arts renown'd,

" For blooming virgins free from loofe defire; .

" A Drake, a Bacon, there a birth-place found,

" And chafte Eliza time fhall e'er admire :

" The hero wields the fword and poet's lyre ;

" This Sidney knew, who ftill with luftre fhines,

" For whom Dan Spenfer wak'd the warbling quire,

" And many more whofe names might grace his lines;

" There round the warriour's palm the lover's myrtle
                                                    [twines."
XXXIII.

At this I woke, and now refolv'd to brave

The utmoft perils for my Columbel;

For, know, I mean to crofs the briny wave,

Where Albion's chalky cliffs the fea repel :

And,

And, if no mage have laid a magic spell,
Perchaunce my lot may be at length to find
Three hundred nymphs, who wicked love can quell;
If not, I must defert all womankind,
And, what me moft amates, leave Columbel behind.

XXXIV.

The Squire of Dames furceafed here his fay,
And forth he yode to feek the Britifh ifle,
Sir Satyrane prick'd on his dapple-grey,
Ne ought forefwonk he travell'd many a mile
To fpend his days in hardiment and toil:
But firft in courteous guife they bid farewell,
As well befits men bred in courtly foil,
Now how the Squire has fped, or ill, or well,
A future canto may, perhaps, at leifure tell.

XXXV.

For fee, how Phœbus welketh in the weft,
My oxen from their yoke I muft untye,
The collar much has chauf'd their tender cheft,
Who labours much the fweets of reft fhould try.
To their warm nefts the daws and ravens fly
Deep in the ruin'd dome or dufky wood;
And beafts and birds faft lock'd in flumber lye,
Save the fell bat, that flutters out for food,
And the foothfaying owl, with her unlovely brood.

CANTO

CANTO II.

ARGUMENT.

The Squire he lights on Bon-vivant,
    Who wons in Fairy *foil,*
Then views in Merlin's *magic glafs*
    A fight that ends his toil.

I.

TO gain the point to which our foul afpires
    We nourifh toil, and reek hard labour fweet;
For this, thro' Greenland's frofts, or India's fires,
The hardy failors death and dangers meet;
And the prow chieftain, bolder than difcreet,
In blood imbru'd purfues the martial fray,
And lovers eke through life's loud tempefts beat,
Led on by hope, that never-dying ray;
Hope wantons in their breaft, and ftrews with flow'rs the
                                                    [way.

II.

And fure of all mankind the Squire of Dames
Shall ftand the firft enfample of true love,
Who aye, untouch'd by any foreign flames,
Preferv'd his paffion for his gentle dove;

Blufh,

Blush, modern youths, whose pulses quickly move,
Fondly you glote upon the witching fair ;
Yet, when a sweet enjoyment once you prove,
You leave the nymph intangled in the snare,
Her tears flow trickling down, her singults pierce the air.

III.

Oh think of transports which ye whilom tasted,
And let the glad remembrance charm your mind,
Be not the fruits of joyment quickly wasted,
And to your heart her happy image bind :
Think what she merits who whilear was kind,
Nor by inconstancy her peace destroy ;
Inconstancy, that monster fell and blind :
That vainly fond of every passing toy,
Treads down its late delight, and poisons rapt'rous joy.

IV.

Return we now unto our gentle youth,
Whose little bark daunc'd lightly on the main,
His breast divided atween joy and ruth ;
Now gay ideas wanton in his brain,
Now woe-begon his heart is rent in twain,
On his success depends his Columbel ;
And now he hopes, and now desponds again ;
The various turns of mind, when thoughts rebel,
Sure pen mote ne'er describe, and none but lovers tell.

                                   V. Methinks

V.

Methinks I see him on the beechy strond,
Where Neptune's waves affrap the sturdy pier;
His hardy steed neighs at the sight of lond,
In all adventures a most faithful seer;
And through that city he doth quickly steer,
Which Ethelbert to holy Austin gave:
The kings of Kent did erst inhabit here,
Here haughty Becket sunk into the grave,
Here thro' the smiling meads, Stoure rolls his dimpling
[wave.

VI.

Long travell'd he, ne ventur'd to assay
The nymphs he met, for much he was affray'd
To bribes or pray'rs few women would cry nay;
At flatt'ry's tongue full oft will virtue fade;
What shall he do? to win his lovely maid
He must three hundred virtuous females find,
Perdie, quoth he, my fortune be essay'd,
I'll boldly try the strength of womankind:
For craven heart, they say, ne'er won fair lady's mind.

VII.

So on he prick'd, and from a rising ground
Discern'd before him, in a distant vale,
A castle fair: and auncient oaks around
Did to the breeze their lofty heads avail;

A silver

A filver ftream refrefh'd the fragrant dale ;
Their ledden loud fat oxen did repeat,
And nibbling fheep difplay'd their fleeces pale,
The woodbine fhed an odor matchlefs fweet,
And to their patient dams the frifking lambkins bleat,

VIII.

To that fame caftle our advent'rer yode,
The merry birds him welcom'd on the way,
An hundred flow'rs aumail'd the winding road,
And all was bright, and all was paffing gay,
You would have fworn it was the month of May.
Withouten drad he thunders at the gate,
Who wons within, or giant, knight or fay,
Shall ne'er, in footh, our imp of fame amate :
Unto the fummons loud the portal opens ftreit.

IX.

And forth there iffued the fenefchal,
Of middle age he was, if right I ween,
He was in perfonage both plump and tall,
Ne feemed he to tafte of dol'rous teen,
Ne wrinkle deep was on his forehead feen,
But jovifaunce fat bafking on his brow,
At every word he fpoke, he fmil'd at-ween,
His temples were ycrown'd with myrtle bough,
And virelays he fong with matchlefs grace, I vow.

X. " Who-

X.

" Whoe'er thou art, thrice welcome to thefe plains,

" Where bitter dole ne'er fhows her hateful head,

" Good-fellowfhip wons here, and free from pains

" Both youth and eld the paths of pleafure tread ;

" Catch flying blifs, ne be by ought forefaid ;

" Think that this life is but a little fpan ;

" Then laugh, and fport, and fhun all dreryhed,

" Thy rolling days in prefent pleafures plan,

" Come, fpend thy hours in joy, thou fon of mortal
[man.

XI.

" Know'ft thou my name ! I am l'Allegro hight,

" Let me conduct thee to our jovial hall,

" Where Bon-vivant in revels fpends the night,

" Who bids a hearty welcome unto all,

" Or wear he red crofs-ftoles, or paynim pall."

With that he lad him with a courtly air

Into a chamber deck'd for feaft and ball ;

And though no tedes or tapers glimmer'd there,

Yet all within was bright, as all without was fair.

XII.

As at the clofe of an hot fummer's day,

When Phœbus in the weft deferts the fky,

Bright ftreams of light along the æther play,

And though his fi'ry orb forfake our eye,

The

The beamy gushes gild each object nigh;
The painted meads are ting'd with golden light,
And rivers roll their glitt'ring waters by;
So in this house of joy with ease you might
Perceive celestial rays, that cherish'd human sight.

XIII.

The Squire of Dames his jolly host salew'd,
And Bon-vivant his hond in friendship press'd;
" Come, sit thee down, and taste our choicest food;
" We entertake, quoth he, no vulgar guest.
" Enur'd to toil, come taste the sweets of rest,
" Doff thy hard arms, this samite garment wear,
" This better far than mail shall bind thy breast,
" This coronal shall deck thy auburn hair;
" Push the brisk goblet round, and drown intruding care.

XIV.

" For us the lark attunes his morning song,
" For us the spring depeints her every flower,
" To sooth our sleep yon fountain purls along,
" And oaks to shade us, twine into a bow'r,
" The pensive bard sits many a watchful hour,
" In ditty sweet, to carol forth our praise:
" While valour spends his days in dole and stour,
" We, wiser we, undying trophies raise
" To ever-blooming bliss, ne reck what wisdom says.

I

XV. " With

XV.

" With fprightly notes we make the welkin ring,

" In mazy daunce we tread the chequer'd ground,

" To yielding nymphs tranfported fhepherds fing,

" Ne hard misfare emongft our train is found.

" The fimple fwain, who looks with cark aftoun'd

" Becaufe his leman ill rewards his care,

" Oh, let him ftond to all a lout renown'd,

" Ne gibing fcorn her twitting bords forbear ;

" Are there not other nymphs lefs coy, and full as fair ?"

XVI.

At this the Squire wex'd pale, " Ne eath it is,

" Moft courteous knight, he cry'd, far to remove

" The thoughts of her in whom we place all blifs."

Quoth Bon-vivant, " What, then thou art in love ?"

" That I am fo thefe many fingults prove,"

Return'd the Squire. L'Allegro then reply'd,

" Thou'dft better wend to yonder willow grove,

" Where fhoals of lovers hanging fide by fide,

" Feed the vile carrion crows, and highten female pride."

XVII.

With that he braft into a fcornful laugh,

And much abafh'd appear'd our conftant Squire ;

The others fportful the brifk vintage quaff.

While thus the fpringal : " Yes, I do afpire

" To

" To love the faireft of the female quire.

" Three hundred virtuous damfels in this ifle

" I came to find." " Perdie, your odd defire,.

" Quoth Bon-vivant, will afk thee muchel toil ;

" And thou fhalt travel too full many a weary mile.

XVIII.

" 'Tis not enough the conduct of the fair

" Is form'd by frowning virtue's ftricteft leer :

" The blatant-beaft does here in pieces tear

" The fame of thofe ybred in fchool fevere ;

" His rankling tongue throughout the rolling year

" With baleful venom every thing confumes ;

" Where beauty's fplendor gilds our northern fphere

" He flyly creeps, and to deftruction dooms

" The honour of the fpring, and wifdom's early blooms.

XIX.

" The brindled lyon in the lonely wood

" Hides his grim afpect from the fight of men ;

" The pardelis and libbard's fpotted brood

" Refide contented in fequefter'd den ;

" Not fo the blatant-beaft, he lives in ken

" Of the proud city or well-peopled town ;

" Thence with detefted fury he will ren,

" Ne fpare the prelate's lawn, or monarch's crown:

" All fares alike with him, for all he tumbleth down.

XX. " What

XX.

" What then avails it to be fair or wife?

" Or what avails it to be warlike knight?

" Where-e'er the monfter cafts his fi'ry eyes,

" Each grace, each virtue fickens at the fight.

" Then, goodly Squire, until the morning's light

" Quaff the thick darknefs of the night away;

" And, when the morn fhall rife, in arms bedight

" Proceed, and luck attend you on your way;

" Algates we wifh in truth with us you'd ever ftay."

XXI.

The Squire agrees, but vows, when rifing morn

Shall gild the glitt'rand portals of the eaft,

Himfelf he will in habergeon adorn,

And feek around the ifle the blatant-beaft:

Mean while in buxom mirth they fpend the feaft.

Ill fares the mortal man too much who knows;

Oft fhall he wifh himfelf from thought releaft;

The fatal knowledge in his bofom glows,

And mars his golden reft, and murders foft repofe.

XXII.

Sir Chaunticleer now ey'd the rifing day,

And call'd dame Partlet from her vetchy bed;

Now wakeful Phofpher fpreads his gleamy ray,

And the pale moon conceal'd her filver head;

The

The cattle brouze the lawn with dew befpread,
While every bird from out the bufkets flies.
Then to the field our lover iffued;
But fleep had feal'd l'Allegro's droufy eyes,
And Bon-vivant alfo in downy flumber lies.

XXIII.

Our Squire, withouten drad, purfu'd his way,
And look'd around to fpy this monfter fell,
And many a well conceited roundelay.
He fung in honour of his Columbel:
Mote he, perchaunce, deftroy this fpawn of hell,
How eafy were the tafk to him affign'd!
The lond of Fairy doth each lond excel;
View there the paragons of womankind;
View the bright virgins there, and leave thy heart behind.

XXIV.

Ah! lever fhould'ft thou try the females there
Than thus unwife another courfe purfue;
There every nymph is innocent as fair:
Try what I here advance, you'll find it true:
Hard is our fate while blifs in hopes we few,
Some deadly fiend to blaft our joy appears;
Contentment fweet, alas, is known to few.
Thus for awhile the fun the welkin chears,
But foon he hides his head, and melts in dropping tears.

XXV. Life

XXV.

Life is a fcene of conteck and diftrefs,
Ne is it longer than a winter's day ;
And fhall we make our few enjoyments lefs ?
Far from my cot, thou blatant-beaft away.
No hufband's noul will I with horns array,
Ne fhall my tongue its venom'd malice wreak
On tuneful bards, whom laurel crowns apay ;
Ne will I 'gainft the comely matron fpeak,
Or draw one pearly drop down beauty's rofy cheek.

XXVI.

The Squire of Dames rode on with muchel tine,
And, as he caft afkaunce his greedy look,
He faw empight beneath an auncient pine
A hoary fhepherd leaning on his crook ;
His falling tears increas'd the fwelling brook :
And he did figh as he would break his heart.
" O thou deep-read in forrow's baleful book,
" The Squire exclaim'd, areed thy burning fmart ;
" Our dolors grow more light when we the tale impart."

XXVII.

To whom the fwain reply'd, " O gentle youth,
" Yon fruitful meads my num'rous herds poffefs'd,
" My days roll'd on unknown to pain or ruth,
" And one fair daughter my old age yblefs'd.
" Oh,

" Oh, had you feen her for the wake ydrefs'd

" With kirtle ty'd with many a colour'd ftring,

" Thy tongue to all the world had then confefs'd

" That fhe was fheener than the pheafant's wing,

" And, when fhe rais'd her voice, ne lark fo foot could
                              [fing.

XXVIII.

" In virtue's thews I bred the lovely maid,

" And fhe right well the leffons did purfue;

" Too wife fhe was to be by man betray'd;

" But the curft blatant-beaft her form did view,

" And round our plains did fpread a tale untrue,

" That Rofabella, fpurning marriage band,

" Had felt thofe pangs which virgin never knew,

" And that Sir Topas my poor girl trepann'd;

" He, who in fable ftole doth in our pulpit ftand.

XXIX.

" Nay, more, the hellifh monfter has invented,

" How a young fwain on Shannon's banks yborn

" (Had not my care the deep-laid plot prevented)

" Would from my arms my Rofabel have born.

" Have I not caufe to weep from rifing morn

" 'Till Phœbus welketh in the weftern main,

" To fee my dearling's fame thus vildly torn?

" Have I not caufe to nourifh endlefs pain?"

At this he deeply figh'd, and wept full fore again.

XXX. " Curft

XXX.

" Curſt be this blatant-beaſt, reply'd the Squire,

" That thus infeſts your ſea-begirted iſle ;

" Shew me his face, that I may wreak mine ire

" Upon this imp of hell, this monſter vile."

" Away from hence not paſſing ſure a mile,

" Might I advife you, you had better wend,"

Return'd the ſwain, " deep-read in magic-ſtyle

" There Merlin wons, ſue him to be your friend ;

" And left you miſs your way, myſelf will you attend."

XXXI.

Together now they ſeek the hermitage

Deep in the covert of a duſky glade,

Where in his dortour wons the hoary ſage.

The moſs-grown trees did form a gloomy ſhade,

Their ruſtling leaves a ſolemn muſic made,

And fairies nightly tripp'd the aweful green,

And if the tongue of fame have truth diſplay'd,

Full many a ſpeſtre was at midnight ſeen,

Torn from his earthly grave, a horrid ſight! I ween.

XXXII.

Ne roſe, ne vi'let glads the chearleſs bow'r,

Ne fringed pink from earth's green boſom grew.

But hemlock dire, and every baleful flow'r

Might here be found, and knots of myſtic rue.

Clofe to the cell fprong up an auncient yew,
And ftore of imps were on its boughs ypight,
At his behefts they from its branches flew,
And, in a thoufand various forms bedight,
Frifk'd to the moon's pale wain, and revell'd all the night,

XXXIII.

Around the cave a cluft'ring ivy fpread
In wide embrace his over-twining arms,
Within, the walls with characters befpread
Declar'd the pow'rful force of magic charms,
Here drugs were plac'd deftructive of all harms,
And books that deep futurity could fcan:
Here ftood a fpell that of his rage difarms
The mountain lyon 'till he yields to man;
With many fecrets more, which fcarce repeat I can.

XXXIV.

The Squire of Dames deep enters in the cell;
What will not valiant heart for beauty dare?
His borrel fere here bids his friend farewell,
And home he wends renewing cark and care.
When, louting low with a becoming air,
The youth cry'd out, " O thrice renowned mage,
" Vouchfafe to cure me of my black difpair;
" For thou not only art grown wife through age,
" But art of mortal man by far the wifeft fage."

I

XXXV. Then

XXXV.

Then Merlin with a look benign reply'd,
(For he was bred with every courteous thew)'
" I know to make fair Columbel your bride
" The blatant-beaft you through the lond purfue;
" The fate of empires now demands my view,
" And for awhile denys my prefence here;
" Soon in this cell I'll thee again falew,
" What moft thou lik'ft partake withouten fear,
" Share all my cave affords, nor think I grudge my chear.

XXXVI.

" Yet mark my counfel, open not that door,
" Left thou repent thy follies when too late,
" Ten thoufand pangs fhall make thy heart full fore,
" For horror fcouls behind that heben gate,
" And future ills fhall thy dear peace amate;
" There ftands a mirror, wrought by magic leer,
" In which are read the dark decrees of fate,
" And whom you wifh to fee will ftreit appear,
" Devoid of art's falfe mafk, to human eye-fight clear.

XXXVII.

" Ah how unlike the godlike man he feem'd
" In this my glafs the patriot I've defcry'd,
" By the vile rabblement a faint efteem'd?
" He's oft a wretch compos'd of floth and pride:

" And

" And Kefars too, not feldom deify'd,

" With other men their vice and follies fhare ;

" And by my mirror if the nymph be try'd,

" It will without referve the truth declare,

" Ne flatter head that's crown'd, ne flatter face that's fair.

XXXVIII.

" Once more let me advife thee, gentle Squire,

" Forbear to look at this fame magic glafs ;

" Do not too rafhly into fate enquire—

" But I to foreign ftronds awhile muft pafs."

Th' unweeting youth cry'd to himfelf, " Alas !

" Would I could know the lot to me affign'd !"

" Patience, quoth Merlin, doth all things furpafs."

Then to his car were winged dragons join'd,

With which he fails thro' air, and far outftrips the wind.

XXXIX.

And now the Squire furveys the lonefome cave,

His wav'ring mind is in a whirlwind toft,

And now the mirror he refolves to brave,

And now he finds his boafted courage loft.

At length determin'd whatfoe'er it coft,

To fee the glafs, he darts into the cell ;

And, left his eyes by vild retrait be croft,

Thrice he invokes his lovely Columbel.

As Adam fell of yore, the Squire of Dames yfell.

XL. The

XL.

The heben doors full widely he diſplay'd,
And ſaw the lovely queen of all his heart,
Fair as the lilly in the watry glade,
Bright as the morn, and bright withouten art.
Through every vein he feels a thrillant ſmart:
For the dear maid lay on her bed undreſs'd,
And, may I unreprov'd the truth impart,
She hugg'd a luſty ſtripling to her breaſt,
Whom ſhe full cloſely clipp'd, and wantonly careſs'd.

XLI.

" O faytor falſe, O wicked imp of night!
Exclaim'd the Squire aſtound, " ah! wealaway!
" Let Erebus in pitchy ſtole bedight
" With fouleſt ſprites the ſons of men affray,
" And blot for ever the fair face of day.
" Ye haggard ſiſters, found my paſſing-bell;
" Oh! ne'er believe, ye youths, what women ſay.
" O loſel looſe, O impious Columbel!"
Then like a ſtean to earth, full heavily he fell.

XLII.

There ſhall we leave him, for my leaky boat
Lets in the water, and I muſt recure
Her much-worn hulk, that ſcarcely now can float,
And moor'd in harbour ſhe ſhall ride ſecure;

Then

Then if I can a pilot wife procure,

Mayhap I may again hoift forth my fail,

And other hardy voyages endure

Through fhelves and fhallows : now the adverfe gale

Gives me fome time to reft, and lond with joy I hail.

GLOSSARY.

Amail, enamel
Avale, bow
Brond-iron, a fword
Blatant-beaft, detraction or envy
Bufkets, bufhes
Borrel fere, clownifh companion
Crumeual, purfe
Coronal, crown or garland
Fortilage, fort
Flight, arrow

Keftrel, an hawk
Levin-brond, thunder-bolt
Ledden, language
Pannikel, crown of the head
To royne, to bite, or gnaw
Recure, to repair
Sib, an uncle
Springal, a youth
Wimble, fhifting to and fro
Yode, went.

On the DEATH of a Lady's OWL.

By the Same.

THE Owl expires ! death gave the dreadful word,
  And lovely Anna weeps her fav'rite bird.
Ye feather'd choir in willing throngs repair,
And footh the forrows of the melting fair ;

In founds of woe the dear-departed greet,

With cyprefs ftrew, ye doves, the green retreat;

The fateful raven tolls the paffing-bell,

The folemn dirge be fung by Philomel;

Sir Chanticlear, a chief of hardy race,

Shall guard from kites and daws the facred place.

With your juft tears a bard fhall mix his own,

And thus, in artlefs verfe, infcribe the ftone.

E P I T A P H.

INTERR'D within this little fpace
   The bird of wifdom lies ;
Learn hence, how vain is every grace,
   How fruitlefs to be wife.

Can mortal ftop the arm of Death
   Who ne'er compaffion knew ?
He * Venus' lover robb'd of breath,
   He, Anna's darling flew.

Ah happy bird, to raife thofe fighs
   Which man could ne'er obtain !
Ah happy bird, to cloud thofe eyes
   That fir'd each kneeling fwain !

   * Adonis.

L 4

Thrice

Thrice blefs'd thy life, her joy, her blifs,
Thrice blefs'd thy happy doom;
She gave thee many a melting kifs,
She wept upon thy tomb.

The VANITY of HUMAN WISHES.

THE

Tenth Satire of JUVENAL,

IMITATED

By Mr. SAMUEL JOHNSON.

LET * obfervation with extenfive view,
Survey mankind, from China to Peru;
Remark each anxious toil, each eager ftrife,
And watch the bufy fcenes of crowded life;
Then fay how hope and fear, defire and hate,
O'erfpread with fnares the clouded maze of fate,
Where wav'ring man, betray'd by vent'rous pride,
To tread the dreary paths without a guide;

* Ver. 1 — 11.

As

As treach'rous phantoms in the mist delude,
Shuns fancied ills, or chafes airy good.
How rarely reafon guides the ftubborn choice,
Rules the bold hand, or prompts the fuppliant voice,
How nations fink, by darling fchemes opprefs'd,
When vengeance liftens to the fool's requeft.
Fate wings with every wifh th' afflictive dart,
Each gift of nature, and each grace of art,
With fatal heat impetuous courage glows,
With fatal fweetnefs elocution flows,
Impeachment ftops the fpeaker's pow'rful breath,
And reftlefs fire precipitates on death.

   [b] But fcarce obferv'd the knowing and the bold,
Fall in the gen'ral maffacre of gold;
Wide-wafting peft! that rages unconfin'd,
And crowds with crimes the records of mankind;
For gold his fword the hireling ruffian draws,
For gold the hireling judge diftorts the laws;
Wealth heap'd on wealth, nor truth nor fafety buys,
The dangers gather as the treafures rife.

   Let hift'ry tell where rival kings command,
And dubious title fhakes the madded land,
When ftatutes glean the refufe of the fword,
How much more fafe the vaffal than the lord,

[b] Ver. 12—22.

Low

Low sculks the hind beneath the rage of pow'r,
And leaves the wealthy traytor in the Tow'r,
Untouch'd his cottage, and his slumbers found,
Though confiscation's vulturs hover round.

The needy traveller, serene and gay,
Walks the wild heath, and sings his toil away.
Does envy seize thee? crush th' upbraiding joy,
Increase his riches and his peace destroy,
New fears in dire vicissitude invade,
The rustling brake alarms, and quiv'ring shade,
Nor light nor darkness bring his pain relief,
One shews the plunder, and one hides the thief.

Yet ᶜ still one gen'ral cry the skies assails,
And gain and grandeur load the tainted gales;
Few know the toiling statesman's fear or care,
Th' insidious rival and the gaping heir.

Once ᵈ more, Democritus, arise on earth,
With chearful wisdom and instructive mirth,
See motly life in modern trappings dress'd,
And feed with varied fools th' eternal jest:
Thou who couldst laugh where want enchain'd caprice,
Toil crush'd conceit, and man was of a piece;
Where wealth unlov'd without a mourner dy'd;
And scarce a sycophant was fed by pride;

ᶜ Ver. 23 — 27.   ᵈ Ver. 28 — 55.

Where

Where ne'er was known the form of mock debate;
Or feen a new-made mayor's unwieldy ftate ;
Where change of fav'rites made no change of laws,
And fenates heard before they judg'd a caufe ;
How wouldft thou fhake at Britain's modifh tribe,
Dart the quick taunt, and edge the piercing gibe ?
Attentive truth and nature to decry,
And pierce each fcene with philofophic eye.
To thee were folemn toys or empty fhew,
The robes of pleafure and the veils of woe :
All aid the farce, and all thy mirth maintain,
Whofe joys are caufelefs, and whofe griefs are vain.

   Such was the fcorn that fill'd the fage's mind,
Renew'd at every glance on humankind ;
How juft that fcorn ere yet thy voice declare,
Search every ftate, and canvafs every prayer.

   * Unnumber'd fuppliants crowd Preferment's gate,
Athirft for wealth, and burning to be great ;
Delufive Fortune hears th' inceffant call,
They mount, they fhine, evaporate, and fall.
On every ftage the foes of peace attend,
Hate dogs their flight, and infult mocks their end.
Love ends with hope, the finking ftatefman's door
Pours in the morning worfhipper no more ;

    * Ver. 56 — 107.

For

For growing names the weekly fcribbler lies,
To growing wealth the dedicator flies,
From every room defcends the painted face,
That hung the bright Palladium of the place,
And fmoak'd in kitchens, or in auctions fold,
To better features yields the frame of gold;
For now no more we trace in every line
Heroic worth, benevolence divine :
The form diftorted juftifies the fall,
And deteftation rids th' indignant wall.

    But will not Britain hear the laft appeal,
Sign her foes doom, or guard her fav'rites zeal ;
Through Freedom's fons no more remonftrance rings,
Degrading nobles, and controuling kings;
Our fupple tribes reprefs their patriot throats,
And afk no queftions but the price of votes;
With weekly libels and feptennial ale,
Their wifh is full to riot and to rail.

    In full-blown dignity, fee Wolfey ftand,
Law in his voice, and fortune in his hand :
To him the church, the realm, their pow'rs confign;
Through him the rays of regal bounty fhine,
Still to new heights his reftlefs wifhes tow'r,
Claim leads to claim, and pow'r advances pow'r;

'Till

'Till conqueſt unreſiſted ceas'd to pleaſe,
And rights ſubmitted, left him none to ſeize.
At length his ſov'reign frowns — the train of ſtate
Mark the keen glance, and watch the ſign to hate.
Where-e'er he turns he meets a ſtranger's eye,
His ſuppliants ſcorn him, and his followers fly ;
At once is loſt the pride of aweful ſtate,
The golden canopy, the glitt'ring plate,
The regal palace, the luxurious board,
The liv'ried army, and the menial lord.
With age, with cares, with maladies oppreſs'd,
He ſeeks the refuge of monaſtic reſt.
Grief aids diſeaſe, remember'd folly ſtings,
And his laſt ſighs reproach the faith of kings.

   Speak thou, whoſe thoughts at humble peace repine,
Shall Wolſey's wealth, with Wolſey's end be thine?
Or liv'ſt thou now, with ſafer pride content,
The wiſeſt juſtice on the banks of Trent?
For why did Wolſey near the ſteeps of fate,
On weak foundations raiſe th' enormous weight?
Why but to ſink beneath Misfortune's blow,
With louder ruin to the gulphs below?

   What [f] gave great Villiers to th' aſſaſſin's knife,
And fix'd diſeaſe on Harley's cloſing life?

[f] Ver. 108 — 113.

                        What

What murder'd Wentworth, and what exil'd Hyde,
By kings protected, and to kings ally'd?
What but their wish indulg'd in courts to shine,
And pow'r too great to keep, or to resign?

When [g] first the college rolls receive his name,
The young enthusiast quits his ease for fame;
Through all his veins the fever of renown
Spreads from the strong contagion of the gown;
O'er Bodley's dome his future labours spread,
And [h] Bacon's manfion trembles o'er his head.
Are these thy views? proceed, illustrious youth,
And Virtue guard thee to the throne of Truth!
Yet should thy soul indulge the gen'rous heat,
'Till captive Science yields her last retreat,
Should Reason guide thee with her brightest ray,
And pour on misty Doubt resistless day;
Should no false Kindness lure to loose delight,
Nor Praise relax, nor Difficulty fright;
Should tempting Novelty thy cell refrain,
And Sloth effuse her opiate fumes in vain;
Should Beauty blunt on fops her fatal dart,
Nor claim the triumph of a letter'd heart;

[g] Ver. 114 — 132.
[h] There is a tradition, that the study of friar Bacon, built on
an arch over the bridge, will fall, when a man greater than Bacon
shall pass under it.

Should

Should no Difeafe thy torpid veins invade,
Nor Melancholy's phantoms haunt thy fhade;
Yet hope not life from grief or danger free,
Nor think the doom of man revers'd for thee:
Deign on the paffing world to turn thine eyes,
And paufe awhile from letters, to be wife;
There mark what ills the fcholar's life affail,
Toil, envy, want, the patron, and the jail.
See nations flowly wife, and meanly juft,
To buried merit raife the tardy buft.
If dreams yet flatter, once again attend,
Hear Lydiat's life, and Galileo's end.

    Nor deem, when Learning her laft prize beftows,
The glitt'ring eminence exempt from woes;
See when the vulgar 'fcape, defpis'd or aw'd,
Rebellion's vengeful talons feize on Laud.
From meaner minds, though fmaller fines content
The plunder'd palace or fequefter'd rent;
Mark'd out by dangerous parts he meets the fhock;
And fatal Learning leads him to the block:
Around his tomb let Art and Genius weep,
But hear his death, ye blockheads, hear and fleep.

    The [1] feftal blazes, the triumphal fhow,
The ravifh'd ftandard, and the captive foe,

---

[1] Ver. 133 — 146.

The

The fenate's thanks, the gazette's pompous tale,
With force refiftlefs o'er the brave prevail.
Such bribes the rapid Greek o'er Afia whirl'd,
For fuch the fteady Romans fhook the world;
For fuch in diftant lands the Britons fhine,
And ftain with blood the Danube or the Rhine;
This pow'r has praife, that virtue fcarce can warm,
'Till fame fupplies the univerfal charm.
Yet Reafon frowns on War's unequal game,
Where wafted nations raife a fingle name,
And mortgag'd ftates their grandfires wreaths regret,
From age to age in everlafting debt;
Wreaths which at laft the dear-bought right convey
To ruft on medals, or on ftones decay.

On [k] what foundation ftands the warrior's pride,
How juft his hopes let Swedifh Charles decide;
A frame of adamant, a foul of fire,
No dangers fright him, and no labours tire;
O'er love, o'er fear extends his wide domain,
Unconquer'd lord of pleafure and of pain;
No joys to him pacific fcepters yield,
War founds the trump, he rufhes to the field;
Behold furrounding kings their pow'r combine,
And one capitulate, and one refign;

[k] Ver. 147 — 167.

Peace

Peace courts his hand, but fpreads her charms in vain;

" Think nothing gain'd, he cries, 'till nought remain,

" On Mofcow's walls 'till Gothic ftandards fly,

" And all be mine beneath the polar fky."

The march begins in military ftate,

And nations on his eye fufpended wait;

Stern Famine guards the folitary coaft,

And Winter barricades the realm of Froft;

He comes, not want and cold his courfe delay; —

Hide, blufhing Glory, hide Pultowa's day:

The vanquifh'd hero leaves his broken bands,

And fhews his miferies in diftant lands;

Condemn'd a needy fupplicant to wait,

While ladies interpofe, and flaves debate.

But did not Chance at length her error mend?

Did no fubverted empire mark his end?

Did rival monarchs give the fatal wound?

Or hoftile millions prefs him to the ground?

His fall was deftin'd to a barren ftrand,

A petty fortrefs, and a dubious hand;

He left the name, at which the world grew pale,

To point a moral, or adorn a tale.

All[1] times their fcenes of pompous woes afford,

From Perfia's tyrant to Bavaria's lord.

[1] Ver, 168 — 187.

In gay hoftility, and barb'rous pride,
With half mankind embattled at his fide,
Great Xerxes comes to feize the certain prey,
And ftarves exhaufted regions in his way;
Attendant Flatt'ry counts his myriads o'er,
'Till counted myriads footh his pride no more;
Frefh praife is try'd 'till madnefs fires his mind,
The waves he lafhes, and enchains the wind;
New pow'rs are claim'd, new pow'rs are ftill beftow'd,
'Till rude refiftance lops the fpreading god;
The daring Greeks deride the martial fhow,
And heap their vallies with the gaudy foe;
Th' infulted fea with humbler thoughts he gains,
A fingle fkiff to fpeed his flight remains;
Th' incumber'd oar fcarce leaves the dreaded coaft
Through purple billows and a floating hoft.

The bold Bavarian, in a lucklefs hour,
Tries the dread fummits of Cefarean pow'r,
With unexpected legions burfts away,
And fees defencelefs realms receive his fway;
Short fway! fair Auftria fpreads her mournful charms,
The queen, the beauty, fets the world in arms;
From hill to hill the beacons roufing blaze
Spreads wide the hope of plunder and of praife;

The fierce Croatian, and the wild Huffar,
And all the fons of ravage crowd the war ;
The baffled prince in honour's flatt'ring bloom
Of hafty greatnefs finds the fatal doom,
His foes derifion, and his fubjects blame,
And fteals to death from anguifh and from fhame.

   Enlarge * my life with multitude of days,
In health, in ficknefs, thus the fuppliant prays ;
Hides from himfelf his ftate, and fhuns to know,
That life protracted is protracted woe.
Time hovers o'er, impatient to deftroy,
And fhuts up all the paffages of joy :
In vain their gifts the bounteous feafons pour,
The fruit autumnal, and the vernal flow'r,
With liftlefs eyes the dotard views the ftore,
He views, and wonders that they pleafe no more ;
Now pall the taftelefs meats, and joylefs wines,
And Luxury with fighs her flave refigns.
Approach, ye minftrels, try the foothing ftrain,
And yield the tuneful lenitives of pain :
No founds, alas ! would touch th' impervious ear,
Though dancing mountains witnefs Orpheus near,
Nor lute nor lyre his feeble pow'rs attend,
Nor fweeter mufic of a virtuous friend,

^m Ver. 188 — 288.

M 2

But

But everlasting dictates crowd his tongue,
Perversely grave or positively wrong.
The still returning tale, and ling'ring jest,
Perplex the fawning niece and pamper'd guest,
While growing hopes scarce awe the gath'ring sneer,
And scarce a legacy can bribe to hear;
The watchful guests still hint the last offence,
The daughter's petulance, the son's expence,
Improve his heady rage with treach'rous skill,
And mould his passions 'till they make his will.

Unnumber'd maladies his joints invade,
Lay siege to life and press the dire blockade;
But unextinguish'd Av'rice still remains,
And dreaded losses aggravate his pains;
He turns, with anxious heart and crippled hands,
His bonds of debt, and mortgages of lands;
Or views his coffers with suspicious eyes,
Unlocks his gold, and counts it 'till he dies.

But grant, the virtues of a temp'rate prime
Bless with an age exempt from scorn or crime;
An age that melts in unperceiv'd decay,
And glides in modest innocence away;
Whose peaceful day Benevolence endears,
Whose night congratulating Conscience chears;

The

The gen'ral fav'rite, as the gen'ral friend;
Such age there is, and who could wish its end?
   Yet ev'n on this her load Misfortune flings,
To prefs the weary minutes flagging wings:
New forrow rifes as the day returns,
A fifter fickens, or a daughter mourns.
Now kindred Merit fills the fable bier,
Now lacerated friendfhip claims a tear.
Year chafes year, decay purfues decay,
Still drops fome joy from with'ring life away;
New forms arife, and diff'rent views engage,
Superfluous lags the vet'ran on the ftage,
'Till pitying Nature figns the laft releafe,
And bids afflicted worth retire to peace.
   But few there are whom hours like thefe await,
Who fet unclouded in the gulphs of Fate.
From Lydia's monarch fhould the fearch defcend,
By Solon caution'd to regard his end,
In life's laft fcene what prodigies furprife,
Fears of the brave, and follies of the wife?
From Marlb'rough's eyes the ftreams of dotage flow,
And Swift expires a driv'ler and a fhow.
   The [n] teeming mother, anxious for her race,
Begs for each birth the fortune of a face:

[n] Ver. 289 — 345.

Yet

Yet Vane could tell what ills from beauty fprings,
And Sedley curs'd the form that pleas'd a king.
Ye nymphs of rofy lips and radiant eyes,
Whom Pleafure keeps too bufy to be wife,
Whom Joys with foft varieties invite,
By day the frolic, and the dance by night,
Who frown with vanity, who fmile with art,
And afk the latent fafhion of the heart,
What care, what rules your heedlefs charms fhall fave,
Each nymph your rival, and each youth your flave?
Againft your fame with fondnefs hate combines,
The rival batters, and the lover mines.
With diftant voice neglected Virtue calls,
Lefs heard and lefs, the faint remonftrance falls;
Tir'd with contempt, fhe quits the flipp'ry reign,
And Pride and Prudence take her feat in vain.
In crowd at once, where none the pafs defend,
The harmlefs Freedom, and the private Friend.
The guardians yield, by force fuperior ply'd;
By Int'reft, Prudence; and by Flatt'ry, Pride.
Now beauty falls betray'd, defpis'd, diftrefs'd,
And hiffing Infamy proclaims the reft.

Where ° then fhall Hope and Fear their objects find?
Muft dull Sufpence corrupt the ftagnant mind?

° Ver. 346 — 366.

Muft

Muſt helpleſs man, in ignorance ſedate,
Roll darkling down the torrent of his fate?
Muſt no diſlike alarm, no wiſhes riſe,
No cries attempt the mercies of the ſkies?
·Enquirer, ceaſe, petitions yet remain,
Which heav'n may hear, nor deem religion vain.
Still raiſe for good the ſupplicating voice,
But leave to heav'n the meaſure and the choice.
Safe in his pow'r, whoſe eyes diſcern afar
The ſecret ambuſh of a ſpecious pray'r.
Implore his aid, in his deciſions reſt,
Secure whate'er he gives, he gives the beſt.
Yet when the ſenſe of ſacred preſence fires,
And ſtrong devotion to the ſkies aſpires,
Pour forth thy fervours for a healthful mind,
Obedient paſſions, and a will reſign'd;
For love, which ſcarce collective man can fill;
For patience, ſov'reign o'er tranſmuted ill;
For faith, that panting for a happier ſeat,
Counts death kind Nature's ſignal to retreat:
Theſe goods for man the laws of heav'n ordain,
Theſe goods he grants, who grants the pow'r to gain;
With theſe celeſtial Wiſdom calms the mind,
And makes the happineſs ſhe does not find.

THE

In gay hoftility, and barb'rous pride,
With half mankind embattled at his fide,
Great Xerxes comes to feize the certain prey,
And ftarves exhaufted regions in his way ;
Attendant Flatt'ry counts his myriads o'er,
'Till counted myriads footh his pride no more ;
Frefh praife is try'd 'till madnefs fires his mind,
The waves he lafhes, and enchains the wind ;
New pow'rs are claim'd, new pow'rs are ftill beftow'd,
'Till rude refiftance lops the fpreading god ;
The daring Greeks deride the martial fhow,
And heap their vallies with the gaudy foe ;
Th' infulted fea with humbler thoughts he gains,
A fingle fkiff to fpeed his flight remains ;
Th' incumber'd oar fcarce leaves the dreaded coaft
Through purple billows and a floating hoft.

The bold Bavarian, in a lucklefs hour,
Tries the dread fummits of Cefarean pow'r,
With unexpected legions burfts away,
And fees defencelefs realms receive his fway ;
Short fway ! fair Auftria fpreads her mournful charms,
The queen, the beauty, fets the world in arms ;
From hill to hill the beacons roufing blaze
Spreads wide the hope of plunder and of praife ;

Vain hope! no more in choral bands unite
   Her virgin vot'ries, and at early dawn,
Sacred to May and Love's myfterious rite,
   Brufh the light dew-drops * from the fpangled lawn.

To her no more Augufta's [b] wealthy pride
   Pour's the full tribute from Potofi's mine ;
Nor frefh-blown garlands village maids provide,
   A purer off'ring, at her ruftic fhrine.

No more the Maypole's verdant height around
   To Valour's games th' ambitious youth advance ;
No merry bells and tabors' fprightlier found
   Wake the loud carol, and the fportive dance.

Sudden in penfive fadnefs droop'd her head,
   Faint on her cheeks the blufhing crimfon dy'd—
" O! chafte victorious triumphs, whither fled ?
   " My maiden honours, whither gone ?" fhe cry'd.

Ah! once to fame and bright dominion born,
   The Earth and fmiling Ocean faw me rife,
With time coeval and the ftar of morn,
   The firft, the faireft daughter of the fkies.

* Alluding to the country cuftom of gathering May-dew.
[b] The plate garlands of London.

Then,

But everlafting dictates crowd his tongue,
Perverfely grave or pofitively wrong.
The ftill returning tale, and ling'ring jeft,
Perplex the fawning niece and pamper'd gueft,
While growing hopes fcarce awe the gath'ring fneer,
And fcarce a legacy can bribe to hear;
The watchful guefts ftill hint the laft offence,
The daughter's petulance, the fon's expence,
Improve his heady rage with treach'rous fkill,
And mould his paffions 'till they make his will.

Unnumber'd maladies his joints invade,
Lay fiege to life and prefs the dire blockade;
But unextinguifh'd Av'rice ftill remains,
And dreaded loffes aggravate his pains;
He turns, with anxious heart and crippled hands,
His bonds of debt, and mortgages of lands;
Or views his coffers with fufpicious eyes,
Unlocks his gold, and counts it 'till he dies.

But grant, the virtues of a temp'rate prime
Blefs with an age exempt from fcorn or crime;
An age that melts in unperceiv'd decay,
And glides in modeft innocence away;
Whofe peaceful day Benevolence endears,
Whofe night congratulating Confcience chears;

The

The gen'ral fav'rite, as the gen'ral friend;
Such age there is, and who could wifh its end?

Yet ev'n on this her load Misfortune flings,
To prefs the weary minutes flagging wings:
New forrow rifes as the day returns,
A fifter fickens, or a daughter mourns.
Now kindred Merit fills the fable bier,
Now lacerated friendfhip claims a tear.
Year chafes year, decay purfues decay,
Still drops fome joy from with'ring life away;
New forms arife, and diff'rent views engage,
Superfluous lags the vet'ran on the ftage,
'Till pitying Nature figns the laft releafe,
And bids afflicted worth retire to peace.

But few there are whom hours like thefe await,
Who fet unclouded in the gulphs of Fate.
From Lydia's monarch fhould the fearch defcend,
By Solon caution'd to regard his end,
In life's laft fcene what prodigies furprife,
Fears of the brave, and follies of the wife?
From Marlb'rough's eyes the ftreams of dotage flow,
And Swift expires a driv'ler and a fhow.

The [n] teeming mother, anxious for her race,
Begs for each birth the fortune of a face:

[n] Ver. 289—345.

M 3

Yet

Yet Vane could tell what ills from beauty fprings,
And Sedley curs'd the form that pleas'd a king.
Ye nymphs of rofy lips and radiant eyes,
Whom Pleafure keeps too bufy to be wife,
Whom Joys with foft varieties invite,
By day the frolic, and the dance by night,
Who frown with vanity, who fmile with art,
And afk the latent fafhion of the heart,
What care, what rules your heedlefs charms fhall fave,
Each nymph your rival, and each youth your flave?
Againft your fame with fondnefs hate combines,
The rival batters, and the lover mines.
With diftant voice neglected Virtue calls,
Lefs heard and lefs, the faint remonftrance falls;
Tir'd with contempt, fhe quits the flipp'ry reign,
And Pride and Prudence take her feat in vain.
In crowd at once, where none the pafs defend,
The harmlefs Freedom, and the private Friend.
The guardians yield, by force fuperior ply'd;
By Int'reft, Prudence; and by Flatt'ry, Pride.
Now beauty falls betray'd, defpis'd, diftrefs'd,
And hiffing Infamy proclaims the reft.

Where ° then fhall Hope and Fear their objects find?
Muft dull Sufpence corrupt the ftagnant mind?

° Ver. 346 — 366.

Muft

Muſt helpleſs man, in ignorance ſedate,
Roll darkling down the torrent of his fate?
Muſt no diſlike alarm, no wiſhes riſe,
No cries attempt the mercies of the ſkies?
Enquirer, ceaſe, petitions yet remain,
Which heav'n may hear, nor deem religion vain.
Still raiſe for good the ſupplicating voice,
But leave to heav'n the meaſure and the choice.
Safe in his pow'r, whoſe eyes diſcern afar
The ſecret ambuſh of a ſpecious pray'r.
Implore his aid, in his deciſions reſt,
Secure whate'er he gives, he gives the beſt.
Yet when the ſenſe of ſacred preſence fires,
And ſtrong devotion to the ſkies aſpires,
Pour forth thy fervours for a healthful mind,
Obedient paſſions, and a will reſign'd;
For love, which ſcarce collective man can fill;
For patience, ſov'reign o'er tranſmuted ill;
For faith, that panting for a happier ſeat,
Counts death kind Nature's ſignal to retreat:
Theſe goods for man the laws of heav'n ordain,
Theſe goods he grants, who grants the pow'r to gain;
With theſe celeſtial Wiſdom calms the mind,
And makes the happineſs ſhe does not find.

THE

The TEARS of OLD MAY-DAY.

LED by the jocund train of vernal hours
    And vernal airs, uprofe the gentle May;
Blufhing fhe rofe, and blufhing rofe the flow'rs
    That fprung fpontaneous in the genial ray.

Her locks with heav'n's ambrofial dews were bright,
    And am'rous zephyrs flutter'd on her breaft:
With every fhifting gleam of morning light
    The colours fhifted of her rainbow veft.

Imperial enfigns grac'd her fmiling form,
    A golden key, and golden wand fhe bore;
This charms to peace each fullen eaftern ftorm,
    And that unlocks the Summer's copious ftore.

Onward in confcious majefty fhe came,
    The grateful honours of mankind to tafte;
To gather faireft wreaths of future fame,
    And blend frefh triumphs with her glories paft.

Vain

Vain hope! no more in choral bands unite
   Her virgin vot'ries, and at early dawn,
Sacred to May and Love's myſterious rite,
   Bruſh the light dew-drops * from the ſpangled lawn.

To her no more Auguſta's ᵇ wealthy pride
   Pour's the full tribute from Potoſi's mine ;
Nor freſh-blown garlands village maids provide,
   A purer off'ring, at her ruſtic ſhrine.

No more the Maypole's verdant height around
   To Valour's games th' ambitious youth advance :
No merry bells and tabors' ſprightlier ſound
   Wake the loud carol, and the ſportive dance.

Sudden in penſive ſadneſs droop'd her head,
   Faint on her cheeks the bluſhing crimſon dy'd—
" O! chaſte victorious triumphs, whither fled ?
   " My maiden honours, whither gone ?" ſhe cry'd.

Ah! once to fame and bright dominion born,
   The Earth and ſmiling Ocean ſaw me riſe,
With time coeval and the ſtar of morn,
   The firſt, the faireſt daughter of the ſkies.

---

* Alluding to the country cuſtom of gathering May-dew.
ᵇ The plate garlands of London.

Then,

But chief in Europe, and in Europe's pride,
    My Albion's favour'd realms, I rofe ador'd;
And pour'd my wealth to other climes deny'd,
    From Amalthea's horn with plenty ftor'd.

Ah me! for now a younger rival claims
    My ravifh'd honours, and to her belong
My choral dances, and victorious games,
    To her my garlands and triumphal fong.

O fay what yet untafted bounties flow,
    What purer joys await her gentle reign?
Do lillies fairer, vi'lets fweeter blow?
    And warbles Philomel a fofter ftrain?

Do morning funs in ruddier glory rife?
    Does ev'ning fan her with ferener gales?
Do clouds drop fatnefs from the wealthier fkies?
    Or wantons Plenty in her happier vales?

Ah! no: the blunted beams of dawning light
    Skirt the pale orient with uncertain day;
And Cynthia, riding on the car of night,
    Through clouds embattled faintly wins her way.

III.

Praife him, ye blefs'd ætherial plains,
Where, in full majefty, he deigns
   To fix his aweful throne :
Ye waters, that above him roll,
From orb to orb, from pole to pole,
   Oh! make his praifes known!

IV.

Ye thrones, dominions, virtues, pow'rs,
Join ye your joyful fongs with ours,
   With us your voices raife ;
From age to age extend the lay,
To heav'n's eternal Monarch pay
   Hymns of eternal praife.

V.

Cœleftial orb! — whofe pow'rful ray
Opes the glad eyelids of the day,
   Whofe influence all things own ;
Praife him, whofe courts effulgent fhine
With light, as far excelling thine,
   As thine the paler moon.

VI.

Ye glitt'ring planets of the fky,
Whofe lamps the abfent fun fupply,
   With him the fong purfue ;

Or hafte to northern Zembla's favage coaft,
  There hufh to filence elemental ftrife;
Brood o'er the region of eternal Froft,
  And fwell her barren womb with heat and life.

Then Britain — here fhe ceas'd. Indignant grief,
  And parting pangs her fault'ring tongue fuppreft;
Veil'd in an amber cloud, fhe fought relief,
  And tears, and filent anguifh told the reft.

SONG for RANELAGH.

By Mr. W. WHITEHEAD.

I.

Y E belles, and ye flirts, and ye pert little things,
    Who trip in this frolicfome round,
Pray tell me from whence this indecency fprings,
  The fexes at once to confound:
What means the cock'd hat, and the mafculine air,
  With each motion defign'd to perplex?
Bright eyes were intended to languifh, not ftare,
  And foftnefs the teft of your fex.

II. The

II.

The girl who on beauty depends for fupport,
   May call every art to her aid:
The bofom difplay'd, and the petticoat fhort,
   Are famples fhe gives of her trade.
But you, on whom Fortune indulgently fmiles,
   And whom Pride has preferv'd from the fnare;
Should flily attack us with coynefs and wiles,
   Not with open and infolent air.

III.

The Venus whofe ftatue delights all mankind,
   Shrinks modeftly back from the view,
And kindly fhould feem by the artift defign'd
   To ferve as a model for you.
Then learn with her beauties to copy her air,
   Nor venture too much to reveal;
Our fancies will paint what you cover with care,
   And double each charm you conceal.

IV.

The blufhes of Morn, and the mildnefs of May,
   Are charms which no art can procure;
O! be but yourfelves, and our homage we pay,
   And your empire is folid and fure.

But

But if Amazon-like you attack your gallants,
  And put us in fear of our lives,
You may do very well for fifters and aunts,
  But believe me, you'll never be wives.

The BENEDICITE Paraphrafed.

By the Rev. Mr. MERRICK.

I.

YE works of God, on him alone,
  In earth his footftool, heaven his throne,
Be all your praife beftow'd;
Whofe hand the beauteous fabric made,
Whofe eye the finifh'd work furvey'd,
  And faw that all was good.

II.

Ye angels, that with loud acclaim
Admiring view'd the new-born frame,
  And hail'd th' eternal King;
Again proclaim your Maker's praife,
Again your thankful voices raife,
  And touch the tuneful ftring.

III. Praife

III.

Praise him, ye bless'd ætherial plains,
Where, in full majesty, he deigns
　To fix his aweful throne :
Ye waters, that above him roll,
From orb to orb, from pole to pole,
　Oh ! make his praises known !

IV.

Ye thrones, dominions, virtues, pow'rs,
Join ye your joyful songs with ours,
　With us your voices raise ;
From age to age extend the lay,
To heav'n's eternal Monarch pay
　Hymns of eternal praise.

V.

Cœleftial orb ! — whofe pow'rful ray
Opes the glad eyelids of the day,
　Whofe influence all things own ;
Praife him, whofe courts effulgent fhine
With light, as far excelling thine,
　As thine the paler moon.

VI.

Ye glitt'ring planets of the fky,
Whofe lamps the abfent fun fupply,
　With him the fong purfue ;

And let himfelf fubmiffive own,
He borrows from a brighter Sun,
 The light he lends to you.

VII.

Ye fhow'rs, and dews, whofe moifture fhed,
Calls into life the op'ning feed,
 To him your praifes yield;
Whofe influence wakes the genial birth,
Drops fatnefs on the pregnant earth,
 And crowns the laughing field.

VIII.

Ye winds, that oft tempeftuous fweep
The ruffled furface of the deep,
 With us confefs your God;
See, through the heav'ns, the King of kings,
Up-borne on your expanded wings,
 Comes flying all abroad.

IX.

Ye floods of fire, where-e'er ye flow,
With juft fubmiffion humbly bow
 To his fuperior pow'r;
Who ftops the tempeft on its way,
Or bids the flaming deluge ftray,
 And gives it ftrength to roar.

X. Ye

X.

Ye fummer's heat, and winter's cold,
By turns in long fucceffion roll'd,
   The drooping world to chear ;
Praife him, who gave the fun and moon,
To lead the various feafons on,
   And guide the circling year.

XI.

Ye frofts, that bind the wat'ry plain,
Ye filent fhow'rs of fleecy rain,
   Purfue the heav'nly theme ;
Praife him, who fheds the driving fnow,
Forbids the harden'd waves to flow,
   And ftops the rapid ftream.

XII.

Ye days and nights, that fwiftly born,
From morn to eve, from eve to morn,
   Alternate glide away ;
Praife him, whofe never-varying light,
Abfent, adds horror to the night,
   But prefent gives the day.

XIII.

Light, — from whofe rays all beauty fprings,
Darknefs, — whofe wide-expanded wings
   Involve the dufky globe ;

          Praife

Praife him, by whom ye all are fed,
Praife him, without whofe heav'nly aid
  Ye languifh, faint, and die.

XXI.

Ye birds, exalt your Maker's name,
Begin, and with th' important theme
  Your artlefs lays improve;
Wake with your fongs the rifing day,
Let mufic found on every fpray,
  And fill the vocal grove.

XXII.

Praife him, ye beafts, that nightly roam,
Amid the folitary gloom,
  Th' expected prey to feize;
Ye flaves of the laborious plough,
Your ftubborn necks fubmiffive bow,
  And bend your weary'd knees.

XXIII.

Ye fons of men, his praife difplay,
Who ftampt his image on your clay,
  And gave it pow'r to move;
Ye, that in Judah's confines dwell,
From age to age fucceffive tell
  The wonders of his love.

XXIV. Let

XXIV.

Let Levi's tribe the lay prolong,
'Till angels listen to the song,
  And bend attentive down;
Let wonder seize the heav'nly train,
Pleas'd, while they hear a mortal strain,
  So sweet, so like their own.

XXV.

And you, your thankful voices join,
That oft at Salem's sacred shrine
  Before his altars kneel;
Where, throned in majesty he dwells,
And from the mystic cloud reveals
  The dictates of his will.

XXVI.

Ye spirits of the just and good,
That, eager for the blest abode,
  To heav'nly mansions soar:
O! let your songs his praise display,
'Till heav'n itself shall melt away,
  And time shall be no more.

XXVII.

Praise him, ye meek and humble train,
Ye saints, whom his decrees ordain
  The boundless bliss to share;

O! praise

And while my outward senses sleep,
Loft in contemplation deep,
Sudden I ftop, and turn my ear,
And lift'ning hear, or think I hear.
Firft a dead and fullen found
Walks along the holy ground;
Then through the gloom alternate breaks
Groans, and the fhrill fcreech-owl's fhriek.
Lo! the moon hath hid her head,
And the graves give up their dead:
By me pafs the ghaftly crowds,
Wrapt in vifionary fhrouds;
Maids, who died with love forlorn,
Youths, who fell by maidens' fcorn,
Helplefs fires, and matrons old
Slain for fordid thirft of gold,
And babes, who owe their fhorten'd date
To cruel ftep-dames ruthlefs hate;
Each their fev'ral errands go,
To haunt the wretch that wrought their woe:
From their fight the caitiff flies,
And his heart within him dies;
While a horror damp and chill
Through his frozen blood doth thrill,

And

And his hair for very dread
Bears itself upon his head,
When the early breath of day
Hath made the shadows flee away;
Still possess'd by thee I rove
Bosom'd in the shelt'ring grove,
There, with heart and lyre new strung,
Meditate the lofty song.
And if thou my voice inspire,
And with wonted frenzy fire,
Aided by thee I build the rhyme
Such, as nor the flight of time,
Nor wasting flame, nor eating show'r,
Nor light'ning's blast can e'er devour.
Or if chance some moral page
My attentive thoughts engage,
On I walk, with silent tread,
Under the thick-woven shade,
While the thrush, unheeded by,
Tunes her artless minstrelsy.
Lift'ning to their sacred lore,
I think on ages long past o'er,
When Truth and Virtue hand in hand
Walk'd upon the smiling land.

Thence

Thence my eyes on Britain glance,
And, awaken'd from my trance,
While my busy thoughts I rear,
Oft I wipe the falling tear.
When the night again descends
And her shadowy cone extends,
O'er the fields I walk alone,
By the silence of the moon.
Hark! upon my left I hear
Wild music wand'ring in the air;
Led by the sound I onward creep,
And through the neighb'ring hedge I peep;
There I spy the Fairy band
Dancing on the level land,
Now with step alternate bound,
Join'd in one continu'd round;
Now their plighted hands unbind,
And such tangled mazes wind
As the quick eye can scarce pursue,
And would have puzzled that fam'd clue,
Which led th' Athenian's unskill'd feet
Through the Labyrinth of Crete.
At the near approach of day,
Sudden the music dies away,

Wafting

Wafting in the fea of air,
And the phantoms difappear,
All (as the glow-worm waxes dim)
Vanifh like a morning dream,
And of their revels leave no trace,
Save the ring upon the grafs.
When the elfin fhow is fled,
Home I hafte me to my bed;
There, if thou with magic wand
On my temples take thy ftand,
I fee in mix'd diforder rife
All that ftruck my waking eyes;
So when I ftand, and round me gaze,
Where the fam'd Lodona ftrays,
On the woods and thickets brown,
That its fedgy margin crown,
And watch the vagrant clouds that fly
Through the vaft defart of the fky,
When adown I caft my look
On the fmooth unruffled brook,
(While its current clear doth run,
And holds its mirrour to the fun,)
There I fee th' inverted fcene
Fall, and meet the eye again,

✕✕✕✕✕✕✕✕✕✕✕✕✕✕✕✕ ✕ ✕✕✕✕✕✕✕✕✕✕✕✕✕✕✕✕

The MONKIES, a TALE.

By the Same.

WHOE'ER with curious eye has rang'd
 Through Ovid's tales, has seen
How Jove, incens'd, to monkies chang'd
 A tribe of worthless men.

Repentant foon th' offending race
 Intreat the injur'd pow'r,
To give them back the human face,
 And reason's aid reftore.

Jove, footh'd at length, his ear inclin'd,
 And granted half their pray'r;
But t' other half he bade the wind
 Difperfe in empty air.

Scarce had the thund'rer giv'n the nod
 That fhook the vaulted fkies,
With haughtier air the creatures ftrode,
 And ftretch'd their dwindled fize.

The

The hair in curls, luxuriant now,
    Around their temples spread ;
The tail that whilom hung below,
    Now dangled from the head.

The head remains unchang'd within,
    Nor alter'd much the face ;
It still retains its native grin,
    And all its old grimace.

Thus half transform'd and half the same,
    Jove bade them take their place,
(Restoring them their ancient claim)
    Among the human race.

Man with contempt the brute survey'd,
    Nor would a name bestow ;
But woman lik'd the motley breed,
    And call'd the thing a Beau.

An

✖✖✖✖✖✖✖✖✖✖✖✖✖✖✖✖✖✖✖✖✖✖✖✖✖✖✖✖

The MONKIES, a TALE.

By the Same.

WHOE'ER with curious eye has rang'd
    Through Ovid's tales, has seen
How Jove, incens'd, to monkies chang'd
    A tribe of worthless men.

Repentant soon th' offending race
    Intreat the injur'd pow'r,
To give them back the human face,
    And reason's aid restore.

Jove, sooth'd at length, his ear inclin'd,
    And granted half their pray'r;
But t' other half he bade the wind
    Disperse in empty air.

Scarce had the thund'rer giv'n the nod
    That shook the vaulted skies,
With haughtier air the creatures strode,
    And stretch'd their dwindled size.

                  The

The hair in curls, luxuriant now,
  Around their temples fpread ;
The tail that whilom hung below,
  Now dangled from the head.

The head remains unchang'd within,
  Nor alter'd much the face ;
It ftill retains its native grin,
  And all its old grimace.

Thus half transform'd and half the fame,
  Jove bade them take their place,
(Reftoring them their ancient claim)
  Among the human race.

Man with contempt the brute furvey'd,
  Nor would a name beftow ;
But woman lik'd the motley breed,
  And call'd the thing a Beau.

An E P I T A P H.

QUÆ te fub tenerâ rapuerunt, Pæta, juventâ,
　　O utinam me crudelia fata vocent;
Ut linquam terras invifaque lumina folis,
　Utque tuus rurfum corpore fim pofito.
Tu cave Lethæo contingas ora liquore,
　Et ciò venturi fis memor, oro, viri.
Te fequar obfcurum per iter: dux ibit eunti
　Fidus amor, tenebras lampade difcutiens.

Thus TRANSLATED.

THEE, Pæta, death's relentlefs hand
　　Cut off in earlieft bloom,
Oh! had the fates for me ordain'd
　To fhare an equal doom;

With joy this bufy world I'd leave,
　This hated light refign,
To lay me in the peaceful grave,
　And be for ever thine:

For fure my Pollio and Mæcenas
Were as good ftatefmen, Mr. Dean, as
Either your Bolingbroke or Harley,
Though they made Lewis beg a parley:
And as for Mordaunt, your lov'd hero,
I'll match him with my Drufus Nero.
You'll boaft perhaps your fav'rite Pope,
But Virgil is as good I hope.
I own indeed I can't get any
To equal Helfham and Delany;
Since, Athens brought forth Socrates,
A Grecian ifle Hippocrates;
Since, Tully liv'd before my time,
And Galen blefs'd another clime.

 You'll plead perhaps to my requeft,
To be admitted as a gueft,
Your hearing's bad — but why fuch fears?
I fpeak to eyes, and not to ears;
And for that reafon, wifely took
The form you fee me in, a book.
Attack'd, by flow-devouring moths,
By rage of barb'rous Huns and Goths;
By Bentley's notes, my deadlieft foes,
By Creech's rhimes and Dunfter's profe;

I found

I found my boasted wit and fire
In their rude hands almost expire;
Yet still they but in vain affail'd,
For had their violence prevail'd,
And in a blast deftroy'd my fame,
They would have partly mifs'd their aim;
Since all my fpirit in thy page
Defies the Vandals of this age.
'Tis yours to fave thefe fmall remains
From future pedants muddy brains,
And fix my long-uncertain fate,
You beft know how,—which way ?—tranflate.

XXXXXXXXXXXXXXXXXXXXXXXXXXXXXX

VERSES written in a GARDEN.

By Lady M. W. M.

SEE how that pair of billing doves
With open murmurs own their loves;
And heedlefs of cenforious eyes,
Purfue their unpolluted joys:
No fears of future want moleft
The downy quiet of their neft;

No int'reft join'd the happy pair,
Securely bleft in Nature's care,
While her dear dictates they purfue:
For conftancy is nature too.

    Can all the doctrine of our fchools,
Our maxims, our religious rules,
Can learning to our lives enfure
Virtue fo bright, or blifs fo pure?
The great Creator's happy ends,
Virtue and pleafure ever blends:
In vain the church and court have try'd
Th' united effence to divide;
Alike they find their wild miftake,
The pedant prieft, and giddy rake.

XXXXXXXXXXXXXXX*XXXXXXXXXXXXXX

An ANSWER to a LOVE-LETTER.

By the Same.

IS it to me, this fad lamenting ftrain:
Are heaven's choiceft gifts beftow'd in vain?
A plenteous fortune, and a beauteous bride,
Your love rewarded, gratify'd your pride:

Yet

Yet leaving her — 'tis me that you purfue
Without one fingle charm, but being new.
How vile is man! how I deteſt their ways
Of artful falſhood, and deſigning praiſe!
Taſteleſs, an eaſy happineſs you ſlight,
Ruin your joy, and miſchief your delight.
Why ſhould poor pug (the mimic of your kind)
Wear a rough chain, and be to box confin'd?
Some cup, perhaps, he breaks, or tears a fan, —
While roves unpuniſh'd the deſtroyer, man.
Not bound by vows, and unreſtrain'd by ſhame,
In ſport you break the heart, and rend the fame.
Not that your art can be ſucceſsful here,
Th' already plunder'd need no robber fear:
Nor ſighs, nor charms, nor flatteries can move,
Too well fecur'd againſt a fecond love.
Once, and but once, that devil charm'd my mind;
To reaſon deaf, to obſervation blind;
I idly hop'd (what cannot love perſuade!)
My fondneſs equal'd, and my love repay'd;
Slow to diſtruſt, and willing to believe,
Long huſh'd my doubts, and did, myſelf, deceive:
But oh! too ſoon — this tale would ever laſt;
Sleep, ſleep, my wrongs, and let me think 'em paſt.

For

For you, who mourn with counterfeited grief,
And aſk ſo boldly like a begging thief,
May ſoon ſome other nymph inflict the pain,
You know ſo well with cruel art to feign.
Though long you ſported have with Cupid's dart,
You may ſee eyes, and you may feel a heart.
So the briſk wits, who ſtop the evening coach,
Laugh at the fear that follows their approach;
With idle mirth, and haughty ſcorn deſpiſe
The paſſenger's pale cheek, and ſtaring eyes:
But ſeiz'd by Juſtice, find a fright no jeſt,
And all the terror doubled in their breaſt.

In Anſwer to a LADY who adviſed RETIREMENT.

By the Same.

YOU little know the heart that you adviſe;
I view this various ſcene with equal eyes:
In crowded courts I find myſelf alone,
And pay my worſhip to a nobler throne.
Long ſince the value of this world I know,
Pity the madneſs, and deſpiſe the ſhow.

Well

Well as I can my tedious part I bear,
And wait for my difmiffion without fear.
Seldom I mark mankind's detefted ways,
Not hearing cenfure, nor affecting praife;
And, unconcern'd, my future ftate I truft
To that fole Being, merciful and juft.

❀❀❀❀❀❀❀❀❀❀❀❀❀❀❀❀❀❀❀❀❀❀❀

An Addrefs of the STATUES at STOWE, to Lord COBHAM, on his Return to his Gardens.

FROM every Mufe and every art thy own,
   Thy bow'rs our theatres, thy mind our throne.
Hail! to thy virtues manumiz'd from ftate;
Hail! to thy leifure to be wifely great.

   Fetter'd by duties and to forms enflav'd,
How timely have thy years a remnant fav'd!
To tafte that freedom which thy fword maintain'd,
And lead in letter'd eafe, a life unpain'd:
So Scipio (Carthage fall'n) refign'd his plume,
And fmil'd at the forgetfulnefs of Rome.
O greatly blefs'd! whofe evening fweeteft fhines,
And, in unclouded flownefs, calm declines!
While free reflection with reverted eye,
Wan'd from hot noon-tide and a troubled fky,

                                        Divides

Divides life well: the largeſt part, long known
Thy country's claim; the laſt and beſt thy own.

Here while detach'd, thy ſelf-ſupported ſoul
Reſumes dominion, and eſcapes controul;
Moves with a grandeur, monarchs wiſh in vain,
Above all fears, ſtorms, dangers, hopes or pain;
A glance ſometimes from thy ſafe ſummit throw,
And ſee the duſty world look dim below:
Through the dark throng diſcern huge ſlaves of pride
Should'ring unheeded Happineſs aſide;
Thwarted and puſh'd and lab'ring into name,
And dignify'd with all the dirt of fame;
Then with a ſmile ſuperior, turn away,
And lop th' exub'rance of ſome ſtraggling ſpray;
Wind through thy mazes to ſerene delight,
And from the burſting bubbles ſhade thy ſight.

Yet where thou ſhin'ſt, like heav'n behind a cloud,
Moving like light, all piercing, though not loud;
The Muſe ſhall find thee in thy bleſt retreat,
And breathe this honeſt wiſh at Cobham's feet:
Freſh as thy lakes, may all thy pleaſures flow!
And breezy like thy groves, thy paſſions blow!
Wide as thy fancy, be thy ſpreading praiſe!
And long and lovely as thy walks, thy days!

An

{3✲✲✲✲✲✲✲✲✲✲✲✲✲✲✲✲✲✲✲✲✲✲✲✲✲✲✲✲✲3}

An O D E

ON THE

DEATH of Mr. PELHAM.

By Mr. GARRICK.

An honeſt man's the nobleſt work of God! POPE.

LET others hail the rifing fun,
 I bow to that whofe courfe is run,
 Which fets in endlefs night ;
Whofe rays benignant blefs'd this ifle,
Made peaceful Nature round us fmile
 With calm, but cheerful light.

No bounty paft provokes my praife,
No future profpects prompt my lays,
 From real grief they flow ;
I catch th' alarm from Britain's fears,
My forrows fall with Britain's tears,
 And join a nation's woe.

See

See — as you pass the crowded street,
Despondence clouds each face you meet,
　　All their lost friend deplore :
You read in every pensive eye,
You hear in every broken sigh,
　　That Pelham is no more.

If thus each Briton be alarm'd,
Whom but his distant influence warm'd,
　　What grief their breasts must rend,
Who in his private virtues bless'd,
By Nature's dearest tyes possess'd
　　The Husband, Father, Friend!

What! mute ye bards? — no mournful verse,
No chaplets to adorn his hearse,
　　To crown the good and just?
Your flowers in warmer regions bloom,
You seek no pensions from the tomb,
　　No laurels from the dust.

When pow'r departed with his breath,
The sons of Flatt'ry fled from death :
　　Such insects swarm at noon.

Not

Not for herfelf my Mufe is griev'd,
She never afk'd, nor e'er receiv'd,
   One minifterial boon.

Hath fome peculiar ftrange offence,
Againft us arm'd Omnipotence,
   To check the nation's pride ?
Behold th' appointed punifhment!
At length the vengeful bolt is fent,
   It fell — when Pelham dy'd !

Uncheck'd by fhame, unaw'd by dread,
When Vice triumphant rears her head,
   Vengeance can fleep no more ;
The evil angel ftalks at large,
The good fubmits, refigns his charge,
   And quits th' unhallow'd fhore.

The fame fad morn * to church and ftate,
(So for our fins 'twas fix'd by fate)
   A double ftroke was giv'n ;

---

* The 6th of March, 1754, was remarkable for the publica-
tion of the works of a late Lord, and the death of Mr. Pelham.

Black

Black as the whirlwinds of the north,
St. J—n's fell Genius iffu'd forth,
    And Pelham fled to heav'n !

By angels watch'd in Eden's bow'rs,
Our parents pafs'd their peaceful hours,
    Nor guilt nor pain they knew ;
But on the day which ufher'd in
The hell-born train of mortal fin,
    The heav'nly guards withdrew.

Look down, much honour'd fhade, below,
Still let thy pity aid our woe ;
    Stretch out thy healing hand ;
Refume thofe feelings, which on earth
Proclaim'd thy patriot love and worth,
    And fav'd a finking land.

Search with thy more than mortal eye,
The breafts of all thy friends : defcry
    What there has got poffeffion.
See if thy unfufpecting heart,
In fome for truth miftook not art,
    For principle, profeffion.

From

V E R S E S

Written at MONTAUBAN in FRANCE, 1750.

By the Rev. Mr. JOSEPH WARTON.

TARN, how delightful wind thy willow'd waves;
But ah! they fructify a land of flaves!
In vain thy bare-foot, fun-burnt peafants hide
With lufcious grapes yon' hill's romantic fide;
No cups nectareous fhall their toils repay,
The prieft's, the foldier's, and the fermier's prey:
Vain glows this fun in cloudlefs glory dreft,
That ftrikes frefh vigour through the pining breaft;
Give me, beneath a colder, changeful fky,
My foul's beft, only pleafure, LIBERTY!
What millions perifh'd near thy mournful flood [b]
When the red papal tyrant cry'd out — " Blood ! "
Lefs fierce the Saracen, and quiver'd Moor,
That dafh'd thy infants 'gainft the ftones of yore,
Be warn'd, ye nations round; and trembling fee
Dire fuperftition quench humanity!

[b] Alluding to the perfecutions of the proteftants, and the wars of the Saracens, carried on in the Southern provinces of France.

By

By all the chiefs in Freedom's battle dead ;

By wise and virtuous ALFRED's aweful ghost ;

By old GALGACUS' scythed, iron car,

That swiftly whirling through the walks of war,

Dash'd Roman blood, and crush'd the foreign throngs ;

By holy Druids' courage-breathing songs ;

By fierce BONDUCA's shield, and foaming steeds ;

By the bold peers that met on Thames's meads ;

By the fifth HENRY's helm, and lightning spear ;

O LIBERTY, my warm petition hear ;

Be ALBION still thy joy ! with her remain,

Long as the surge shall lash her oak-crown'd plain !

***

The Revenge of A M E R I C A.

By the Same.

WHEN fierce PISARRO's legions flew
    O'er ravag'd fields of rich Peru,
Struck with his bleeding people's woes,
Old India's aweful Genius rose.
He sat on Andes' topmost stone,
And heard a thousand nations groan ;
For grief his feathery crown he tore,
To see huge PLATA foam with gore ;

He broke his arrows, ftampt the ground,
To view his cities fmoaking round.
  What woes, he cry'd, hath luft of gold
O'er my poor country widely roll'd ;
Plunderers proceed ! my bowels tear,
But ye fhall meet deftruction there ;
From the deep-vaulted mine fhall rife
Th' infatiate fiend, pale Avarice !
Whofe fteps fhall trembling Juftice fly,
Peace, Order, Law, and Amity !
I fee all Europe's children curft
With lucre's univerfal thirft :
The rage that fweeps my fons away,
My baneful gold fhall well repay.

The Dying INDIAN.

By the Same.

THE dart of Izdabel prevails ! 'twas dipt
  In double poifon— I fhall foon arrive
At the bleft ifland, where no tigers fpring
On heedlefs hunters ; where anana's bloom

Thrice

Thrice in each moon; where rivers fmoothly glide,
Nor thundering torrents whirl the light canoe
Down to the fea; where my forefathers feaft
Daily on hearts of Spaniards!—O my fon,
I feel the venom bufy in my breaft,
Approach, and bring my crown, deck'd with the teeth
Of that bold chriftian who firft dar'd deflour
The virgins of the fun; and, dire to tell!
Robb'd PACHACAMAC's altar of its gems!
I mark'd the fpot where they interr'd this traitor,
And once at midnight ftole I to his tomb,
And tore his carcafe from the earth, and left it
A prey to poifonous flies. Preferve this crown
With facred fecrecy: if e'er returns
Thy much-lov'd mother from the defart woods,
Where, as I hunted late, I haplefs loft her,
Cherifh her age. Tell her I ne'er have worfhip'd
With thofe that eat their God. And when difeafe
Preys on her languid limbs, then kindly ftab her
With thine own hands, nor fuffer her to linger,
Like chriftian cowards, in a life of pain.
I go! great COPAC beckons me! farewel!

ODE

ODE occafion'd by Reading Mr. WEST's
Tranflation of PINDAR.

By the Same.

I. 1.

ALBION exult! thy fons a voice divine have heard,
    The man of Thebes hath in thy vales appear'd!
Hark! with frefh rage and undiminifh'd fire,
The fweet enthufiaft fmites the Britifh lyre;
The founds that echoed on Alphéus' ftreams,
Reach the delighted ear of liftening Thames;
        Lo! fwift acrofs the dufty plain
        Great Theron's foaming courfers ftrain!
        What mortal tongue e'er roll'd along
Such full impetuous tides of nervous fong?

I. 2.

The fearful, frigid lays of cold and creeping Art,
    Nor touch, nor can tranfport th' unfeeling heart;
Pindar, our inmoft bofom piercing, warms
With glory's love, and eager thirft of arms:
When Freedom fpeaks in his majeftic ftrain,
The patriot-paffions beat in every vein:

We

We long to fit with heroes old,

  'Mid groves of vegetable gold,

    [a] Where Cadmus and Achilles dwell,

And ftill of daring deeds and dangers tell.

I. 3.

  Away, enervate bards, away,

  Who fpin the courtly, filken lay,

    [b] As wreaths for fome vain Louis' head,

  Or mourn fome foft Adonis dead:

  No more your polifh'd lyrics boaft,

In Britifh Pindar's ftrength o'erwhelm'd and loft:

    As well might ye compare

  The glimmerings of a waxen flame,

  (Emblem of verfe correctly tame)

[c] To his own Ætna's fulphur-fpouting caves,

When to heav'n's vault the fiery deluge raves,

When clouds and burning rocks dart thro'the troubled air.

II. 1.

In roaring cataracts down Andes' channel'd fteeps

  Mark how enormous Orellana fweeps!

  Monarch of mighty floods! fupremely ftrong,

  Foaming from cliff to cliff he whirls along,

[a] See 2. Olym. Od.
[b] Alluding to the French and Italian lyric poets.
[c] See 1. Pyth. Od.

          Swoln

Swoln with an hundred hills' collected fnows !
Thence over namelefs regions widely flows,
 Round fragrant ifles, and citron-groves,
 Where ftill the naked Indian roves,
 And fafely builds his leafy bow'r,
From flavery far, and curft Iberian pow'r ;

II. 2.

So rapid Pindar flows. — O parent of the lyre,
Let me for ever thy fweet fons admire !
O ancient Greece, but chief the bard whofe lays
The matchlefs tale of Troy divine emblaze ;
And next Euripides, foft Pity's prieft,
Who melts in ufeful woes the bleeding breaft ;
 And him, who paints th' inceftuous king,
 Whofe foul amaze and horror wring ;
 Teach me to tafte their charms refin'd,
The richeft banquet of th' enraptur'd mind :

II. 3.

 For the bleft man, the Mufe's child [4],
 On whofe aufpicious birth fhe fmil'd,
 Whofe foul fhe form'd of purer fire,
 For whom fhe tun'd a golden lyre,
 Seeks not in fighting fields renown :
No widows' midnight fhrieks, nor burning town,

[4] Hor. Od. 3. L. 4.

The

The peaceful poet pleafe;

Nor ceafelefs toils for fordid gains,

Nor purple pomp, nor wide domains,

Nor heaps of wealth, nor power, nor ftatefman's fchemes,

Nor all deceiv'd Ambition's feverifh dreams,

Lure his contented heart from the fweet vale of eafe.

⁕⁕⁕⁕⁕⁕⁕⁕⁕⁕⁕⁕⁕⁕⁕⁕⁕⁕⁕⁕⁕⁕⁕⁕⁕⁕⁕⁕⁕⁕

THE

PLEASURES of MELANCHOLY.

Written in the Year 1745.

By Mr. THOMAS WARTON.

MOTHER of mufings, Contemplation fage,
Whofe grotto ftands upon the topmoft rock
Of Teneriff: 'mid the tempeftuous night,
On which, in calmeft meditation held,
Thou hear'ft with howling winds the beating rain
And drifting hail defcend; or if the fkies
Unclouded fhine, and through the blue ferene
Pale Cynthia rolls her filver-axled car,
Whence gazing ftedfaft on the fpangled vault
Raptur'd thou fit'ft, while murmurs indiftinct
Of diftant billows footh thy penfive ear

With

With hoarfe and hollow founds ; fecure, felf-bleft,
There oft thou liften'ft to the wild uproar
Of fleets encount'ring, that in whifpers low
Afcends the rocky fummit, where thou dwell'ft
Remote from man, converfing with the fpheres !
O lead me, queen fublime, to folemn glooms
Congenial with my foul ; to cheerlefs fhades,
To ruin'd feats, or twilight cells and bow'rs,
Where thoughtful Melancholy loves to mufe,
Her fav'rite midnight haunts.   The laughing fcenes
Of purple Spring, where all the wanton train
Of Smiles and Graces feem to lead the dance
In fportive round, while from their hands they fhow'r
Ambrofial blooms and flow'rs, no longer charm ;
Tempe, no more I court thy balmy breeze,
Adieu green vales ! ye broider'd meads, adieu !

   Beneath yon ruin'd abbey's mofs-grown piles
Oft let me fit, at twilight hour of eve,
Where through fome weftern window the pale moon
Pours her long-levell'd rule of ftreaming light ;
While fullen facred filence reigns around,
Save the lone fcreech-owl's note, who builds his bow'r
Amid the mould'ring caverns, dark and damp,
Or the calm breeze, that ruftles in the leaves

Of

Of flaunting ivy, that with mantle green
Invefts fome wafted tow'r.   Or let me tread
Its neighb'ring walk of pines, where mus'd of old
The cloyfter'd brother : through the gloomy void
That far extends beneath their ample arch
As on I pace, religious horror wraps
My foul in dread repofe.   But when the world
Is clad in Midnight's raven-colour'd robe,
'Mid hollow charnels let me watch the flame
Of taper dim, fhedding a livid glare
O'er the wan heaps ; while airy voices talk
Along the glimm'ring walls : or ghoftly fhape
At diftance feen, invites with beck'ning hand
My lonefome fteps, through the far-winding vaults.
Nor undelightful is the folemn noon
Of night, when haply wakeful from my couch
I ftart : lo, all is motionlefs around !
Roars not the rufhing wind ; the fons of men
And every beaft in mute oblivion lie ;
All nature's hufh'd in filence and in fleep.
O then how fearful is it to reflect,
That through the ftill globe's aweful folitude,
No being wakes but me ! 'till ftealing fleep
My drooping temples bathes in opiate dews.

Nor

Nor then let dreams, of wanton folly born,
My fenfes lead through flowery paths of joy;
But let the facred Genius of the night
Such myftic vifions fend, as Spenfer faw,
When through bewild'ring Fancy's magic maze,
To the fell houfe of Bufyrane, he led
Th' unfhaken Britomart; or Milton knew,
When in abftracted thought he firft conceiv'd
All heav'n in tumult, and the Seraphim
Come tow'ring, arm'd in adamant and gold.

   Let others love foft fummer's ev'ning fmiles,
As, lift'ning to the diftant water-fall,
They mark the blufhes of the ftreaky weft;
I choofe the pale December's foggy glooms.
Then, when the fullen fhades of ev'ning clofe,
Where through the room a blindly-glimm'ring gleam
The dying embers fcatter, far remote
From Mirth's mad fhouts, that thro' th' illumin'd roof
Refound with feftive echo, let me fit,
Bleft with the lowly cricket's drowfy dirge.
Then let my thought contemplative explore
This fleeting ftate of things, the vain delights,
The fruitlefs toils, that ftill our fearch elude,
As through the wildernefs of life we rove.

This

This fober hour of filence will unmafk
Falfe Folly's fmiles, that like the dazzling fpells
Of wily Comus cheat th' unweeting eye
With blear illufion, and perfuade to drink
That charmed cup, which Reafon's mintage fair
Unmoulds, and ftamps the monfter on the man.
Eager we tafte, but in the lufcious draught
Forget the pois'nous dregs that lurk beneath.

Few know that elegance of foul refin'd,
Whofe foft fenfation feels a quicker joy
From Melancholy's fcenes, than the dull pride
Of taftelefs fplendor and magnificence
Can e'er afford.   Thus Eloife, whofe mind
Had languifh'd to the pangs of melting love,
More genuine tranfport found, as on fome tomb
Reclin'd, fhe watch'd the tapers of the dead;
Or through the pillar'd iles, amid pale fhrines
Of imag'd faints, and intermingled graves,
Mus'd a veil'd votarefs : than Flavia feels,
As through the mazes of the feftive ball,
Proud of her conquering charms, and beauty's blaze,
She floats amid the filken fons of drefs,
And fhines the faireft of th' affembled fair.

When azure noon-tide cheers the dædal globe,

And

And the bleſt regent of the golden day
Rejoices in his bright meridian bow'r,
How oft my wiſhes aſk the night's return,
That beſt befriends the melancholy mind!
Hail, ſacred Night! thou too ſhalt ſhare my ſong!
Siſter of Ebon-ſcepter'd Hecat, hail!
Whether in congregated clouds thou wrap'ſt
Thy viewleſs chariot, or with ſilver crown
Thy beaming head encircleſt, ever hail!
What though beneath thy gloom the ſorcereſs-train,
Far in obſcured haunt of Lapland-moors,
With rhymes uncouth the bloody cauldron bleſs;
Though Murder wan, beneath thy ſhrouding ſhade
Summons her ſlow-ey'd vot'ries to deviſe
Of ſecret ſlaughter, while by one blue lamp
In hideous conf'rence ſits the liſtening band,
And ſtart at each low wind, or wakeful ſound:
What though thy ſtay the pilgrim curſeth oft,
As all benighted in Arabian waſtes
He hears the wilderneſs around him howl
With roaming monſters, while on his hoar head
The black deſcending tempeſt ceaſeleſs beats;
Yet more delightful to my penſive mind
Is thy return, than bloomy morn's approach,

Ev'n

Ev'n then,. in youthful pride of opening May,
When from the portals of the faffron eaft
She fheds frefh rofes, and ambrofial dews.
Yet not ungrateful is the morn's approach,
When dropping wet fhe comes, and clad in clouds,
While through the damp air fcowls the louring fouth,
Blackening the landfcape's face, that grove and hill
In formlefs vapours undiftinguifh'd fwim:
Th' afflicted fongfters of the fadden'd groves
Hail not the fullen gloom; the waving elms
That hoar through time, and rang'd in thick array,
Enclofe with ftately row fome rural hall,
Are mute, nor echo with the clamors hoarfe
Of rooks rejoicing on their airy boughs;
While to the fhed the dripping poultry crowd,
A mournful train; fecure the village-hind
Hangs o'er the crackling blaze, nor tempts the ftorm;
Fix'd in th' unfinifh'd furrow refts the plough:
Rings not the high wood with enliv'ning fhouts
Of early hunter: all is filence drear;
And deepeft fadnefs wraps the face of things.

Thro' Pope's foft fong tho' all the Graces breathe,
And happieft art adorn his Attic page;
Yet does my mind with fweeter tranfport glow,

As

As at the root of mossy trunk reclin'd,
In magic SPENSER's wildly-warbled song
I see deserted Una wander wide
Through wasteful solitudes, and lurid heaths
Weary, forlorn; than when the * fated fair,
Upon the bosom bright of silver Thames,
Launches in all the lustre of brocade,
Amid the splendors of the laughing Sun.
The gay description palls upon the sense,
And coldly strikes the mind with feeble bliss.

Ye Youths of Albion's beauty-blooming isle,
Whose brows have worn the wreath of luckless love,
Is there a pleasure like the pensive mood,
Whose magic wont to sooth your soften'd souls?
O tell how rapturous the joy, to melt
To Melody's assuasive voice; to bend
Th' uncertain step along the midnight mead,
And pour your sorrows to the pitying moon,
By many a slow trill from the bird of woe
Oft interrupted; in embowering woods
By darksome brook to muse, and there forget
The solemn dulness of the tedious world,
While Fancy grasps the visionary fair:

* Belinda. See Rape of the Lock.

And

And now no more th' abftracted ear attends
The water's murm'ring lapfe, th' entranced eye
Pierces no longer through th' extended rows
Of thick-rang'd trees ; 'till haply from the depth
The woodman's ftroke, or diftant-tinkling team,
Or heifer ruftling through the brake alarms
Th' illuded fenfe, and mars the golden dream.
Thefe are delights that abfence drear has made
Familiar to my foul, e'er fince the form
Of young Sapphira, beauteous as the Spring,
When from her vi'let-woven couch awak'd
By frolic Zephyr's hand, her tender cheek
Graceful fhe lifts, and blufhing from her bow'r,
Iffues to cloath in gladfome-glift'ring green
The genial globe, firft met my dazzled fight:
Thefe are delights unknown to minds profane,
And which alone the penfive foul can tafte.

   The taper'd choir, at the late hour of pray'r,
Oft let me tread, while to th' according voice
The many-founding organ peals on high,
The clear flow-dittyed chaunt, or varied hymn,
'Till all my foul is bath'd in ecftafies,
And lap'd in Paradife.   Or let me fit
Far in fequefter'd iles of the deep dome,

There

There lonefome liften to the facred founds,
Which, as they lengthen through the Gothic vaults,
In hollow murmurs reach my ravifh'd ear.
Nor when the lamps expiring yield to night,
And folitude returns, would I forfake
The folemn manfion, but attentive hear
The due clock fwinging flow with fweepy fway,
Meafuring Time's flight with momentary found.

   Nor let me fail to cultivate my mind
With the foft thrillings of the tragic Mufe,
Divine Melpomene, fweet Pity's nurfe,
Queen of the ftately ftep, and flowing pall.
Now let Monimia mourn with ftreaming eyes
Her joys inceftuous, and polluted love :
Now let foft Juliet in the gaping tomb
Print the laft kifs on her true Romeo's lips,
His lips yet reeking from the deadly draught.
Or Jaffeir kneel for one forgiving look.
Nor feldom let the Moor of Defdemone
Pour the mifguided threats of jealous rage.
By foft degrees the manly torrent fteals
From my fwoln eyes; and at a brother's woe
My big heart melts in fympathizing tears.

   What are the fplendors of the gaudy court,

Its

Its tinfel trappings, and its pageant pomps?
To me far happier feems the banifh'd Lord
Amid Siberia's unrejoicing wilds
Who pines all lonefome, in the chambers hoar
Of fome high caftle fhut, whofe windows dim
In diftant ken difcover tracklefs plains,
Where Winter ever whirls his icy car;
While ftill-repeated objects of his view,
The gloomy battlements, and ivied fpires
That crown the folitary dome, arife;
While from the topmoft turret the flow clock,
Far heard along th' inhofpitable waftes,
With fad-returning chime awakes new grief;
Ev'n he far happier feems than is the proud,
The potent Satrap, whom he left behind.
'Mid Mofcow's golden palaces, to drown
In eafe and luxury the laughing hours.

  Illuftrious objects ftrike the gazer's mind
With feeble blifs, and but allure the fight,
Nor rouze with impulfe quick th' unfeeling heart.
Thus feen by fhepherd from Hymettus' brow,
What dædal landfcapes fmile! here balmy groves,
Refounding once with Plato's voice, arife,
Amid whofe umbrage green her filver head

Th' unfading olive lifts; her vine-clad hills
Lay forth their purple ftores, and funny vales
In profpect vaft their level laps expand,
Amid whofe beauties glift'ring Athens tow'rs.
Though through the blifsful fcenes Iliffus roll
His fage-infpiring flood, whofe winding marge
The thick-wove laurel fhades; though rofeate Morn
Pour all her fplendors on th' empurpled fcene;
Yet feels the hoary Hermit truer joys,
As from the cliff that o'er his cavern hangs
He views the piles of fall'n Perfepolis
In deep arrangement hide the darkfome plain.
Unbounded wafte! the mould'ring obelifc
Here, like a blafted oak, afcends the clouds;
Here Parian domes their vaulted halls difclofe
Horrid with thorn, where lurks th' unpitying thief,
Whence flits the twilight-loving bat at eve,
And the deaf adder wreathes her fpotted train,
The dwellings once of elegance and art.
Here temples rife, amid whofe hallow'd bounds
Spires the black pine, while through the naked ftreet,
Once haunt of tradeful merchants, fprings the grafs:
Here columns heap'd on proftrate columns, torn
From their firm bafe, increafe the mould'ring mafs.

Far

Far as the fight can pierce, appear the fpoils
Of funk magnificence! a blended fcene
Of moles, fanes, arches, domes, and palaces,
Where, with his brother Horror, Ruin fits.

O come then, Melancholy, queen of thought!
O come with faintly look, and ftedfaft ftep,
From forth thy cave embower'd with mournful yew,
Where to the diftant curfeu's folemn found
Lift'ning thou fitt'ft, and with thy cyprefs bind
Thy votary's hair, and feal him for thy fon.
But never let Euphrófyne beguile
With toys of wanton mirth my fixed mind,
Nor in my path her primrofe-garland caft.
Though 'mid her train the dimpled Hebe bare
Her rofy bofom to th' enamour'd view;
Though Venus, mother of the Smiles and Loves,
And Bacchus, ivy-crown'd, in citron-bow'r
With her on nectar-ftreaming fruitage feaft:
What though 'tis her's to calm the low'ring fkies,
And at her prefence mild th' embattel'd clouds
Difperfe in air, and o'er the face of heav'n
New day diffufive gleam at her approach;
Yet are thefe joys that Melancholy gives,

Q 2

Than all her witlefs revels happier far;
Thefe deep-felt joys, by Contemplation taught.
   Then ever, beauteous Contemplation, hail!
From thee began, aufpicious maid, my fong,
With thee fhall end : for thou art fairer far
Than are the nymphs of Cirrha's moffy grot;
To loftier rapture thou canft wake the thought,
Than all the fabling Poet's boafted pow'rs.
Hail, queen divine! whom, as tradition tells,
Once, in his ev'ning-walk a Druid found,
Far in a hollow glade of Mona's woods;
And piteous bore with hofpitable hand
To the clofe fhelter of his oaken bow'r.
There foon the fage admiring mark'd the dawn
Of folemn mufing in your penfive thought;
For when a fmiling babe, you lov'd to lie
Oft deeply lift'ning to the rapid roar
Of wood-hung Meinai, ftream of Druids old,
That lav'd his hallow'd haunt with dafhing wave.

A SON-

A SÓNNET; written at W——DE
in the Abſence of——.

By the Same.

W——DE, thy beechen ſlopes with waving grain
 Border'd, thine azure views of wood and lawn,
Whilom could charm, or when the joyous Dawn
'Gan Night's dun robe with fluſhing purple ſtain,
Or Evening drove to fold her woolly train;
 Her faireſt landſcapes whence my Muſe has drawn,
 Too free with ſervile courtly phraſe to fawn,
Too weak to try the Buſkin's ſtately ſtrain;
 Yet now no more thy ſlopes of beech and corn
Nor proſpects charm, ſince HE far-diſtant ſtrays
 With whom I trac'd their ſweets each eve and morn,
From Albion far, to cull Heſperian bays;
 In this alone they pleaſe, howe'er forlorn,
That ſtill they can recall thoſe happier days.

On

✖✖✖✖✖✖✖✖✖✖✖✖✖✖✖✖✖✖✖✖✖✖✖✖✖✖✖✖✖✖✖

On BATHING,

A SONNET.

By the Same.

WHEN late the trees were ſtript by Winter pale;
  Fair HEALTH, a Dryad-maid in veſture green,
 Rejoyc'd to rove 'mid the bleak ſylvan ſcene,
On airy-uplands caught the fragrant gale,
And ere freſh morn the low-couch'd lark did hail
 Watching the ſound of earlieſt horn was ſeen.
 But ſince gay Summer, thron'd in chariot ſheen,
Is come to ſcorch each primroſe ſprinkled dale,
She chooſes that delightful cave beneath
 The cryſtal treaſures of meek Iſis' ſtream;
And now all glad the temperate air to breathe,
 While cooling drops diſtil from arches dim,
Binding her dewy locks with ſedgy wreath
 She ſits amid the quire of Naiads trim.

To

To Lady H——y. By Mr. de VOLTAIRE.

H——Y would you know the paffion
    You have kindled in my breaft,
Trifling is the inclination
    That by words can be exprefs'd.

In my filence fee the lover,
    True love is by filence known;
In my eyes you'll beft difcover
    All the power of your own.

On Sir ROBERT WALPOLE's Birth-day,
AUGUST the 26th.

By the Honourable Mr. D——TON.

ALL hail, aufpicious day, whofe wifh'd return
    Bids every breaft with grateful ardor burn,
While pleas'd Britannia that great man furveys
The Prince may truft, and yet the People praife:
One bearing greateft toils with greateft eafe,
One born to ferve us, and yet born to pleafe;

Q 4

His

His foul capacious, yet his judgment clear,
His tongue is flowing, and his heart fincere:
His counfels guide, his temper cheers our ifle,
And fmiling gives three kingdoms caufe to fmile.
Auguft, how bright thy golden fcenes appear,
Thou faireft daughter of the various year,
On thee the fun with all his ardor glows,
On thee in dowry all its fruits beftows,
The greateft Prince, the foremoft fon of fame,
To thee bequeath'd the glories of his name;
Nature and Fortune thee their darling chofe,
Nor could they grace thee more, 'till Walpole rofe.
By fteps to mighty things Fate makes her way,
The fun and Cæfar but prepar'd this day.

The Lawyer's Farewell to his Mufe.

Written in the Year 1744.

AS, by fome tyrant's ftern command,
A wretch forfakes his native land,
In foreign climes condemn'd to roam
An endlefs exile from his home;

Penfive

Penfive he treads the deftin'd way,
And dreads to go, nor dares to ftay;
'Till on fome neighb'ring mountain's brow
He ftops, and turns his eyes below ;
There, melting at the well-known view,
Drops a laft tear, and bids adieu :
So I, thus doom'd from thee to part,
Gay queen of Fancy and of Art,
Reluctant move, with doubtful mind,
Oft ftop, and often look behind.

   Companion of my tender age,
Serenely gay, and fweetly fage,
How blithfome were we wont to rove
By verdant hill, or fhady grove,
Where fervent bees, with humming voice,
Around the honey'd oak rejoice,
And aged elms with aweful bend
In long cathedral walks extend !
Lull'd by the lapfe of gliding floods,
Cheer'd by the warbling of the woods,
How bleft my days, my thoughts how free,
In fweet fociety with thee !
Then all was joyous, all was young,
And years unheeded roll'd along :

But

But now the pleafing dream is o'er,
Thefe fcenes muft charm me now no more;
Loft to the field, and torn from you, —
Farewel ! — a long, a laft adieu.

   Me wrangling courts, and ftubborn Law,
To fmoak, and crowds, and cities draw ;
There felfifh Faction rules the day,
And Pride and Av'rice throng the way :
Difeafes taint the murky air,
And midnight conflagrations glare ;
Loofe Revelry and Riot bold
In frighted ftreets their orgies hold ;
Or, when in filence all is drown'd,
Fell Murder walks her lonely round :
No room for peace, no room for you,
Adieu, celeftial Nymph, adieu !

   Shakefpear no more, thy fylvan fon,
Nor all the art of Addifon,
Pope's heav'n-ftrung lyre, nor Waller's eafe,
Nor Milton's mighty felf muft pleafe :
Inftead of thefe, a formal band
In furs and coifs around me ftand ;
With founds uncouth and accents dry
That grate the foul of harmony,

Each

Each pedant fage unlocks his ftore
Of myftic, dark, difcordant lore;
And points with tott'ring hand the ways
That lead me to the thorny maze.

    There, in a winding, clofe retreat,
Is Juftice doom'd to fix her feat,
There, fenc'd by bulwarks of the Law,
She keeps the wond'ring world in awe,
And there, from vulgar fight retir'd,
Like eaftern queens, is more admir'd.

    O let me pierce the fecret fhade
Where dwells the venerable maid!
There humbly mark, with rev'rent awe,
The guardian of Britannia's Law,
Unfold with joy her facred page,
(Th' united boaft of many an age,
Where mix'd, yet uniform, appears
The wifdom of a thoufand years)
In that pure fpring the bottom view,
Clear, deep, and regularly true,
And other doctrines thence imbibe
Than lurk within the fordid fcribe;
Obferve how parts with parts unite
In one harmonious rule of right;

See

See countless wheels diftinctly tend
By various laws to one great end ;
While mighty Alfred's piercing foul
Pervades, and regulates the whole.

 Then welcome bufinefs, welcome ftrife,
Welcome the cares, the thorns of life,
The vifage wan, the pore-blind fight,
The toil by day, the lamp at night,
The tedious forms, the folemn prate,
The pert difpute, the dull debate,
The drowfy bench, the babling Hall,
For thee, fair Juftice, welcome all !

 Thus though my noon of life be paft,
Yet let my fetting fun, at laft,
Find out the ftill, the rural cell,
Where fage Retirement loves to dwell !
There let me tafte the homefelt blifs
Of innocence, and inward peace ;
Untainted by the guilty bribe ;
Uncurs'd amid the harpy-tribe ;
No orphan's cry to wound my ear ;
My honour and my confcience clear ;
Thus may I calmly meet my end,
Thus to the grave in peace defcend.

By

By Miſs COOPER (now Mrs. MADAN) in her
Brother's Coke upon Littleton.

O Thou, who labour'ſt in this rugged mine,
  May'ſt thou to gold th' unpoliſh'd ore refine!
May each dark page unfold its haggard brow!
Doubt not to reap, if thou canſt bear to plough.
To tempt thy care, may, each revolving night,
Purſes and maces ſwim before thy ſight!
From hence in times to come, advent'rous deed!
May'ſt thou eſſay, to look and ſpeak like Mead,
When the black bag and roſe no more ſhall ſhade
With martial air the honours of thy head;
When the full wig thy viſage ſhall encloſe,
And only leave to view thy learned noſe:
Safely may'ſt thou defy beaux, wits, and ſcoffers;
While tenants, in fee ſimple, ſtuff thy coffers.

SOLITUDE.

S O L I T U D E.

An O D E.

By Dr. GRAINGER.

I.

O Solitude, romantic maid,
　　Whether by nodding towers you tread;
Or haunt the defart's trackless gloom,
Or hover o'er the yawning tomb,
Or climb the Andes' clifted side,
Or by the Nile's coy fource abide,
Or ftarting from your half-year's fleep
From Hecla view the thawing deep,
Or at the purple dawn of day,
Tadmor's marble waftes furvey;
　You, Reclufe, again I woo,
　And again your fteps purfue.

II.

Plum'd Conceit himfelf furveying,
Folly with her fhadow playing,

Purfe-

Purſe-proud, elbowing Inſolence,
Bloated empiric, puff'd Pretence,
Noiſe that through a trumpet ſpeaks,
Laughter in loud peals that breaks,
Intruſion with a fopling's face,
(Ignorant of time and place)
Sparks of fire Diſſention blowing,
Ductile, court-bred Flattery, bowing,
Reſtraint's ſtiff neck, Grimace's leer,
Squint-ey'd Cenſure's artful ſneer,
Ambition's buſkins ſteep'd in blood,
Fly thy preſence, Solitude.

III.

Sage Reflection bent with years,
Conſcious Virtue void of fears,
Muffled Silence, wood-nymph ſhy,
Meditation's piercing eye,
Halcyon Peace on moſs reclin'd,
Retroſpect that ſcans the mind,
Rapt earth-gazing Reſvery,
Bluſhing artleſs Modeſty,
Health that ſnuffs the morning air,
Full-ey'd Truth with boſom bare,

Inſpiration,

Infpiration, Nature's child,
Seek the folitary wild.

IV.

You with the tragic Mufe [f] retir'd
The wife Euripides infpir'd,
You taught the fadly-pleafing air
That [g] Athens fav'd from ruins bare.
You gave the Cean's tears to flow,
And [h] unlock'd the fprings of woe;
You penn'd what exil'd Nafo thought,
And pour'd the melancholy note.
With Petrarch o'er Valclufe you ftray'd,
When Death fnatch'd his [i] long-lov'd maid;
You taught the rocks her lofs to mourn,
You ftrew'd with flowers her virgin urn.
And late in [k] Hagley you were feen,
With blood-fhed eyes, and fombre mien,
Hymen his yellow veftment tore,
And Dirge a wreath of cyprefs wore.
But chief your own the folemn lay
That wept Narciffa young and gay,

[f] In the ifland Salamis.
[g] See Plutarch in the life of Lyfander.
[h] Simonides.
[i] Laura, twenty years, and ten after her death.
[k] Monody on the death of Mrs. Lyttelton.

Darknefs

Darkneſs clap'd her ſable wing,
While you touch'd the mournful ſtring,
Anguiſh left the pathleſs wild,
Grim-fac'd Melancholy ſmil'd,
Drowſy Midnight ceas'd to yawn,
The ſtarry hoſt put back the dawn,
Aſide their harps ev'n Seraphs flung
To hear thy ſweet Complaint, O Young.

V.

When all Nature's huſh'd aſleep,
Nor Love nor Guilt their vigils keep,
Soft you leave your cavern'd den,
And wander o'er the works of men.
But when Phoſphor brings the dawn,
By her dappled courſers drawn,
Again you to the wild retreat
And the early huntſman meet,
Where as you penſive pace along,
You catch the diſtant ſhepherd's ſong,
Or bruſh from herbs the pearly dew,
Or the riſing primroſe view.
Devotion lends her heav'n-plum'd wings,
You mount, and Nature with you ſings.

R But

But when mid-day fervors glow,
To upland airy fhades you go,
Where never funburnt woodman came,
Nor fportfman chas'd the timid game ;
And there beneath an oak reclin'd,
With drowfy waterfalls behind,
You fink to reft.
'Till the tuneful bird of night
From the neighb'ring poplar's height,
Wake you with her folemn ftrain,
And teach pleas'd Echo to complain.

VI.

With you rofes brighter bloom,
Sweeter every fweet perfume,
Purer every fountain flows,
Stronger every wilding grows.

VII.

Let thofe toil for gold who pleafe,
Or for fame renounce their eafe.
What is fame? an empty bubble,
Gold? a tranfient, fhining trouble.
Let them for their country bleed,
What was Sidney's, Raleigh's meed?

Man's

Man's not worth a moment's pain,
Bafe, ungrateful, fickle, vain.
Then let me, fequefter'd fair,
To your Sibyl grot repair,
On yon hanging cliff it ftands
Scoop'd by Nature's falvage hands,
Bofom'd in the gloomy fhade
Of cyprefs not with age decay'd.
Where the owl ftill-hooting fits,
Where the bat inceffant flits,
There in loftier ftrains I'll fing
Whence the changing feafons fpring,
Tell how ftorms deform the fkies,
Whence the waves fubfide and rife,
Trace the comet's blazing tail,
Weigh the planets in a fcale;
Bend, great God, before thy fhrine,
The bournlefs macrocofm's thine.

VIII.

Save me ! what's yon fhrouded fhade,
That wanders in the dark-brown glade ?
It beckons me ! — vain fears adieu,
Myfterious ghoft, I follow you.

R 2   Ah

Ah me! too well that gait I know,
My youth's firſt friend, my manhood's woe!
Its breaſt it bares! what! ſtain'd with blood?
Quick let me ſtanch the vital flood.
O ſpirit, whither art thou flown?
Why left me comfortleſs alone?
O Solitude, on me beſtow
The heart-felt harmony of woe,
Such, ſuch, as on th' Auſonian ſhore,
Sweet [1] Dorian Moſchus trill'd of yore:
No time ſhould cancel thy deſert,
More, more, than [m] Bion was, thou wert.

IX.

O goddeſs of the tearful eye,
The never-ceaſing ſtream ſupply.
Let us with Retirement go
To charnels, and the houſe of woe,
O'er Friendſhip's herſe low-drooping mourn,
Where the ſickly tapers burn,
Where Death and nun-clad Sorrow dwell,
And nightly ring the ſolemn knell.

[1] See Idyll.
[m] Alluding to the death of a friend.

The

The gloom difpels, the charnel fmiles,
Light flafhes through the vaulted iles.
Blow filky foft, thou weftern gale,
O goddefs of the defart, hail !
She burfts from yon cliff-riven cave,
Infulted by the wintry wave ;
Her brow an ivy garland binds,
Her treffes wanton with the winds,
A lion's fpoils, without a zone,
Around her limbs are carelefs thrown ;
Her right-hand wields a knotted mace,
Her eyes roll wild, a ftride her pace ;
Her left a magic mirror holds,
In which fhe oft herfelf beholds.
O goddefs of the defart, hail !
And fofter blow, thou weftern gale !

   Since in each fcheme of life I've fail'd,
And difappointment feems entail'd ;
Since all on earth I valued moft,
My guide, my ftay, my friend is loft ;
You, only you, can make me bleft,
And hufh the tempeft in my breaft.
Then gently deign to guide my feet
To your hermit-trodden feat,

Where

Where I may live at laft my own,
Where I at laft may die unknown.

I fpoke, fhe twin'd her magic ray,
And thus fhe faid, or feem'd to fay:

Youth, you're miftaken, if you think to find
In fhades a medicine for a troubled mind;
Wan Grief will haunt you wherefoe'er you go,
Sigh in the breeze, and in the ftreamlet flow,
There pale Inaction pines his life away,
And, fatiate, curfes the return of day:
There naked Frenzy laughing wild with pain,
Or bares the blade, or plunges in the main:
There Superftition broods o'er all her fears,
And yells of dæmons in the Zephyr hears.
But if a hermit you're refolv'd to dwell,
And bid to focial life a laft farewell;
'Tis impious.—
God never made an independent man,
'Twould jar the concord of his general plan:
See every part of that ftupendous whole,
" Whofe body Nature is, and God the foul;"
To one great end, the general good, confpire,
From matter, brute, to man, to feraph, fire.

Should

Should man through Nature folitary roam,
His will his fovereign, every where his home,
What force would guard him from the lion's jaw?
What fwiftnefs wing him from the panther's paw?
Or fhould Fate lead him to fome fafer fhore,
Where panthers never prowl, nor lions roar;
Where liberal Nature all her charms beftows,
Suns fhine, birds fing, flowers bloom, and water flows,
Fool, doft thou think he'd revel on the ftore,
Abfolve the care of Heaven, nor afk for more?
Tho' waters flow'd, flow'rs bloom'd, and Phœbus fhone,
He'd figh, he'd murmur that he was alone.
For know, the Maker on the human breaft
A fenfe of kindred, country, man, impreft;
And focial life to better, aid, adorn,
With proper faculties each mortal's born.

   Though Nature's works the ruling mind declare,
And well deferve enquiry's ferious care,
The God (whate'er Mifanthropy may fay)
Shines, beams in man with moft unclouded ray.
What boots it thee to fly from pole to pole,
Hang o'er the fun, and with the planets roll?
What boots through fpace's furtheft bourns to roam,
If thou, O man, a ftranger art at home?

Then

Then know thyſelf, the human mind ſurvey,
The uſe, the pleaſure will the toil repay.
Hence Inſpiration plans his manner'd lays;
Hence Homer's crown, and, Shakeſpear, hence thy bays.
Hence he, the pride of Athens, and the ſhame,
The beſt and wiſeſt of mankind became.
Nor ſtudy only, practiſe what you know,
Your life, your knowledge, to mankind you owe.
With Plato's olive wreath the bays entwine :
Thoſe who in ſtudy, ſhould in practice ſhine.
Say, does the learned Lord of Hagley's ſhade,
Charm man ſo much by moſſy fountains laid,
As when arouz'd, he ſtems Corruption's courſe,
And ſhakes the ſenate with a Tully's force ?
When Freedom gaſp'd beneath a Cæſar's feet,
Then public Virtue might to ſhades retreat ;
But where ſhe breathes, the leaſt may uſeful be,
And Freedom, Britain, ſtill belongs to thee.
Though man's ungrateful, or though Fortune frown ;
Is the reward of worth a ſong, or crown ?
Nor yet unrecompens'd are Virtue's pains,
Good Allen lives, and bounteous Brunſwick reigns.
On each condition diſappointments wait,
Enter the hut, and force the guarded gate.

Nor dare repine, though early Friendſhip bleed,
From love, the world, and all its cares he's freed.
But know, Adverſity's the child of God;
Whom Heaven approves of moſt, moſt feel her rod.
When ſmooth old Ocean and each ſtorm's aſleep,
Then Ignorance may plough the watery deep;
But when the dæmons of the tempeſt rave,
Skill muſt conduct the veſſel through the wave.
Sidney, what good man envies not thy blow?
Who would not wiſh ᵃ Anytus for a foe?
Intrepid Virtue triumphs over Fate,
The good can never be unfortunate.
And be this maxim graven in thy mind,
The height of virtue is to ſerve mankind.

But when old age has ſilver'd o'er thy head,
When memory fails, and all thy vigour's fled,
Then may'ſt thou ſeek the ſtillneſs of retreat,
Then hear aloof the human tempeſt beat,
Then will I greet thee to my woodland cave,
Allay the pangs of age, and ſmooth thy grave.

ᵃ One of the accuſers of Socrates.

★☆★☆★☆★☆★☆★☆★☆★☆★☆★☆★☆★☆★☆★☆★☆★☆★☆★

An O D E

To the Right Honourable

STEPHEN POYNTZ, Efq; &c. &c.

By the Honourable

Sir CHARLES HAN. WILLIAMS, Kt. of the Bath.

Senfere quid mens rite, quid indoles
Nutrita fauftis fub penetralibus
Poffet ——————
Doctrina fed vim promovet infitam,
Rectique cultus pectora roborant.

HOR. Lib. IV. Od. 4.

I.

WHILST William's deeds and William's praife
 Each Englifh breaft with tranfport raife,
 Each Englifh tongue employ;
Say, Poyntz, if thy elated heart
Affumes not a fuperior part,
 A larger fhare of joy?

II.

But that thy country's high affairs
Employ thy time, demand thy cares,
 You fhould renew your flight;

You

You only fhould this theme purfue—
Who can for William feel like you ?
   Or who like you can write ?

III.

Then to rehearfe the Hero's praife,
To paint this funfhine of his days,
   The pleafing tafk be mine —
To think on all thy cares o'erpaid,
To view the Hero you have made,
   That pleafing part be thine.

IV.

Who firft fhould watch, and who call forth
This youthful Prince's various worth,
   You had the public voice ;
Wifely his royal Sire confign'd
To you, the culture of his mind,
   And England bleft the choice.

V.

You taught him to be early known
By martial deeds of courage fhewn:
   From this, near Mona's flood,
By his victorious Father led,
He flefh'd his maiden fword, he fhed,
   And prov'd th' illuftrious blood.

VI. Of

VI.

Of Virtue's various charms you taught,
With happinefs and glory fraught,
 How her unfhaken pow'r
Is independent of fuccefs;
That no defeat can make it lefs,
 No conqueft make it more.

VII.

This, after Tournay's fatal day,
'Midft forrow, cares, and dire difmay,
 Brought calm, and fure relief;
He fcrutiniz'd his noble heart,
Found Virtue had perform'd her part,
 And peaceful flept the Chief.

VIII.

From thee he early learnt to feel
The Patriot's warmth for England's weal;
 (True Valour's nobleft fpring)
To vindicate her Church diftreft;
To fight for Liberty oppreft;
 To perifh for his King.

IX.

Yet fay, if in thy fondeft fcope
Of thought, you ever dar'd to hope
 That bounteous heaven fo foon

Would

Would pay thy toils, reward thy care,
Confenting bend to every pray'r,
 And all thy wifhes crown?

X.

We faw a wretch, with trait'rous aid,
Our King's and Church's rights invade:
 And thine, fair Liberty!
We faw thy Hero fly to war,
Beat down Rebellion, break her fpear,
 And fet the nation free.

XI.

Culloden's field, my glorious theme,
My rapture, vifion, and my dream,
 Gilds the young Hero's days:
Yet can there be one Englifh heart
That does not give thee, Poyntz, thy part,
 And own thy fhare of praife?

XII.

Nor is thy fame to thee decreed
For life's fhort date: when William's head,
 For victories to come,
The frequent laurel fhall receive:
Chaplets for thee our fons fhall weave,
 And hang 'em on thy tomb.

       ODE

ༀ⌖ༀ⌖ༀ⌖ༀ⌖ༀ⌖ༀ⌖ༀ⌖ༀ⌖ༀ⌖ༀ⌖ༀ⌖ༀ⌖

O D E on the Death of MATZEL, a favourite
Bull-finch, addreſs'd to Mr. ST ——— PE, to
whom the Author had given the Reverſion of
it when he left Dreſden.

By the Same.

I.

TRY not, my St— pe, 'tis in vain
 To ſtop your tears, to hide your pain,
  Or check your honeſt rage ;
Give ſorrow and revenge their ſcope,
My preſent joy, your future hope,
  Lies murder'd in his cage.

II.

Matzel's no more, ye graces, loves,
Ye linnets, nightingales and doves,
  Attend th' untimely bier ;
Let every ſorrow be expreſt,
Beat with your wings each mournful breaſt,
  And drop the nat'ral tear.

III. In

III.

In height of song, in beauty's pride,
By fell Grimalkin's claws he died—
  But vengeance shall have way;
On pains and tortures I'll refine;
Yet, Matzel, that one death of thine,
  His nine will ill repay.

IV.

For thee, my bird, the sacred Nine,
Who lov'd thy tuneful notes, shall join
  In thy funereal verse:
My painful task shall be to write
Th' eternal dirge which they indite,
  And hang it on thy hearse.

V.

In vain I lov'd, in vain I mourn
My bird, who never to return
  Is fled to happier shades,
Where Lesbia shall for him prepare
The place most charming, and most fair
  Of all th' Elysian glades.

VI.

There shall thy notes in cypress grove
Sooth wretched ghosts that died for love;
  There shall thy plaintive strain

I   Lull

Lull impious Phædra's endless grief,
To Procris yield some short relief,
    And soften Dido's pain.

VII.

'Till Proserpine by chance shall hear
Thy notes, and make thee all her care,
    And love thee with my love;
While each attendant's soul shall praise
The matchless Matzel's tuneful lays,
    And all his songs approve.

MARTIALIS EPIGRAMMA.

Lib. VI. Ep. 34. Imitated.

By the Same.

COME, Chloe, and give me sweet kisses,
    For sweeter sure never girl gave:
But why in the midst of my blisses
  Do you ask me how many I'd have?
I'm not to be stinted in pleasure,
    Then pr'ythee my charmer be kind,
For whilst I love thee above measure,
  To numbers I'll ne'er be confin'd.

Count

Count the bees that on Hybla are playing,
  Count the flow'rs that enamel its fields,
Count the flocks that on Tempe are ftraying,
  Or the grain that rich Sicily yields;
Go number the ftars in the heaven,
  Count how many fands on the fhore,
When fo many kiffes you've given
  I ftill fhall be craving for more.
To a heart full of love let me hold thee,
  To a heart which, dear Chloe, is thine;
With my arms I'll for ever enfold thee,
  And twift round thy limbs like a vine.
What joy can be greater than this is?
  My life on thy lips fhall be fpent;
But the wretch that can number his kiffes
  With few will be ever content.

The Progrefs of DISCONTENT.

A POEM.

Written at Oxford in the Year 1746.

WHEN now mature in claffic knowledge,
  The joyful youth is fent to college,

His father comes, a vicar plain,
At Oxford bred — in Anna's reign,
And thus in form of humble suitor
Bowing accosts a reverend tutor.
" Sir, I'm a Glo'stershire divine,
" And this my eldest son of nine;
" My wife's ambition and my own
" Was that this child should wear a gown:
" I'll warrant that his good behaviour
" Will justify your future favour:
" And for his parts, to tell the truth,
" My son's a very forward youth;
" Has Horace all by heart — you'd wonder—
" And mouths out Homer's Greek like thunder.
" If you'd examine — and admit him,
" A scholarship would nicely fit him:
" That he succeeds 'tis ten to one;
" Your vote and interest, Sir!" — 'Tis done.
Our pupil's hopes, though twice defeated,
Are with a scholarship compleated:
A scholarship but half maintains,
And college rules are heavy chains:
In garret dark he smokes and puns,
A prey to discipline and duns;

And

And now intent on new defigns,
Sighs for a fellowfhip — and fines.

   When nine full tedious winters paft,
That utmoft wifh is crown'd at laft :
But the rich prize no fooner got,
Again he quarrels with his lot :
" Thefe fellowfhips are pretty things,
" We live indeed like petty kings :
" But who can bear to wafte his whole age
" Amid the dullnefs of a college,
" Debarr'd the common joys of life,
" And that prime blifs — a loving wife !
" O ! what's a table richly fpread
" Without a woman at its head !
" Would fome fnug benefice but fall,
" Ye feafts, ye dinners ! farewel all !
" To offices I'd bid adieu,
" Of dean, vice præs. — of burfar too ;
" Come joys, that rural quiet yields,
" Come, tythes, and houfe, and fruitful fields !"
   Too fond of liberty and eafe
A patron's vanity to pleafe,
Long time he watches, and by ftealth,
Each frail incumbent's doubtful health ;

At

At length — and in his fortieth year,
A living drops — two hundred clear!
With breaft elate beyond expreffion,
He hurries down to take poffeffion,
With rapture views the fweet retreat —
" What a convenient houfe! how neat!
" For fuel here's fufficient wood :
" Pray God the cellars may be good!
" The garden — that muft be new plann'd —
" Shall thefe old-fafhion'd yew-trees ftand ?
" O'er yonder vacant plot fhall rife
" The flow'ry fhrub of thoufand dies : —
" Yon' wall, that feels the fouthern ray,
" Shall blufh with ruddy fruitage gay ;
" While thick beneath its afpeft warm
" O'er well-rang'd hives the bees fhall fwarm,
" From which, ere long, of golden gleam
" Metheglin's lufcious juice fhall ftream :
" This aukward hut o'er-grown with ivy,
" We'll alter to a modern privy :
" Up yon' green flope, of hazels trim,
" An avenue fo cool and dim,
" Shall to an arbour, at the end,
" In fpite of gout, intice a friend.

" M

" My predeceffor lov'd devotion —
" But of a garden had no notion."
    Continuing this fantaftic farce on,
He now commences country parfon.
To make his character entire,
He weds — a coufin of the 'fquire ;
Not over-weighty in the purfe,
But many doctors have done worfe :
And though fhe boaft no charms divine,
Yet fhe can carve, and make birch wine.
    Thus fixt, content he taps his barrel,
Exhorts his neighbours not to quarrel :
Finds his church-wardens have difcerning
Both in good liquor and good learning ;
With tythes his barns replete he fees,
And chuckles o'er his furplice fees ;
Studies to find out latent dues,
And regulates the ftate of pews ;
Rides a fleek mare with purple houfing,
To fhare the monthly club's caroufing ;
Of Oxford pranks facetious tells,
And — but on Sundays — hears no bells ;
Sends prefents of his choiceft fruit,
And prunes himfelf each fablefs fhoot,

Plants

II.

From the gay world we'll oft retire
To our own family and fire,
    Where love our hours employs;
No noify neighbour enters here,
No intermeddling ftranger near,
    To fpoil our heart-felt joys.

III.

If folid happinefs we prize,
Within our breaft this jewel lies;
    And they are fools who roam:
The world has nothing to beftow,
From our own felves our joys muft flow,
    And that dear hut, our home.

IV.

Of reft was Noah's dove bereft,
When with impatient wing fhe left
    That fafe retreat, the ark;
Giving her vain excurfion o'er,
The difappointed bird once more
    Explor'd the facred bark.

V.

Though fools fpurn Hymen's gentle pow'rs,
We, who improve his golden hours,
    By fweet experience know,

That

That marriage, rightly underftood,
Gives to the tender and the good
    A paradife below.

VI.

Our babes fhall richeft comforts bring,
If tutor'd right, they'll prove a fpring,
    Whence pleafures ever rife:
We'll form their minds with ftudious care,
To all that's manly, good, and fair,
    And train them for the fkies.

VII.

While they our wifeft hours engage,
They'll joy our youth, fupport our age,
    And crown our hoary hairs:
They'll grow in virtue every day,
And thus our fondeft loves repay,
    And recompenfe our cares.

VIII.

No borrow'd joys! they're all our own,
While to the world we live unknown,
    Or by the world forgot:
Monarchs! we envy not your ftate,
We look with pity on the great,
    And blefs our humbler lot.

IX. Our

Plants colliflow'rs, and boasts to rear
The earliest melons of the year;
Thinks alteration charming work is,
Keeps Bantam cocks, and feeds his turkies;
Builds in his copse a favourite bench,
And stores the pond with carp and tench. —

But ah! too soon his thoughtless breast
By cares domestic is oppress;
And a third butcher's bill, and brewing,
Threaten inevitable ruin:
For children fresh expences yet,
And Dicky now for school is fit.
" Why did I sell my college life
" (He cries) for benefice and wife?
" Return, ye days! when endless pleasure
" I found in reading, or in leisure!
" When calm around the common room
" I puff'd my daily pipe's perfume!
" Rode for a stomach, and inspected,
" At annual bottlings, corks selected:
" And din'd untax'd, untroubled, under
" The pourtrait of our pious founder!
" When impositions were supply'd
" To light my pipe — or sooth my pride —

" No

" No cares were then for forward peas,

" A yearly-longing wife to pleafe :

" My thoughts no chrift'ning dinner croft,

" No children cry'd for butter'd toaft ;

" And every night I went to bed,

" Without a Modus in my head !"

   Oh ! trifling head, and fickle heart !

Chagrin'd at whatfoe'er thou art ;

A dupe to follies yet untry'd,

And fick of pleafures, fcarce enjoy'd !

Each prize poffefs'd, thy tranfport ceafes,

And in purfuit alone it pleafes.

The FIRE-SIDE.

By Dr. COTTON.

I.

DEAR Chloe, while the bufy crowd,

  The vain, the wealthy, and the proud,

    In Folly's maze advance ;

Though fingularity and pride

Be call'd our choice, we'll ftep afide,

    Nor join the giddy dance.

    II. From

II.

From the gay world we'll oft retire
To our own family and fire,
    Where love our hours employs;
No noify neighbour enters here,
No intermeddling ftranger near,
    To fpoil our heart-felt joys.

III.

If folid happinefs we prize,
Within our breaft this jewel lies;
    And they are fools who roam:
The world has nothing to beftow,
From our own felves our joys muft flow,
    And that dear hut, our home.

IV.

Of reft was Noah's dove bereft,
When with impatient wing fhe left
    That fafe retreat, the ark;
Giving her vain excurfion o'er,
The difappointed bird once more
    Explor'd the facred bark.

V.

Though fools fpurn Hymen's gentle pow'rs,
We, who improve his golden hours,
    By fweet experience know,

That

That marriage, rightly underſtood,
Gives to the tender and the good
  A paradiſe below.

VI.

Our babes ſhall richeſt comforts bring,
If tutor'd right, they'll prove a ſpring,
  Whence pleaſures ever riſe:
We'll form their minds with ſtudious care,
To all that's manly, good, and fair,
  And train them for the ſkies.

VII.

While they our wiſeſt hours engage,
They'll joy our youth, ſupport our age,
  And crown our hoary hairs:
They'll grow in virtue every day,
And thus our fondeſt loves repay,
  And recompenſe our cares.

VIII.

No borrow'd joys! they're all our own,
While to the world we live unknown,
  Or by the world forgot:
Monarchs! we envy not your ſtate,
We look with pity on the great,
  And bleſs our humbler lot.

IX. Our

IX.

Our portion is not large indeed,
But then, how little do we need!
　For Nature's calls are few!
In this the art of living lies,
To want no more than may suffice,
　And make that little do.

X.

We'll therefore relish with content
Whate'er kind Providence has sent,
　Nor aim beyond our pow'r;
For if our stock be very small,
'Tis prudence to enjoy it all,
　Nor lose the present hour.

XI.

To be resign'd, when ills betide,
Patient, when favours are deny'd,
　And pleas'd with favours giv'n;
Dear Chloe, this is wisdom's part,
This is that incense of the heart,
　Whose fragrance smells to heav'n.

XII.

We'll ask no long protracted treat,
(Since winter life is seldom sweet;)
　But when our feast is o'er,

Gratefu

Grateful from table we'll arife,
Nor grudge our fons with envious eyes,
 The relics of our ftore.
XIII.
Thus hand in hand through life we'll go,
Its checker'd paths of joy and woe
 With cautious fteps we'll tread;
Quit its vain fcenes without a tear,
Without a trouble or a fear,
 And mingle with the dead.
XIV.
While Confcience, like a faithful friend,
Shall through the gloomy vale attend,
 And cheer our dying breath;
Shall, when all other comforts ceafe,
Like a kind angel whifper peace,
 And fmooth the bed of death.

T O - M O R R O W.
By the Same.
Pereunt et Imputantur.

TO-morrow, didft thou fay!
 Methought I heard Horatio fay, To-morrow.

Go to — I will not hear of it — To-morrow !
'Tis a sharper, who stakes his penury
Against thy plenty — who takes thy ready cash,
And pays thee nought but wishes, hopes, and promises,
The currency of ideots. — Injurious bankrupt,
That gulls the easy creditor ! — To-morrow !
It is a period no where to be found ·
In all the hoary registers of Time,
Unless perchance in the fool's calendar.
Wisdom disclaims the word, nor holds society
With those who own it. No, my Horatio,
'Tis Fancy's child, and Folly is its father ;
Wrought of such stuff as dreams are ; and baseless
As the fantastic visions of the evening.

   But soft, my friend — arrest the present moments ;
For be assur'd, they all are arrant tell-tales ;
And though their flight be silent, and their path
Trackless, as the wing'd couriers of the air,
They post to heav'n, and there record thy folly.
Because, though station'd on th' important watch,
Thou, like a sleeping, faithless centinel,
Didst let them pass unnotic'd, unimprov'd.
And know, for that thou slumber'dst on the guard,
Thou shalt be made to answer at the bar

For

For every fugitive: and when thou thus
Shalt ftand impleaded at the high tribunal
Of hood-wink'd Juftice, who fhall tell thy audit !
  Then ftay the prefent inftant, dear Horatio ;
Imprint the marks of wifdom on its wings.
'Tis of more worth than kingdoms ! far more precious
Than all the crimfon treafures of life's fountain.
Oh ! let it not elude thy grafp, but like
The good old patriarch upon record,
Hold the fleet angel faft, until he blefs thee.

On Lord C o b h a m's Gardens.

By the Same.

IT puzzles much the fages' brains,
  Where Eden ftood of yore ;
Some place it in Arabia's plains,
  Some fay, it is no more.
But Cobham can thefe tales confute,
  As all the curious know ;
For he has prov'd beyond difpute,
  That paradife is Stow.

To

To a Child of Five Years old.

By the Same.

FAIREST flow'r, all flow'rs excelling,
　　Which in Eden's garden grew ;
Flow'rs of Eve's imbower'd dwelling *,
　　Are, my Fair-one, types of you.
Mark, my Polly, how the rofes
　　Emulate thy damafk cheek ;
How the bud its fweets difclofes,
　　Buds thy opening bloom befpeak.
Lilies are, by plain direction,
　　Emblems of a double kind ;
Emblems of thy fair complexion,
　　Emblems of thy fairer mind.
But, dear girl, both flow'rs and beauty
　　Bloffom, fade, and die away ;
Then purfue good fenfe and duty,
　　Evergreens, that ne'er decay.

* Alluding to Milton's defcription of Eve's bower.

Father

Father FRANCIS's Prayer.

Written in Lord WESTMORLAND's Hermitage.

NE gay attire, ne marble hall,
   Ne arched roof, ne pictur'd wall;
Ne cook of Fraunce, ne dainty board,
Beftow'd with pypes of perigord;
Ne power, ne fuch like idle fancies,
Sweet Agnes grant to father Francis;
Let me ne more myfelf deceive;
Ne more regret the toys I leave;
The world I quit, the proud, the vain,
Corruption's and Ambition's train;
But not the good, perdie nor fair,
'Gainft them I make ne vow, ne pray'r;
But fuch aye welcome to my cell,
And oft, not always, with me dwell;
Then caft, fweet Saint, a circle round,
And blefs from fools this holy ground;
From all the foes to worth and truth,
From wanton old, and homely youth;

The gravely dull, and pertly gay,
Oh banifh thefe; and be my fay,
Right well I ween that in this age,
Mine houfe fhall prove an hermitage.

An Infcription on the Cell.

Beneath thefe mofs-grown roots, this ruftic cell,
Truth, Liberty, Content, fequefter'd dwell;
Say you, who dare our hermitage difdain,
What drawing-room can boaft fo fair a train?

An Infcription in the Cell.

Sweet bird that fing'ft on yonder fpray,
Purfue unharm'd thy fylvan lay;
While I beneath this breezy fhade,
In peace repofe my carelefs head;
And joining thy enraptur'd fong,
Inftruct the world-enamour'd throng,
That the contented harmlefs breaft
In folitude itfelf is bleft.

XXXXXXXXXXXXXXXXXXXXXXXXXX

To the Right Hon. HENRY PELHAM, Efq.

THE humble Petition of the worfhipful company
of Poets and News-writers,

SHEWETH,

THAT your honour's petitioners (dealers in rhymes,
And writers of fcandal, for mending the times)
By loffes in bus'nefs, and England's well-doing,
Are funk in their credit, and verging on ruin.

That thefe their misfortunes, they humbly conceive,
Arife not from dulnefs, as fome folks believe,
But from rubs in their way, that your honour has laid,
And want of materials to carry on trade.

That they always had form'd high conceits of their ufe,
And meant their laft breath fhould go out in abufe;
But now (and they fpeak it with forrow and tears)
Since your honour has fate at the helm of affairs,
No party will join 'em, no faction invite
To heed what they fay, or to read what they write;
Sedition, and Tumult, and Difcord are fled,
And Slander fcarce ventures to lift up her head —

In ſhort, public buſ'neſs is ſo carry'd on,
That their country is ſav'd, and the patriots undone;

To perplex 'em ſtill more, and ſure famine to bring
(Now ſatire has loſt both its truth and its ſting)
If, in ſpite of their natures, they bungle at praiſe,
Your honour regards not, and nobody pays.

YOUR Petitioners therefore moſt humbly entreat.
(As times will allow, and your honour thinks meet)
That meaſures be chang'd, and ſome cauſe of complaint
Be immediately furniſh'd, to end their reſtraint;
Their credit thereby, and their trade to retrieve,
That again they may rail, and the nation believe.

Or elſe (if your wiſdom ſhall deem it all one)
Now the parliament's riſing, and buſ'neſs is done,
That your honour would pleaſe, at this dangerous criſis,
To take to your boſom a few private vices,
By which your petitioners, haply, might thrive,
And keep both themſelves and contention alive.

In compaſſion, good Sir! give 'em ſomething to ſay,
And your honour's petitioners ever ſhall pray.

An ODE

Performed in the

Senate-House at Cambridge July 1, 1749,

At the Installation of his Grace

THOMAS HOLLES Duke of NEWCASTLE,

CHANCELLOR of the University.

—— canit erràntèm Permeſſi ad flumina Gallum
Aonas in montes ut duxerit una ſororum ;
Utque viro Phœbi chorus aſſurrexerìt omnis. VIRGIL.

By Mr. MASON, Fellow of Pembroke-Hall.

Set to Muſic by Mr. BOYCE, Compoſer to his Majeſty.

Recitative. HERE all thy active fires diffuſe,
　　　　　Thou genuine Britiſh Muſe ;
　Hither deſcend from yonder orient ſky,
　Cloth'd in thy heav'n-wove robe of harmony.

　　　　　　　　　　Air I.

Air I. Come, imperial queen of song;
   Come with all that free-born grace,
   Which lifts thee from the servile throng,
  Who meanly mimic thy majestic pace;
   That glance of dignity divine,
   Which speaks thee of celestial line;
   Proclaims thee inmate of the sky,
   Daughter of Jove and Liberty.

II.

Recitative. The elevated soul, who feels
  Thy aweful impulse, walks the fragrant ways
   Of honest unpolluted praise:
   He with impartial justice deals
  The blooming chaplets of immortal lays:
  He flies above ambition's low career;
  And nobly thron'd in Truth's meridian sphere,
  Thence, with a bold and heav'n-directed aim,
Full on fair Virtue's shrine he pours the rays of fame.

III.

Air II. Goddess! thy piercing eye explores
   The radiant range of Beauty's stores,
   The steep ascent of pine-clad hills,
   The silver slope of falling rills,
   Catches each lively-colour'd grace,
   The crimson of the wood-nymph's face,

The

The verdure of the velvet lawn,

The purple in the eaftern dawn,

Or all thofe tints, which rang'd in vivid glow

Mark the bold fweep of the celeftial bow.

IV.

Recitative. But chief fhe lifts her tuneful tranfports high,

When to her intellectual eye

The mental beauties rife in moral dignity :

The facred zeal for Freedom's caufe,

That fires the glowing Patriot's breaft;

The honeft pride that plumes the Hero's creft,

When for his country's aid the fteel he draws;

Or that, the calm, yet active heat,

With which mild Genius warms the Sage's heart,

To lift fair Science to a loftier feat,

Or ftretch to ampler bounds the wide domain of art.

Air III. Thefe, the beft bloffoms of the virtuous mind,

She culls with tafte refin'd;

From their ambrofial bloom

With bee-like fkill fhe draws the rich perfume,

And blends the fweets they all convey,

In the foft balm of her mellifluous lay.

V.

Recitative. Is there a clime, where all thefe beauties rife

In one collected radiance to her eyes ?

Is there a plain, whofe genial foil inhales
 Glory's invigorating gales,
Her brighteft beams where Emulation fpreads,
 Her kindlieft dews where Science fheds,
 Where every ftream of Genius flows,
 Where every flower of Virtue glows ?
 Thither the Mufe exulting flies,
 There fhe loudly cries ———
Chorus I. All hail, all hail,
Majeftic Granta ! hail thy aweful name,
Dear to the Mufe, to Liberty, to Fame.

VI.

Recitative. You too, illuftrious Train, fhe greets
 Who firft in thefe infpiring feats
Caught the bright beams of that ætherial fire,
Which now fublimely prompts you to afpire
To deeds of nobleft note : whether to fhield
Your country's liberties, your country's laws ;
 Or in Religion's hallow'd caufe
To hurl the fhafts of reafon, and to wield
Thofe heav'nly-temper'd arms, whofe rapid force
Arrefts bafe Falfhood in her impious courfe,
And drives rebellious Vice indignant from the field.

VII. *Air*

VII.

Air IV. And now fhe tunes her plaufive fong
   To you her fage domeftic throng;
   Who here, at Learning's richeft fhrine,
   Difpenfe to each ingenuous youth
   The treafures of immortal Truth,
   And open Wifdom's golden mine.

Recitative. Each youth infpir'd by your perfuafive art,
   Clafps the dear form of Virtue to his heart;
      And feels in his tranfported foul
      Enthufiaftic raptures roll,
   Gen'rous as thofe the fons of Cecrops caught
In hoar Lycæum's fhades from Plato's fire-cladthought.

VIII.

Air V. O Granta! on thy happy plain
   Still may thefe Attic glories reign:
   Still mayft thou keep thy wonted ftate,
   In unaffected grandeur great;

Recitative. Great as at this illuftrious hour,
   When He, whom GEORGE's well-weigh'd choice
      And Albion's general voice
   Have lifted to the faireft heights of pow'r,
      When He appears, and deigns to fhine
      The leader of thy learned line;
   And bids the verdure of thy olive bough

T 4   'Mid

'Mid all his civic chaplets twine,
And add frefh glories to his honour'd brow.

IX.

Air VI. Hafte then, and amply o'er his head
The graceful foliage fpread;
Mean while the Mufe fhall fnatch the trump of Fame,
And lift her fwelling accents high,
To tell the world that PELHAM's name
Is dear to Learning as to Liberty.

Full Chorus. The Mufe fhall fnatch the trump of Fame,
And lift her fwelling accents high,
To tell the world that PELHAM's name
Is dear to Learning as to Liberty.

◆◆

ODE to an ÆOLUS's * Harp.

Sent to Mifs SHEPHEARD.

By the Same.

YES, magic lyre! now all compleat
Thy flender frame refponfive rings,
While kindred notes with undulation fweet
Accordant wake from all thy vocal ftrings.

* This inftrument appears to have been invented by KIRCHER: who has given a very accurate defcription of it in his MUSURGIA. After having been neglected above an hundred years, it was again accidentally difcovered by Mr. OSWALD. See Vol. III. p. 9. of this Mifcellany.

Go then to her, whofe foft requeft
Bade my bleft hands thy form prepare;
Ah go, and fweetly footh her tender breaft
With many a warble wild, and artlefs air.

For know, full oft, while o'er the mead
Bright June extends her fragrant reign,
The Fair fhall place thee near her flumb'ring head
To court the gales that cool the fultry plain;

Then fhall the Sylphs, and Sylphids bright,
Mild Genii all, to whofe high care
Her virgin charms are giv'n, in circling flight
Skim fportive round thee in the fields of air.

Some, flutt'ring 'mid thy trembling ftrings,
Shall catch the rich melodious fpoil,
And lightly brufh thee with their purple wings
To aid the zephyrs in their tuneful toil;

While others check each ruder gale,
Expel rough Boreas from the fky,
Nor let a breeze its heaving breath exhale,
Save fuch as foftly pant, and panting die.

Then, as thy fwelling accents rife,
Fair Fancy waking at the found,
Shall paint bright vifions on her raptur'd eyes,
And waft her fpirits to enchanted ground,

To

To myrtle groves, Elyſian greens,
  'Mid which ſome fav'rite youth ſhall rove,
Shall meet, ſhall lead her through the glitt'ring ſcenes,
  And all be muſic, extacy, and love.   -

ODE to HEALTH.

Non eſt vivere, ſed valere, vita.   MARTIAL.

By Mr. DUNCOMBE, Fellow of Corpus Chriſti College,
CAMBRIDGE.

I.

HEALTH! to thee thy vot'ry owes
  All the bleſſings life beſtows,
All the ſweets the ſummer yields,
Melodious woods, and clover'd fields;
By thee he taſtes the calm delights
Of ſtudious days and peaceful nights:
By thee his eye each ſcene with rapture views;
The Muſe ſhall ſing thy gifts, for they inſpire the Muſe.

II.

Does increaſe of wealth impart
Tranſports to a bounteous heart?
Does the ſire with ſmiles ſurvey
His prattling children round him play?

Does

Does love with mutual blushes streak
The swain's and virgin's artless cheek ?
From HEALTH these blushes, smiles and transports flow;
Wealth, children, love itself, to HEALTH their relish owe.

III.

Nymph! with thee, at early Morn,
Let me brush the waving corn;
And, at Noon-tide's sultry hour,
O bear me to the wood-bine bow'r!
When Evening lights her glow-worm, lead
To yonder dew-enamell'd mead;
And let me range at Night those glimm'ring groves,
Where stillness ever sleeps, and Contemplation roves.

IV.

This my tributary lay,
Grateful at thy shrine I pay,
Who for sev'n whole years hast shed
Thy balmy blessings o'er my head;
O! let me still enamour'd view
Those fragrant lips of rosy hue,
Nor think there needs th' allay of sharp disease,
To quicken thy repast, and give it pow'r to please.

V.

Now by swiftest Zephyrs drawn,
Urge thy chariot o'er the lawn;

In

III.

Let Health, gay daughter of the skies,
 On Zephyr's wings descend,
And scatter pleasures as she flies
 Where Surry's downs extend;
There HERRING wooes her friendly power,
There may she all her roses shower,
To heal that shepherd all her balms employ,
So will she sooth our fears, and give a nation joy.

IV.

Ah me! that Virtue's godlike friends
 So soon are claim'd by Fate!
Lo! * PELHAM to the grave descends,
 The bulwark of the state:
When will fair Truth his equal find
Among the best of human kind?
Long be the fatal day with mourning kept!
AUGUSTUS sigh'd sincere, and all the worthy wept.

V.

Thy delegate, kind heaven, restore
 To health, and safely keep;
Let good AUGUSTUS sigh no more,
 No more the worthy weep:

* The Right Honourable Henry Pelham, Esq; died on the 6th of March 1754.

And ftill upon the royal head
The riches of thy bleffings fhed :
Eftablifh'd with his counfellors around,
Long be his profp'rous reign, and all with glory crown'd.

✦✦✦✦✦✦✦✦✦✦✦✦✦✦✦✦✦✦✦✦✦✦✦✦

An AUTUMNAL ODE.

By the Same.

I.

YET once more, glorious God of day,
  While beams thine orb ferene,
O let me warbling court thy ftay
  To gild the fading fcene !
Thy rays invigorate the Spring,
Bright Summer to perfection bring,
The cold, inclement days of Winter cheer,
And make th' Autumnal months the mildeft of the year.

II.

Ere yet the ruffet foliage fall,
  I'll climb the mountain's brow,
My friend, my Hayman, at thy call,
  To view the fcene below :
How fweetly pleafing to behold
Forefts of vegetable gold !

How

How mix'd the many-chequer'd shades between
The tawny mellowing hue, and the gay vivid green !

III.

How splendid all the sky ! how still !
   How mild the dying gale !
How soft the whispers of the rill
   That winds along the dale !
So tranquil Nature's works appear,
It seems the Sabbath of the year ;
As if, the Summer's Labour past, she chose
This season's sober calm for blandishing repose.

IV.

Such is of well-spent life the time,
   When busy days are past,
Man verging gradual from his prime,
   Meets sacred Peace at last :
His flowery Spring of pleasures o'er,
And Summer's full-blown pride no more,
He gains pacific Autumn, meek and bland,
And dauntless braves the stroke of Winter's palsy'd hand.

V.

For yet awhile, a little while,
   Involv'd in wint'ry gloom,
And lo ! another Spring shall smile,
   A Spring eternal bloom ;

Then

Then fhall he fhine, a glorious gueft;
In the bright manfions of the bleft,
Where due rewards on Virtue are beftow'd,
And reap the golden fruits of what his Autumn fow'd.

A S O N G.

I.

AWAY, let nought to love difpleafing,
  My Winifreda, move thy fear,
Let nought delay the heav'nly bleffing,
  Nor fqueamifh pride, nor gloomy care.

II.

What though no grants of royal donors
  With pompous titles grace our blood,
We'll fhine in more fubftantial honours,
  And to be noble we'll be good.

III.

What though from Fortune's lavifh bounty
  No mighty treafures we poffefs,
We'll find within our pittance plenty,
  And be content without excefs.

IV.

Still fhall each kind returning feafon
  Sufficient for our wifhes give,
For we will live a life of reafon,
  And that's the only life to live.

V.

Our name, whilft virtue thus we tender,
  Shall fweetly found where'er 'tis fpoke,
And all the great ones much fhall wonder,
  How they admire fuch little folk.

VI.

Through youth and age in love excelling,
  We'll hand in hand together tread,
Sweet fmiling Peace fhall crown our dwelling,
  And babes, fweet fmiling babes, our bed.

VII.

How fhould I love the pretty creatures,
  Whilft round my knees they fondly clung,
To fee 'em look their mother's features,
  To hear 'em lifp their mother's tongue !

VIII.

And when with envy Time tranfported
  Shall think to rob us of our joys,
You'll in your girls again be courted,
  And I go wooing in my boys.

The

XXXXXXXXXXXXXXX✱XXXXXXXXXXXXX

The G E N I U S.

An ODE, written in 1717, on occafion of the
Duke of MARLBOROUGH's Apoplexy.

I.

AWEFUL hero, Marlb'rough, rife:
 Sleepy charms I come to break:
Higher turn thy languid eyes:
 Lo! thy Genius calls: awake!

II.

Well furvey this faithful plan,
 Which records thy life's great ftory;
'Tis a fhort, but crowded fpan,
 Full of triumphs, full of glory.

III.

One by one thy deeds review,
 Sieges, battles, thick appear;
Former wonders, loft in new,
 Greatly fill each pompous year.

IV.

This is Blenheim's crimfon field,
 Wet with gore, with flaughter ftain'd!
Here retiring fquadrons yield,
 And a bloodlefs wreath is gain'd!

U 2   V. Ponder

V.

Ponder in thy godlike mind
    All the wonders thou haſt wrought;
Tyrants, from their pride declin'd,
    Be the ſubjeƈt of thy thought!

VI.

Reſt thee here, while life may laſt:
    Th' utmoſt bliſs, to man allow'd,
Is to trace his aƈtions paſt,
    And to own them great and good.

VII.

But 'tis gone — a mortal born!
    Swift the fading ſcenes remove —
Let them paſs with noble ſcorn,
    Thine are worlds, which roll above.

VIII.

Poets, prophets, heroes, kings,
    Pleas'd, thy ripe approach foreſee;
Men, who aƈted wond'rous things,
    Though they yield in fame to thee.

IX.

Foremoſt, in the patriot-band,
    Shining with diſtinguiſh'd day!
See thy friend, Godolphin ſtand!
    See! he beckons thee away.

X. Yonde

X.

Yonder feats and fields of light
  Let thy ravifh'd thought explore;
Wifhing, panting for thy flight!
  Half an angel; man no more.

TRANSLATIONS from HORACE.

By Mr. MARRIOTT, of Trinity-Hall, Cambridge.

Book I. Ode XVII.

Invitation to his Miftrefs.

OFT Faunus leaves Arcadia's plain,
  And to the Sabine hill retreats:
He guards my flocks from rufhing rain,
  From piercing winds, and fcorching heats.

Where lurks the thyme, or fhrubs appear,
  My wanton kids fecurely play;
My goats no pois'nous ferpent fear,
  Safe wand'ring through the woodland way.

No hoftile wolf the fold invades;
   Uftica's pendent rocks rebound
My fong; and all the fylvan fhades,
   By Echo taught, return the found.

The gods my verfe propitious hear,
   My head from every danger fhield:
For you, o'erflows the bounteous year,
   And Plenty's horn hath heap'd my field.

Refponfive to the Teian ftring,
   Within the fun-defended vale,
Here, foftly warbling you fhall fing
   Each tender, tuneful, am'rous tale.

No rival, here, fhall burft the bands
   That wreathe my charmer's beauteous hair,
Nor feize her weakly ftruggling hands;
   But Love and Horace guard the fair.

Book II. Ode VI. Imitated.

BEVIL, that with your friend would roam,
   Far from your England's happier home,
Should e'er the Fates that friend detain
In gayer France, or graver Spain;

Know, all my wish is to retreat,
When age shall quench my youthful heat,
In Kentish shades sweet peace to find,
And leave the sons of care behind.

But should this pleasing hope be vain,
May I fair Windsor's seat attain,
Where Leddon's gentle waters glide,
And flocks adorn its flowery side.

Sweet groves, I love your silent shades,
Your ruffet lawns, and op'ning glades,
With fam'd Italia's plains may vie
Your fertile fields, and healthful sky.

Here, let our eve of life be spent;
Here, friend shall live with friend content:
Here, in cold earth my limbs be laid;
And here thy generous tear be paid.

U 4   Book

Book II. Ode XII. Translated.

THE wars of Numantia and Hannibal dire,
   On land, or on ocean the fighting,
Mæcenas, ne'er fuited my peaceable lyre,
  In fubjects much fofter delighting.

You love not of centaurs embattled to hear,
   Nor of giants, a tale of fuch wonder,
Who fhook all the fkies, made Jupiter fear,
  'Till drove by Alcides and thunder.

In profe, my good patron, more nobly you write,
   As your topic than thefe is much better,
How Cæfar with glory can govern and fight,
  And lead haughty kings in his fetter.

Alone my gay Mufe of Licinia would fing,
   The conftant, good-natur'd, and pretty,
So graceful to dance with the maids in a ring,
  So fparkling, fo merry, and witty.

While you play with her hair that is carelefsly curl'd,
   While this way, now that way fhe twitches,
Of your teazing fo kindly complaining, no world
  Could bribe for one lock with its riches.

Thus

Thus bleſt with the nymph, how tranſporting the joy!
  Who whimſical, wanton, amuſes;
Who pleaſingly forward, or prettily coy,
  Oft ſnatches the kiſs ſhe refuſes.

XXXXXXXXXXXXXXXXXXXXXXXXXXXXX

To a L A D Y making a Pin-Baſket.

By the Same.

WHILE objects of a parent's care,
    With joy your fond attention ſhare,
Madam, accept th' auſpicious ſtrain;
Nor riſe your beauteous work in vain.
Oft be your ſecond race ſurvey'd,
And oft a new pin-baſket made.
  When marriage was in all its glory,
So poets, madam, tell the ſtory,
Ere Plutus damp'd love's purer flame,
Or Smithfield bargains had a name,
In heav'n a blooming youth and bride
At Hymen's altars were ally'd;
When Cupid had his Pſyché won,
And, all her deſtin'd labours done,

The

The cruel Fates their rage relented,
And mamma Venus had confented.

  At Jove's command, and Hermes' call,
The train appear'd to fill the hall,
And gods, and goddeffes were dreft,
To do them honour, in their beft.
The little rogues now pafs'd the row,
And look'd, and mov'd I ^don't know how,
And, ambling hand in hand, appear
Before the mighty thunderer.
Low at his throne they bent the knee;
He fmil'd the blufhing pair to fee,
Lay'd his tremendous bolt afide,
And ftrok'd their cheeks, and kifs'd the bride.

  Says Juno, fince our Jove's fo kind,
My dears, fome prefent I muft find.
In greateft pleafures, greateft dangers,
We and the fex were never ftrangers;
With bounteous hand my gifts I fpread,
Prefiding o'er the marriage-bed.
Soon, for the months are on the wing,
To you a daughter fair I bring,
And know, from this your nuptial morn'
Shall Pleafure, fmiling babe, be born.

                              But

But for the babe we muſt prepare ;
That too ſhall be your Juno's care.
Apollo from his golden lyre,
Shall firſt aſſiſt us with the wire ;
Vulcan ſhall make the ſilver pin.
The baſket thus we ſhall begin,
Where we may put the child's array,
And get it ready by the day.
The nymphs themſelves with flowers ſhall dreſs it,
Pallas ſhall weave, and I will bleſs it.

Captain C U P I D.

By the Same.

E R S T, in Cythera's ſacred ſhade,
When Venus claſp'd the god of war,
The laughing loves around them play'd,
One bore the ſhield, and one the ſpear.

The little warriors Cupid led,
The ſhining baldric grac'd his breaſt,
The mighty helmet o'er his head
Nodded its formidable creſt.

Hence

Hence oft', to win fome ftubborn maid,
Still does the wanton God affume
The martial air, the gay cockade,
The fword, the fhoulder-knot and plume.

Phyllis had long his power defy'd,
Refolv'd her conquefts to maintain;
His fruitlefs art each poet try'd:
Each fhepherd tun'd his pipe in vain.

'Till Cupid came, a captain bold:
Of trenches and of palifadoes
He talk'd; and many a tale he told
Of battles, and of ambufcadoes:

How oft' his godfhip had been drunk;
What melting maids he had undone;
How oft' by night had ftorm'd a punk,
Or bravely beat a faucy dun.

He fwore, drank, whor'd, fung, danc'd with fpirit,
And o'er each pleafing topic ran;
'Till Phyllis figh'd, and own'd his merit,
The Captain's fure a charming man.

Ye

Ye bards, on verfe let Phœbus doat,
Ye fhepherds, leave your pipes to Pan,
Nor verfe nor pipe will Phyllis note.
The Captain is the charming man.

ODE on AMBITION,

By the Same.

THE mariner, when firft he fails,
   While his bold oars the fparkling furface fweep,
With new delight, tranfported hails
The blue expanded fkies, and level deep.

Such young Ambition's fearlefs aim,
Pleas'd with the gorgeous fcene of wealth and power,
   In the gay morn of early fame,
Nor thinks of evening's ftorm, and gloomy hour.

Life's opening views bright charms reveal,
Feed the fond wifh, and fan the youthful fire.
   But woes unknown thofe charms conceal,
And fair illufions cheat our fierce defire.

There

There Envy fhows her fullen mien,
With changeful colour, grinning fmiles of hate ;
   There Malice ftabs, with rage ferene ;
In deadly filence, treacherous Friendfhips wait.

   High on a mountain's lofty brow,
'Mid clouds and ftorms, has Glory fix'd her feat ;
   Rock'd by the roaring winds that blow,
The light'nings blaft it, and the tempefts beat.

   Within the fun-gilt vale beneath,
More moderate Hope with fweet Contentment dwells,
   While gentler breezes round them breathe,
And fofter fhowers refrefh their peaceful cells.

   To better genius ever blind,
That points to each in varied life his fhare,
   Man quits the path by heaven defign'd,
To fearch for blifs among the thorns of care.

   Our native powers we fcorn to know ;
With ftedfaft error ftill the wrong purfue ;
   Inftruct our forward ills to grow ;
While fad fucceffes but our pain renew.

In

In vain heaven tempers life with sweet,
With flowers the way, that leads us home, bestrews,
   If dupes to passion, and deceit,
We drink the bitter, and the rugged choose.

   Few can on Grandeur's stage appear,
Each lofty part with true applause sustain,
   No common virtue safe can steer,
Where rocks unnumber'd lurk beneath the main.

   Then happiest he, whose timely hand
To cool Discretion has the helm resign'd;
   Enjoys the calm, in sight of land,
From changing tides secure, and trustless wind.

ODE to FANCY.

By the Same.

I.

GILDING with brighter beams the vernal skies,
   Now hastes the car of day to rise.
   Youth, and Mirth, and Beauty leads
  In golden reins the sprightly steeds,
With wanton Love that rolls his sparkling eyes.

Morpheus,

Morpheus, no more

Thy poppies, cropt on Lethe's margin, fhed

  Around thy languid poet's head.

    Thou drowfy god,

   'Tis time to break thy leaden rod,

     And give thy flumbers o'er.

But come, thou woodland Nymph, along,

  Miftrefs of the vocal fong,

  Fancy ever fair and free ;

Whether on the mountains ftraying,

Or on beds of rofes playing,

  Daughter of fweet Liberty.

II.

  Through all the ivy-circled cave

Soft mufic at thy birth was heard to found.

  The Graces danc'd thy bower around,

And gently dipt thee in the filver wave.

  With bloffoms fair thy cradle dreft,

  And rock'd their fmiling babe to reft.

To kifs thy lips, the bees, a murmuring throng,

  With bufy wings, unnumber'd flew ;

For thee, from every flower their tribute drew,

And lull'd thy flumbers with an airy fong.

  Come in thy heav'nly woven veft,

That

.That Iris' hand has ting'd in every dye,

  With which she paints the sky,

  Flowing o'er thy zonelefs breaft.

III.

  Me, fweet enchantrefs, deign to bear

   O'er the feas, and through the air ;

   . O'er the plains extended wide,

O'er mifty hills, and curling clouds we ride,

  Now mounting high, now finking low,

  Through hail and rain, and vapours go ;

   Where is treafur'd up the fnow :

  Where fleeps the thunder in its cell ;

   Where the fwift-wing'd light'nings dwell ;

Or where the bluft'ring ftorms are taught to blow.

   Now tread the milky way ;

Unnumber'd worlds that float in æther fpy,

  Among the glittering planets ftray,

   To the lunar orbit fly,

  And mountains, fhores, and feas defcry,

  Now catch the mufic of the fpheres ;

   Which, fince the birth of time,

   Have, in according chime,

  And fair proportion, rolling round,

   With each diviner found

Attentive Silence, pierc'd thy lift'ning ears ;

Unheard by all, but thofe alone

　Whom to wifdom's fecret throne

The Mufe, with heav'n-taught guidance, deigns to brin

To trace the facred paths with hallowed feet;

　　Or, Fancy, who the myftic fhade,

　　　In thy airy car, pervade,

Where Plato's raptur'd fpirit holds its folemn feat.

IV.

　　But, Fancy, downward urge thy flight.

　　On fome mountain's towering height,

　With hoary frofts eternal crown'd,

　　　Rapt with dufky vapours round,

　　　Let me fix my ftedfaft feet.

　I feel, I feel the fanning gales;

　The wat'ry mifts beneath retreat.

　The noontide ray now darts its heat,

　　And pours its glories o'er the vales.

　　Glittering to the dancing beams,

Urging their ftubborn way the rocks among,

　I hear, and fee a thoufand ftreams

　Foam, and roar, and rufh along.

　　　But to the plains defcended,

　　　Their fudden rage is ended.

Now loft in deep recefs of darkfome bowers,

Ag:

Again now sparkling through the meads
   Vested soft with vernal flowers,
  Reflecting the majestic towers,
Its peaceful flood the roving channel leads.
    There the rural cots are seen,
From whose low roof the curling smoak ascends,
And dims with blueish volumes all the green.
    There some forest far extends
  Its groves embrown'd with lengthen'd shade ;
  Embosom'd where some Gothic seat,
     Of monarchs once retreat ;
  In wild magnificence array'd,
  The pride of ancient times presents,
  And lifts, in contrast fair display'd,
  Its sun reflecting battlements.

V.

Near, some imperial city seems to reign,
  Triumphant o'er the subject land ;
  With domes of art Vitruvian crown'd.
  See gleam her gilded spires around,
  Her gates in aweful grandeur stand.
Equal to shine in peace, or war sustain ;
  Her mighty bulwarks threat the plain
With many a work of death, and armed mound.
Where rolls her wealthy river deep and wide,

        Tall

Tall groves of crowded mafts arife ;
Their ftreamers waving to the fkies.
The banks are white with fwelling fails,
And diftant veffels ftem the tide,
Circling through pendant cliffs, and watery dales.
The ruffet hills, the valleys green beneath,
The fallows brown, and dufky heath,
The yellow corn, empurpled vine,
In union foft their tints combine,
And, Fancy, all engage thine eye
With a fweet variety.
While clouds the fleeting clouds purfue,
In mutual fhade, and mutual light,
The changing landfcape meets the fight ;
'Till the ken no more can view ;
And heaven appears to meet the ground ;
The rifing lands, and azure diftance drown'd
Amid the gay horizon's golden bound.

VI.

Such are the fcenes that oft invite
To feed thee, Fancy, with delight.
All that nature can create,
Beauteous, aweful, new and great,
Sweet enthufiaft, is thy treafure,
Source of wonder, and of pleafure ;

' Every

Every fenfe to tranfport winning,
Still unbounded and beginning.
Then, Fancy, fpread thy wings again;
Unlock the caverns of the main.
Above, beneath, and all around:
   Let the tumbling billows fpread;
   'Till the coral floor we tread,
Exploring all the wealth that decks the realms profound;
   There, gather gems that long have glow'd
     In the vaft, unknown abode,
The jafper vein'd, the faphire blue,
The ruby bright with crimfon hue,
Whate'er the bed refplendent paves,
Or decks the glittering roofs on high,
Through whofe tranflucent arch are feen the rolling waves.
   Fancy, thefe fhall clafp thy veft,
With thefe thy lovely brows be dreft,
In every gay, and various dye.
But hark! — the feas begin to roar,
The whiftling winds affault my ear,
The louring ftorms around appear —
   Fancy, bear me to the fhore.
There in thy realms, bright goddefs, deign
Secure to fix thy votary's feet:

O give

O give to follow oft thy train:
Still with accuftom'd lay thy power to greet;
To dwell with Peace, and fport with thee,
Fancy, ever fair and free.

⚜⚜⚜⚜⚜⚜⚜⚜⚜⚜⚜⚜⚜⚜⚜⚜

An Addrefs to his Elbow-chair, new cloath'd.

By the late WM. SOMERVILE, Efq; Author of the Chace*.

MY dear companion, and my faithful friend!
If Orpheus taught the liftening oaks to bend;
If ftones and rubbifh, at Amphion's call,
Danc'd into form, and built the Theban wall;
Why fhould'ft not *thou* attend my humble lays,
And hear my grateful harp refound thy praife?
    True, thou art fpruce and fine, a very beau;
But what are trappings, and external fhow?
To real worth alone I make my court;
Knaves are my fcorn, and coxcombs are my fport.
    Once I beheld thee far lefs trim and gay;
Ragged, disjointed, and to worms a prey;
The fafe retreat of every lurking moufe;
Derided, fhun'd; the lumber of my houfe!

* Written towards the clofe of Mr. Somervile's life.

Thy

Thy robe how chang'd from what it was before!
Thy velvet robe, which pleas'd my fires of yore!
'Tis thus capricious Fortune wheels us round;
Aloft we mount — then tumble to the ground.
Yet grateful *then*, my conftancy I prov'd;
I knew thy worth; my friend in rags I lov'd!
I lov'd thee, *more*; nor like a courtier, fpurn'd
My benefactor, when the tide was turn'd.

With confcious fhame, yet frankly, I confefs,
That in my youthful days — I lov'd thee lefs.
Where vanity, where pleafure call'd, I ftray'd;
And every wayward appetite obey'd.
But fage experience taught me how to prize
Myfelf; and how, this world: fhe bade me rife
To nobler flights, regardlefs of a race
Of factious emmets; pointed where to place
My blifs, and lodg'd me in thy foft embrace.

Here on thy yielding down I fit fecure;
And, patiently, what heav'n has fent, endure;
From all the futile cares of bufinefs free;
Not *fond* of life, but yet content to *be:*
Here mark the fleeting hours; regret the paft;
And ferioufly prepare, to meet the laft.

So fafe on fhore the penfion'd failor lies;
And all the malice of the ftorm defies:

X 4

With

With eafe of body bleft, and peace of mind,
Pities the reftlefs crew he left behind;
Whilft, in his cell, he meditates alone
On his great voyage, to the world unknown.

XXXXXXXXXXXXXXXXXXXXXXXXXXXXX

S O N G.

By the Same.

I.

AS o'er Afteria's fields I rove,
The blifsful feat of peace and love,
Ten thoufand beauties round me rife,
And mingle pleafure with furprize,

By nature bleft in every part,
Adorn'd with every grace of art,
This paradife of blooming joys
Each raptur'd fenfe, at once, employs.

II.

But when I view the radiant queen,
Who form'd this fair enchanting fcene;
Pardon ye grots! ye cryftal floods!
Ye breathing flow'rs! ye fhady woods!

Your

Your coolnefs now no more invites;
No more your murmuring ftream delights;
Your fweets decay, your verdure's flown;
My foul's intent on her alone.

XXXXXXXXXXXX﹡XXXXXXXXXXXX

ODE to a FRIEND wounded in a Duel.

HOW long fhall tyrant Cuftom bind
   In flavifh chains the human mind?
How long fhall falfe fantaftic Honour draw
   The vengeful fword, with fury fell,
   And ranc'rous Malice dark as hell,
In fpight of Reafon's rule, and Nature's eldeft law?

Too many gallant youths have bled;
Too much of Britifh blood been fhed
By Britons' fwords, and that foul monfter's laws:
   Youths that might elfe have nobly dar'd;
   More glorious wounds and dangers fhar'd
For Britain's juft defence, and virtue's injur'd caufe.

So

So when the fierce Cadmean youth
Sprung from the dragon's venom'd tooth,
Each chief arose in shining armour dreſt:
With rage inſpir'd, the furious band
Soon found a ready foe at hand,
And plung'd the pointed ſteel each in a brother's breaſt.

Has Britain then no other foes,
That thus her ſons their lives expoſe
To private war, and feuds, and civil fray?
Does Spain inſult her flag no more?
Does Lewis yet his thoughts give o'er
Of univerſal rule, and arbitrary ſway?

'Tis Britons' to ſupport the law;
'Tis theirs ambitious kings to awe,
And equal rights of empire to maintain.
For this our fathers, brave and ſtout,
At Agincourt and Creſſy fought,
And heap'd fam'd Blenheim's field with mountains of the [ſlain.

How will the Gallic monarch ſmile,
To ſee the ſons of Albion's iſle
Their country's blood with ruthleſs weapons drain!
Them-

Themfelves avenge the glorious day
When Marlb'rough fwept whole hofts away,
And fent the frighted Danube purple to the main!

O fay, in this inglorious ftrife
Thy arm had robb'd thy friend of life,
What pangs, what anguifh had thy bofom prov'd?
How hadft thou curs'd the cruel deed,
That caus'd the gallant youth to bleed,
Pierc'd by thy guilty fword, and flain by him he lov'd?

How did the fair Maria blame
Thy high-bred fpirit's eager flame,
That courting danger flighted her foft love?
Far other wreaths for thee fhe twin'd;
Far other cares for thee defign'd;
And for the laurel crown, the myrtle chaplet wove.

If not for her's, for Britain's fake,
Forbear thy precious life to ftake;
Nor taint thy honour with fo foul a deed.
One day thy country may require
Thy gallant arm and martial fire:
Then may'ft thou bravely conquer, or as bravely bleed.

ODE

✖✖✖✖✖✖✖✖✖✖✖✖✖✖✖✖✖✖✖✖✖✖✖✖✖✖✖✖✖✖

ODE to NIGHT.

THE bufy cares of day are done;
   In yonder weftern cloud the fun
Now fets, in other worlds to rife,
And glad with light the nether fkies.
With ling'ring pace the parting day retires,
And flowly leaves the mountain tops, and gilded fpires.

Yon azure cloud, enrob'd with white,
   Still fhoots a gleam of fainter light:
At length defcends a browner fhade;
At length the glimm'ring objects fade :
'Till all fubmit to NIGHT's impartial reign,
And undiftinguifh'd darknefs covers all the plain.

No more the ivy-crowned oak
   Refounds beneath the wood-man's ftroke.
Now Silence holds her folemn fway;
Mute is each bufh, and every fpray:
Nought but the found of murm'ring rills is heard,
Or from the mould'ring tow'r, NIGHT's folitary bird.

                              Hail

Hail sacred hour of peaceful rest !
Of pow'r to charm the troubled breast !
  By thee the captive slave obtains
  Short respite from his galling pains ;
  Nor sighs for liberty, nor native soil ;
But for a while forgets his chains, and sultry toil.

  No horrors hast thou in thy train,
  No scorpion lash, no clanking chain.
  When the pale murd'rer round him spies
  A thousand grisly forms arise,
  When shrieks and groans arouse his palsy'd fear,
'Tis guilt alarms his soul, and conscience wounds his ear.

  The village swain whom Phillis charms,
  Whose breast the tender passion warms,
  Wishes for thy all-shadowing veil,
  To tell the fair his love-sick tale :
  Nor less impatient of the tedious day,
She longs to hear his tale, and sigh her soul away.

  Oft by the covert of thy shade
  LEANDER woo'd the THRACIAN maid ;
  Through foaming seas his passion bore,
  Nor fear'd the ocean's thund'ring roar.

The

The confcious virgin from the fea-girt tow'r
Hung out the faithful torch to guide him to her bow'r.

 Oft at thy filent hour the fage
 Pores on the fair inftructivo page ;
 Or rapt in mufings deep, his foul
 Mounts active to the ftarry pole :
There pleas'd to range the realms of endlefs night,
Numbers the ftars, or marks the comet's devious light.

 Thine is the hour of converfe fweet,
 When fprightly wit and reafon meet :
 Wit, the fair bloffom of the mind,
 But fairer ftill with reafon join'd.
Such is the feaft thy focial hours afford,
When eloquence and GRANVILLE join the friendly board.

 GRANVILLE, whofe polifh'd mind is fraught
 With all that ROME or GREECE e'er taught ;
 Who pleafes and inftructs the ear,
 When he affumes the critic's chair,
Or from the STAGYRITE or PLATO draws
The arts of civil life, the fpirit of the laws.

         O let

O let me often thus employ
The hour of mirth and social joy !
And glean from GRANVILLE's learned ſtore
Fair ſcience and true wiſdom's lore.
Then will I ſtill implore thy longer ſtay,
Nor change thy feſtive hours for ſunſhine and the day.

Written upon leaving a FRIEND's Houſe in WALES.

By the Rev. Dr. M.

THE winds were loud, the clouds deep-hung;
    And dragg'd their ſweepy trains along
The dreary mountain's ſide ;
When, from the hill, one look to throw
On Towy's rambling flood below,
    I turn'd my horſe — and ſigh'd.

But ſoon the guſts of ſleet and hail
Flew thick acroſs the darken'd vale,
    And blurr'd the face of day :
Forlorn and ſad, I jogg'd along ;
And though Tom cry'd, " You're going wrong,"
    Still wander'd from my way.

1   The

The scenes, which once my fancy took,
And my aw'd mind with wonder struck,
  Pass'd unregarded, all!
Nor black Trecarris' steepy height,
Nor waste Trecastle gave delight;
  Nor clamorous Hondy's fall.

Did the bleak day then give me pain?
The driving snow, or pelting rain,
  Or sky with tempests fraught?
No! these unheeded rag'd around:
Nought in them so much Mine I found,
  As claim'd one wandering thought.

Far other cares engross'd my mind,
Cares for the joys I left behind,
  In * Newton's happy groves!
Yet not because its woods disclose
Or grots or lawns more sweet than those
  Which Pan at noon-day loves;

But that, beside its social hearth
Dwells every joy, which youthful mirth
  Or serious age can claim:

* Newton is the name of a seat belonging to Sir John Price.

The

The man too whom my foul firſt knew,
To virtue and to honour true ;
   And friendſhip's ſacred name.

O Newton, could theſe penſive lays
In worthy numbers ſcan thy praiſe,
   Much gratitude would ſay ;
But that the Muſe, ingenuous maid,
Of *flattery* ſeems ſo much afraid,
   She'll ſcarce her *duty* pay.

Brecknock, Oct. 16, 1749.

DENNIS to Mr. THOMSON,

Who had procured him a Benefit Night.

REflecting on thy worth, methinks I find
  Thy various Seaſons in their author's mind.
Spring opes her bloſſoms, various as thy Muſe,
And, like thy ſoft compaſſion, ſheds her dews.
Summer's hot drought in thy expreſſion glows,
And o'er each page a tawny ripeneſs throws.
Autumn's rich fruits th' inſtructed reader gains,
Who taſtes the meaning purpoſe of thy ſtrains.

Winter—but that no femblance takes from thee :
That hoary feafon yields a type of me.
Shatter'd by time's bleak ftorms I withering lay,
Leaflefs, and whitening in a cold decay!
Yet fhall my proplefs ivy, pale and bent,
Blefs the fhort funfhine which thy pity lent.

S O N G. 1753.

I.

HO W eafy was Colin, how blithe and how gay !
Ere he met the fair Chloris, how fprightly his lay !
So graceful her form, fo accomplifh'd her mind,
Sure pity, he thought, with fuch charms muft be join'd ?

II.

Whenever fhe danc'd, or whenever fhe fung,
How juft was her motion, how fweet was her tongue !
And when the youth told her his paffionate flame,
She allow'd him to fancy her heart felt the fame.

III.

With ardour he prefs'd her to think him fincere,
But alas ! fhe redoubled each hope and each fear ;
She would not deny, nor fhe would not approve,
And fhe neither refus'd him, nor gave him her love.

IV. Now

IV.

Now cheer'd by complacence, now froze by difdain,
He languifh'd for freedom, but languifh'd in vain :
'Till Thyrfis, who pity'd fo helplefs a flave,
Eas'd his heart of its pain by the counfel he gave.

V.

Forfake her, faid he, and rejeƈt her awhile ;
If, fhe love you, fhe foon will return with a fmile !
You can judge of her paffion by abfence alone,
And by abfence will conquer her heart or—your own.

VI.

This advice he purfu'd ; but the remedy prov'd
Too fatal, alas ! to the fair one he lov'd ;
Which cur'd his own paffion, but left her in vain
To figh for a heart fhe could never regain.

I. S. H.

✿✿✿✿✿✿✿✿✿✿✿✿✿✿✿✿✿✿✿✿✿✿✿✿✿

The BULFINCH in Town.

By a Lady of Quality.

HARK to the blackbird's pleafing note :
  Sweet ufher of the vocal throng !
Nature direƈts his warbling throat,
  And all that hear admire the fong.

Y 2

Yon'

Yon' bulfinch, with unvary'd tone,
  Of cadence harfh, and accent fhrill,
Has brighter plumage to atone
  For want of harmony and fkill.

Yet, difcontent with nature's boon,
  Like man, to mimic art he flies ;
On opera-pinions hoping foon
  Unrivall'd he fhall mount the fkies.

And while, to pleafe fome courtly fair,
  He one dull tune with labour learns,
A well-gilt cage, remote from air,
  And faded plumes, is all he earns !

Go, haplefs captive ! ftill repeat
  The founds which nature never taught ;
Go, liftening fair ! and call them fweet,
  Becaufe you know them dearly bought.

Unenvy'd both ! go hear and fing
  Your ftudy'd mufic o'er and o'er ;
Whilft I attend th' inviting fpring,
  In fields where birds unfetter'd foar.

SONG

S O N G.

Written in Winter 1745.

By the Same.

I.

THE fun, his gladfome beams withdrawn,
  The hills all white with fnow,
Leave me dejected and forlorn !
  Who can defcribe my woe ?
But not the fun's warm beams could cheer,
  Nor hills, though e'er fo green,
Unlefs my Damon fhould appear,
  To beautify the fcene.

II.

The frozen brooks, and pathlefs vales,
  Disjoin my love and me !
The pining bird his fate bewails
  On yonder leaflefs tree !
But what to me are birds or brooks
  Or any joy that's near ?
Heavy the lute, and dull the books,
  While Damon is not here !

III. The

III.

The Laplander, who, half the year,
    Is wrapt in fhades of night,
Mourns not, like me, his winter drear,
    Nor wifhes more for light.
But what were light, without my love,
    Or objects e'er fo fine ?
The flowery meadow, field, or grove,
    If Damon be not mine ?

IV.

Each moment, from my dear away,
    Is a long age of pain ;
Fly fwift, ye hours, be calm the day,
    That brings my love again !
O hafte and bring him to my arms ;
    Nor let us ever part :
My breaft fhall beat no more alarms,
    When I fecure his heart.

Written

Written to a near Neighbour in a tempeſtuous
Night, 1748.

By the Same.

I.

YOU bid my Muſe not ceaſe to ſing,
　　You bid my ink not ceaſe to flow;
Then ſay it ever ſhall be ſpring,
　　And boiſterous winds ſhall never blow:
When you ſuch miracles can prove,
I'll ſing of friendſhip, or of love.

II.

But now, alone, by ſtorms oppreſt,
　　Which harſhly in my ears reſound;
No cheerful voice with witty jeſt,
　　No jocund pipe to ſtill the ſound;
Untrain'd beſide in verſe-like art,
How ſhall my pen expreſs my heart?

III.

In vain I call th' harmonious Nine,
　　In vain implore Apollo's aid;
Obdurate, they refuſe a line,
　　While ſpleen and care my reſt invade,

Say,

Say, shall we Morpheus next implore,
And try if dreams befriend us more?

IV.

Wisely at least he'll stop my pen,
   And with his poppies crown my brow:
Better by far in lonesome den
   To sleep unheard of — than to glow
With treach'rous wildfire of the brain,
Th' intoxicated poet's bane.

Written at a Ferme Ornee near Birmingham; August 7th, 1749.

By the Same.

'TIS Nature here bids pleasing scenes arise,
   And wisely gives them Cynthio, to revise:
To veil each blemish; brighten every grace;
Yet still preserve the lovely Parent's face.

   How well the bard obeys, each valley tells;
These lucid streams, gay meads, and lonely cells;
Where modest Art in silence lurks conceal'd:
While Nature shines, so gracefully reveal'd,
That she triumphant claims the total plan;
And, with fresh pride, adopts the work of man.

The

The GOLDFINCHES. An Elegy.

By Mr. JAGO.

———Ingenuas didiciſſe fideliter artes
Emollit mores, nec finit eſſe feros.

TO you, whoſe groves protect the feather'd quires,
 Who lend their artleſs notes a willing ear,
To you, whom pity moves, and taſte inſpires,
 The Doric ſtrain belongs; O Shenſtone, hear.

'Twas gentle ſpring, when all the tuneful race,
 By nature taught, in nuptial leagues combine:
A goldfinch joy'd to meet the warm embrace,
 And hearts and fortunes with her mate to join.

Through Nature's ſpacious walks at large they rang'd,
 No ſettled haunts, no fix'd abode their aim;
As chance or fancy led, their path they chang'd,
 Themſelves, in every vary'd ſcene, the ſame.

'Till on a day to weighty cares reſign'd,
 With mutual choice, alternate, they agreed,
On rambling thoughts no more to turn their mind,
 But ſettle ſoberly, and raiſe a breed.

All

All in a garden, on a currant-bush,
  With wond'rous art they built their waving feat:
In the next orchat liv'd a friendly thrush,
  Nor diftant far, a woodlark's foft retreat.

Here bleft with eafe, and in each other bleft,
  With early fongs they wak'd the fprightly groves,
'Till time matur'd their blifs, and crown'd their neft
  With infant pledges of their faithful loves.

And now what tranfport glow'd in either's eye !
  What equal fondnefs dealt th' allotted food !
What joy each other's likenefs to defcry,
  And future fonnets in the chirping brood !

But ah ! what earthly happinefs can laft ?
  How does the faireft purpofe often fail ?
A truant-fchool-boy's wantonnefs could blaft
  Their rifing hopes, and leave them both to wail.

The moft ungentle of his tribe was he ;
  No gen'rous precept ever touch'd his heart :
With concords falfe, and hideous profody
  He fcrawl'd his tafk, and blunder'd o'er his part.

On

On barb'rous plunder bent, with favage eye
   He mark'd where wrapt in down the younglins lay,
Then rufhing feiz'd the wretched family,
   And bore them in his impious hands away.

But how fhall I relate in numbers rude
   The pangs for poor * Chryfomitris decreed!
When from a neighb'ring fpray aghaft fhe view'd
   The favage ruffian's inaufpicious deed!

So wrapt in grief fome heart-ftruck matron ftands,
   While horrid flames furround her children's room!
On heav'n fhe calls, and wrings her trembling hands,
   Conftrain'd to fee, but not prevent their doom.

" O grief of griefs ! with fhrieking voice fhe cry'd,
   " What fight is this that I have liv'd to fee ?
" O ! that I had a maiden-goldfinch died,
   " From love's falfe joys, and bitter forrows free !

" Was it for this, alas ! with weary bill,
   " Was it for this, I pois'd th' unwieldy ftraw ?
" For this I pick'd the mofs from yonder hill ?
   " Nor fhun'd the pond'rous chat along to draw ?

* Chryfomitris, it feems, is the name for a goldfinch.

                                        " Was

" Was it for this, I cull'd the wool with care ;
 " And ftrove with all my fkill our work to crown ?
" For this, with pain I bent the ftubborn hair ;
 " And lin'd our cradle with the thiftle's down ?

" Was it for this my freedom I refign'd ;
 " And ceas'd to rove from beauteous plain to plain ?
" For this I fate at home whole days confin'd,
 " And bore the fcorching heat, and pealing rain ?

" Was it for this, my watchful eyes grow dim ?
 " The crimfon rofes on my cheek turn pale ?
" Pale is my golden plumage, once fo trim ;
 " And all my wonted fpirits 'gin to fail.

" O plund'rer vile ! O more than weezel fell !
 " More treach'rous than the cat with prudifh face !
" More fierce than kites with whom the furies dwell !
 " More pilf'ring than the cuckow's prowling race !

" For thee may plumb or goofb'ry never grow,
 " No juicy currant cool thy clammy throat :
" But bloody birch-twigs work thee fhameful woe,
 " Nor ever goldfinch cheer thee with her note."

Thus

Thus fang the mournful bird her piteous tale,
  The piteous tale her mournful mate return'd :
Then fide by fide they fought the diftant vale,
  And there in filent fadnefs inly mourn'd.

The B L A C K B I R D S. An Elegy.

By the Same.

THE fun had chas'd the mountain fnow,
    And kindly loos'd the frozen foil,
The melting ftreams began to flow,
  And ploughmen urg'd their annual toil.

'Twas then, amid the vocal throng
  Whom nature wakes to mirth and love,
A blackbird rais'd his am'rous fong,
  And thus it echo'd through the grove.

O faireft of the feather'd train !
  For whom I fing, for whom I burn,
Attend with pity to my ftrain,
  And grant my love a kind return.

Foñ

For fee the wintry ftorms are flown,
  And gentle Zephyrs fan the air;
Let us the genial influence own,
  Let us the vernal paftime fhare.

The raven plumes his jetty wing
  To pleafe his croaking paramour;
The larks refponfive ditties fing,
  And tell their paffion as they foar.

But truft me, love, the raven's wing
  Is not to be compar'd with mine;
Nor can the lark fo fweetly fing
  As I, who ftrength with fweetnefs join.

O! let me all thy fteps attend!
  I'll point new treafures to thy fight;
Whether the grove thy wifh befriend,
  Or hedge-rows green, or meadows bright.

I'll fhew my love the cleareft rill
  Whofe ftreams among the pebbles ftray,
Thefe will we fip, and fip our fill,
  Or on the flow'ry margin play.

I'll

I'll lead her to the thickeft brake,
 Impervious to the fchool-boy's eye;
For her the plaifter'd neft I'll make,
 And on her downy pinions lie.

When prompted by a mother's care,
 Her warmth fhall form th' imprifon'd young;
The pleafing tafk I'll gladly fhare,
 Or cheer her labours with my fong.

To bring her food I'll range the fields,
 And cull the beft of every kind;
Whatever nature's bounty yields,
 And love's affiduous care can find.

And when my lovely mate would ftray
 To tafte the fummer fweets at large,
I'll wait at home the live-long day,
 And tend with care our little charge.

Then prove with me the fweets of love,
 With me divide the cares of life;
No bufh fhall boaft in all the grove
 So fond a mate, fo bleft a wife.

He ceas'd his fong.   The melting dame
   With foft indulgence heard the ftrain;
She felt, fhe own'd a mutual flame,
   And hafted to relieve his pain.

He led her to the nuptial bower,
   And neftled clofely to her fide;
The fondeft bridegroom of that hour,
   And fhe, the moft delighted bride.

Next morn he wak'd her with a fong,
   " Behold, he faid, the new-born day!
" The lark his matin peal has rung,
   " Arife, my love, and come away."

Together through the fields they ftray'd,
   And to the murm'ring riv'let's fide;
Renew'd their vows, and hopp'd and play'd,
   With honeft joy and decent pride.

When oh! with grief the Mufe relates
   The mournful fequel of my tale;
Sent by an order from the fates,
   A gunner met them in the vale.

                                        Alarm'd

Alarm'd the lover cry'd, My dear,
 Hafte. hafte away, from danger fly;
Here, gunner, point thy thunder here;
 O fpare my love, and let me die.

At him the gunner took his aim;
 His aim, alas! was all too true:
O! had he chofe fome other game!
 Or fhot — as he was wont to do!

Divided pair! forgive the wrong,
 While I with tears your fate rehearfe;
I'll join the widow's plaintive fong,
 And fave the lover in my verfe.

****

The RAKE.

By a Lady in NEW ENGLAND.

———— *Video meliora proboque,*
Deteriora fequor.   H

A N open heart, a generous mind,
 But paffion's flave, and wild as wind:
In theory, a judge of right;
Though banifh'd from its practice quite:

So loofe, fo proftitute of foul,
His nobler wit becomes the tool
Of every importuning fool :
A thoufand virtues mifapply'd ;
While reafon floats on paffion's tide :
The ruin of the chafte and fair ;
The parent's curfe, the virgin's fnare :
Whofe falfe example leads aftray
The young, the thoughtlefs, and the gay :
Yet, left alone to cooler thought,
He knows, he fees, he feels his fault ;
He knows his fault, he feels, he views,
Detefting what he moft purfues :
His judgment tells him, all his gains
For fleeting joys, are lafting pains :
Reafon with appetite contending,
Repenting ftill, and ftill offending :
Abufer of the gifts of nature,
A wretched, felf-condemning creature,
He paffes o'er life's ill-trod ftage ;
And dies, in youth, the prey of age !
The fcorn, the pity of the wife,
Who love, lament him — and defpife !

FLOWERS.

F L O W E R S.

By ANTHONY WHISTLER, Esq;

—— *Ego apis Matinæ*
More modoque,
Grata carpentis thyma.   Hor.

I.

LET fages, with fuperfluous pains,
  The learned page devour;
While Florio better knowledge drains
  From each inftructive flow'r.

II.

His fav'rite Rofe his fear alarms,
  All opening to the fun;
Like vain coquettes, who fpread their charms,
  And fhine, to be undone.

III.

The Tulip, gaudy in its drefs,
  And made for nought but fhow,
In every fenfe, may well exprefs
  The glittering, empty beau!

IV. The

IV.

The Snow-drop firſt but peeps to light,
 And fearful ſhews its head ;
Thus modeſt merit ſhines more bright,
 By ſelf-diſtruſt miſled.

V.

Th' Auric'la, which through labour roſe,
 Yet ſhines compleat by art,
The force of education ſhows ;
 How much it can impart.

VI.

He marks the Senſitive's nice fit ;
 Nor fears he to proclaim,
If each man's darling vice were hit,
 That he would *act the ſame*.

VII.

Beneath each common hedge, he views
 The Violet, with care ;
Hinting we ſhould not worth refuſe,
 Although we find it *there*.

VIII.

The Tuberoſe that lofty ſprings,
 Nor can ſupport its height,
Well repreſents imperious kings,
 Grown impotent by might.

IX. Fragrant,

IX.

Fragrant, though pale, the Lily blows;
To teach the female breaft,
How virtue can its fweets difclofe
In all complexions dreft.

X.

To every bloom that crowns the year,
Nature fome charm decrees;
Learn hence, ye nymphs, her face to wear,
Ye cannot fail to pleafe.

※※※※※※※※※※※※※※※※※※※※※※※

S O N G. By the Same.

WHILE, Strephon, thus you teize one,
To fay, what won my heart;
It cannot fure be treafon,
If I the truth impart.

'Twas not your fmile, though charming;
'Twas not your eyes, though bright;
'Twas not your bloom, though warming;
Nor beauty's dazzling light.

Z 3

'Twas

'Twas not your drefs, though fhining;
  Nor fhape, that made me figh :
'Twas not your tongue, combining,
  For that I knew — might lye.

No — 'twas your generous nature;
  Bold, foft; fincere, and gay :
It fhone in every feature,
  And ftole my heart away.

<hr />

The CABINET.

Or, Verfes on Roman Medals. To Mr. W.

By Mr. GRAVES.

I.

LO! the rich Cafket's mimic dome!
  Where cells in graceful rows
The triumphs of imperial Rome
  In miniature difclofe.

II. Lefs

II.

Lefs facred far thofe tinfel fhrines,
  In which the fainted bones,
And relics, modern Rome confines,
  Of legendary drones.

III.

In figur'd brafs we here behold
  From time's wide wafte retriev'd,
What patriots firm or heroes bold
  In peace or war atchiev'd.

IV.

Or filver orbs, in feries fair,
  With titles deck'd around,
Prefent each Cæfar's face and air
  With rays or laurels crown'd.

V.

Ages to come fhall hence be taught,
  In lafting lines exprefs'd,
How mighty Julius fpoke or fought,
  Or Cleopatra drefs'd.

VI.

Auguftus here with placid mien,
  Bids raging difcord ceafe;
The gates of War clofe-barr'd are feen,
  And all the world is peace.

VII. A

VII.

A race of tyrants then fucceeds,
  Who frown with brow fevere;
Yet though we fhudder at their deeds,
  Ev'n Nero charms us here.

VIII.

Thus did the blooming Titus look,
  Delight of human kind:
Great Hadrian thus, whofe death befpoke
  His firm yet gentle mind.

IX.

Aurelius too! thy ftoic face
  Indignant we compare
With young Fauftina's wanton grace,
  And meretricious air.

X.

Each paffion here and virtue fhines
  In livelieft emblems drefs'd:
Lefs ftrong in Tully's ethic lines,
  Or Plato's flights exprefs'd.

XI.

With heighten'd grace in verdant ruft,
  Each work of ancient art,
The temple, column, arch or buft
  Their wonted charms impart.

XII. All-

XII.

All-glorious Rome, through martial toil,
    Beneath each zone obey'd,
Shew'd every province, trophy, fpoil,
    On current gold difplay'd.

XIII.

Hence prodigals, that vainly fpend,
    Promote the great defign;
And mifers aid ambition's end,
    Who treafure up the coin.

XIV.

The peafant finds in every clime
    The fcientific ore;
Whilft on the rich remains of time,
    The learn'd with rapture pore.

XV.

Each fading ftroke they now retrace,
    Each legend dark unfold:
Then in hiftoric order place —
    And copper vies with gold.

XVI.

Happy the fage! like you, my friend,
    The evening of whofe days
Heav'n grants in that fair vale to fpend
    Where Thames delighted ftrays.

XVII. To

XVII.

To medals there and books of taste
Thofe moments you confign,
Which barren minds ignobly wafte
On dogs, or cards, or wine.

XVIII.

Whilft I 'mid rocks and favage woods
Enjoy thefe golden dreams;
* Where Avon winds to mix her floods
With Bladud's healing ftreams.

PANACEA:

Or, The Grand RESTORATIVE.

By the Same.

WELCOME to Baiæ's ftreams, ye fons of fpleen,
Who rove from fpa to fpa — to fhift the fcene.
While round the ftreaming fount you idly throng,
Come, learn a wholfome fecret from my fong.
Ye fair, whofe rofes feel th' approaching froft,
And drops fupply the place of fpirits loft:

* Claverton near Bath, 1750.

Ye

Ye 'fquires, who rack'd with gouts, at heav'n repine,
Condemn'd to water for excefs in wine :
Ye portly cits, fo corpulent and full,
Who eat and drink 'till appetite grows dull :
For whets and bitters then unftring the purfe,
Whilft nature more opprefs grows worfe and worfe :
Dupes to the craft of pill-prefcribing leaches :
You nod or laugh at what the parfon preaches : .
Hear then a rhyming quack,—who fpurns your wealth,
And gratis gives a fure receipt for health.
No more thus vainly roam o'er fea and land,
When lo ! a fovereign remedy at hand :
'Tis Temperance—ftale cant !—'Tis Fafting then ;
Heav'n's antidote againft the fins of men.
Foul luxury's the caufe of all your pain :
To fcour th' obftructed glands, abftain ! abftain !
Faft and take reft, ye candidates for fleep,
Who from high food tormenting vigils keep :
Faft and be fat — thou ftarveling in a gown :
Ye bloated, faft—'twill furely bring you down.
Ye nymphs that pine o'er chocolate and rolls,
Hence take frefh bloom, frefh vigour to your fouls.
Faft and fear not — you'll need no drop nor pill :
Hunger *may* ftarve, excefs is *fure* to kill.

The

The HEROINES, or Modern Memoirs.

By the Same.

IN ancient times, some hundred winters past,
   When British dames, for conscience sake, were chaste,
If some frail nymph, by youthful passion sway'd,
From Virtue's paths unhappily had stray'd:
When banish'd reason re-assum'd her place,
The conscious wretch bewail'd her foul disgrace;
Fled from the world, and pass'd her joyless years
In decent solitude and pious tears;
Veil'd in some convent made her peace with heaven,
And almost hop'd — by Prudes to be forgiven.

  Not so of modern wh—res th' illustrious train,
Renown'd Constantia, P—ton and V—ne;
Grown old in sin, and dead to amorous joy,
No acts of penance *their* great souls employ.
Without a blush behold each nymph advance,
The luscious Heroine of her own romance.
Each harlot triumphs in her loss of fame,
And boldly prints and publishes her shame.

1751.

The

The PARTING.

By the Same.

Written some Years after Marriage.

I.

THE rising sun through all the grove
    Diffus'd a gladsome ray:
My Lucy smil'd, and talk'd of love,
    And every thing look'd gay.

II.

But oh! the fatal hour was come
    That forc'd me from my dear:
My Lucy then through grief was dumb,
    Or spoke but by a tear.

III.

Now far from her and bliss I roam,
    All nature wears a change:
The azure sky seems wrapt in gloom,
    And every place looks strange.

IV. Those

IV.

Thofe flow'ry fields, this verdant fcene,
   Yon larks that towering fing,
With fad contraft increafe my fpleen
   And make me loath the fpring.

V.

My books that wont to footh my mind
   No longer now can pleafe:
There only thofe amufement find
   That have a mind at eafe.

VI.

Nay life itfelf is tafteleſs grown
   From Lucy whilft I ftray:
Sick of the world I mufe alone
   And figh the live-long day.   1748.

ODE to MEMORY. 1748.

By WILLIAM SHENSTONE, Efq;

I.

O Memory! celeftial maid!
   Who glean'ft the flow'rets cropt by time;
And, fuffering not a leaf to fade,
   Preferv'ft the bloffoms of our prime;

           Bring,

Bring, bring thofe moments to my mind
When life was new, and Lefbia kind.

II.

And bring that garland to my fight,
   With which my favour'd crook fhe bound;
And bring that wreath of rofes bright
   Which then my feftive temples crown'd.
And to my raptur'd ear convey
The gentle things fhe deign'd to fay.

III.

And fketch with care the Mufe's bow'r,
   Where Ifis rolls her filver tide;
Nor yet omit one reed or flow'r,
   That fhines on Cherwell's verdant fide;
If fo thou may'ft thofe hours prolong,
When polifh'd Lycon join'd my fong.

IV.

The fong it 'vails not to recite—
   But fure, to footh our youthful dreams,
Thofe banks and ftreams appear'd more bright
   Than other banks, than other ftreams:
Or by thy foftening pencil fhewn,
Affume they beauties not their own?

V. And

V,

And paint that fweetly vacant fcene,
 When, all beneath the poplar bough,
My fpirits light, my foul ferene,
 I breath'd in verfe one cordial vow;
That nothing fhould my foul infpire,
But friendfhip warm, and love entire.

VI.

Dull to the fenfe of new delight,
 On thee the drooping Mufe attends;
As fome fond lover, robb'd of fight,
 On thy expreffive pow'r depends;
Nor would exchange thy glowing lines,
To live the lord of all that fhines.

VII.

But let me chafe thofe vows away,
 Which at ambition's fhrine I made;
Nor ever let thy fkill difplay
 Thofe anxious moments, ill repaid:
Oh! from my breaft that feafon rafe,
And bring my childhood in its place.

VIII.

Bring me the bells, the rattle bring,
 And bring the hobby I beftrode;

When

Whea pleas'd, in many a fportive ring,
  Around the room I jovial rode :
Ev'n let me bid my lyre adieu,
And brirg the whiftle that I blew.

IX.

Then will I mufe, and penfive fay,
  Why did not thefe enjoyments laft ?
How fweetly wafted I the day,
  While innocence allow'd to wafte ?
Ambition's toils alike are vain,
But ah ! for pleafure yield us pain.

●●●●●●●●●●●●●●●●●●●●●●●●●●●●

The Princefs E L I Z A B E T H :

A Ballad, alluding to a Story recorded of her, when
fhe was a Prifoner at Woodftock, 1554.

By the Same.

WILL you hear how once repining
  Great Eliza captive lay,
Each ambitious thought refigning,
  Foe to riches, pomp, and fway ?

While

While the nymphs and swains delighted
  Tript around in all their pride ;
Envying joys by others slighted,
  Thus the royal maiden cry'd.

Bred on plains, or born in vallies,
  Who would bid those scenes adieu ?
Stranger to the arts of malice,
  Who would ever courts pursue ?

Malice never taught to treasure,
  Censure never taught to bear ;
Love is all the shepherd's pleasure;
  Love is all the damsel's care.

How can they of humble station
  Vainly blame the pow'rs above ?
Or accuse the dispensation
  Which allows them all to love ?

Love like air is widely given ;
  Pow'r nor chance can these restrain;
Truest, noblest gifts of heaven !
  Only purest on the plain !

Peers

Peers can no fuch charms difcover,
    All in ftars and garters dreft,
As, on Sundays, does the lover
    With his nofegay on his breaft.

Pinks and rofes in profufion,
    Said to fade when Chloe's near;
Fops may ufe the fame allufion,
    But the fhepherd is fincere.

Hark to yonder milk-maid finging
    Cheerly o'er the brimming pail;
Cowflips all around her fpringing,
    Sweetly paint the golden vale.

Never yet did courtly maiden
    Move fo fprightly, look fo fair;
Never breaft with jewels laden
    Pour a fong fo void of care,

Would indulgent heav'n had granted
    Me fome rural damfel's part!
All the empire I had wanted
    Then had been my fhepherd's heart,

Then,

Then, with him, o'er hills and mountains,
   Free from fetters, might I rove:
Fearlefs tafte the cryftal fountains;
   Peaceful fleep beneath the grove.

Ruftics had been more forgiving;
   Partial to my virgin bloom:
None had envy'd me when living;
   None had triumph'd o'er my tomb.

O D E to a Young Lady,

Somewhat too follicitous about her manner of Expreffion.

By the Same.

SURVEY, my fair! that lucid ftream
   Adown the fmiling valley ftray;
Would art attempt, or fancy dream,
   To regulate its winding way?

So pleas'd I view thy fhining hair
   In loofe difhevell'd ringlets flow:
Not all thy art, nor all thy care
   Can there one fingle grace beftow.

Survey

Survey again that verdant hill,
   With native plants enamell'd o'er;
Say, can the painter's utmoſt ſkill
   Inſtruct one flow'r to pleaſe us more?

As vain it were, with artful dye,
   To change the bloom thy cheeks diſcloſe,
And oh may Laura, ere ſhe try,
   With freſh vermilion paint the roſe.

Hark, how the wood-lark's tuneful throat
   Can every ſtudy'd grace excel;
Let art conſtrain the rambling note,
   And will ſhe, Laura, pleaſe ſo well?

Oh ever keep thy native eaſe,
   By no pedantic laws confin'd!
For Laura's voice is form'd to pleaſe,
   So Laura's words be not unkind.

      VERSES

(✷✷✷✷✷✷✷✷✷✷✷✷✷✷✷✷✷✷✷✷✷✷✷✷✷✷)

V E R S E S

Written towards the clofe of the Year 1748,
to WILLIAM LYTTELTON, Efq;

By the Same.

HOW blithely pafs'd the fummer's day !
　　How bright was every flow'r !
While friends arriv'd, in circles gay,
　To vifit Damon's bow'r,

But now, with filent ftep, I range
　Along fome lonely fhore ;
And Damon's bow'r, alas the change !
　Is gay with friends no more.

Away to crowds and cities borne
　In queft of joy they fteer ;
Whilft I, alas ! am left forlorn,
　To weep the parting year !

　　　　　　　　　　　　O penfive

O penfive Autumn! how I grieve
  Thy forrowing face to fee!
When languid funs are taking leave
  Of every drooping tree.

Ah let me not, with heavy eye,
  This dying fcene furvey!
Hafte, Winter, hafte; ufurp the fky;
  Compleat my bow'r's decay.

Ill can I bear the motley caft
  Yon' fickening leaves retain;
That fpeak at once of pleafure paft,
  And bode approaching pain.

At home unbleft, I gaze around,
  My diftant fcenes require;
Where all in murky vapours drown'd
  Are hamlet, hill, and fpire.

Though Thomfon, fweet defcriptive bard!
  Infpiring Autumn fung:
Yet how fhould we the months regard,
  That ftopp'd his flowing tongue?

          Ah

Ah luckless months, of all the reft,
  To whofe hard fhare it fell !
For fure he was the gentleft breaft
  That ever fung fo well,

And fee, the fwallows now difown
  The roofs they lov'd before ;
Each, like his tuneful genius, flown
  To glad fome happier fhore.

The wood-nymph eyes, with pale affright,
  The fportfman's frantic deed ;
While hounds and horns and yells unite
  To drown the Mufe's reed,

Ye fields with blighted herbage brown !
  Ye fkies no longer blue !
Too much we feel from fortune's frown,
  To bear thefe frowns from you.

Where is the mead's unfullied green ?
  The zephyr's balmy gale ?
And where fweet friendfhip's cordial mien,
  That brighten'd every vale ?

What

What though the vine difclofe her dyes,
    And boaft her purple ftore;
Not all the vineyard's rich fupplies
    Can foothe our forrows more.

He! he is gone, whofe moral ftrain
    Could wit and mirth refine;
He! he is gone, whofe focial vein
    Surpafs'd the pow'r of wine.

Faft by the ftreams he deign'd to praife,
    In yon' fequefter'd grove,
To him a votive urn I raife;
    To him, and friendly love.

Yes there, my friend! forlorn and fad,
    I grave your Thomfon's name;
And there, his lyre; which fate forbad
    To found your growing fame.

There fhall my plaintive fong recount
    Dark themes of hopelefs woe;
And, fafter than the dropping fount,
    I'll teach mine eyes to flow.

There

There leaves, in fpite of Autumn, green,
  Shall fhade the hallow'd ground;
And Spring will then again be feen,
  To call forth flowers around.

But no kind funs will bid me fhare,
  Once more, His focial hour;
Ah Spring! thou never canft repair
  This lofs, to Damon's bow'r.

S O N G S.

By the Same.

I.

IN a vale fring'd with woodland, where grottos abound,
  And rivulets murmur, and echoes refound,
I vow'd to the Mufes my time and my care;
Since neither could win me the fmiles of my fair.

As freedom infpir'd me, I rang'd and I fung;
And Daphne's dear name never fell from my tongue:
But if once a fmooth accent delighted my ear,
I fhould wifh, unawares, that my Daphne might hear.

With

With faireſt ideas my boſom I ſtor'd;
Alluſions to none but the nymph I ador'd;
And the more I with ſtudy my fancy refin'd,
The deeper impreſſion ſhe made on my mind.

Ah! whilſt I the beauties of nature purſue,
I ſtill muſt my Daphne's fair image renew:
The Graces have choſen with Daphne to rove,
And the Muſes are all in alliance with Love.

II. DAPHNE's Viſit.

YE birds! for whom I rear'd the grove,
 With melting lay ſalute my love:
My Daphne with your notes detain:
Or I have rear'd my grove in vain.

Ye flow'rs before her footſteps riſe;
Diſplay at once your brighteſt dyes;
That ſhe your opening charms may ſee:
Or what were all your charms to me?

Kind Zephyr! bruſh each fragrant flow'r,
And ſhed its odours round my bow'r:
Or never more, O gentle wind,
Shall I, from thee, refreſhment find.

Ye

Ye ſtreams! if e'er your banks I lov'd,
If e'er your native ſounds improv'd,
May each ſoft murmur ſoothe my fair:
Or oh! 'twill deepen my deſpair.

And thou, my grot! whoſe lonely bounds
The melancholy pine ſurrounds,
May Daphne praiſe thy peaceful gloom,
Or thou ſhalt prove her Damon's tomb.

III.   The R o s e-B u d.

SEE, Flavia, ſee that budding roſe,
     How bright beneath the buſh it glows;
How ſafely there it lurks conceal'd;
How quickly blaſted, when reveal'd!

The ſun with warm attractive rays
Tempts it to wanton in the blaze:
A blaſt deſcends from eaſtern ſkies,
And all its bluſhing radiance dies.

Then guard, my fair! your charms divine;
And check the fond deſire to ſhine
Where fame's tranſporting rays allure,
While here more happy, more ſecure.

The

The breath of fome neglected maid
Shall make you figh you left the fhade :
A breath to beauty's bloom unkind,
As, to the rofe, an eaftern wind.

The nymph reply'd, " You firft, my fwain,
" Confine your fonnets to the plain ; ,
" One envious tongue alike difarms,
" You, of your wit, me, of my charms.

" What is, unheard, the tuneful thrill ?
" Or what, unknown, the poet's fkill ?
" What, unadmir'd, a charming mien,
" Or what the rofe's blufh, unfeen ?"

IV. Written in a Collection of Bacchanalian Songs.

ADIEU, ye jovial youths, who join
To plunge old Care in floods of wine;
And, as your dazzled eye-balls roll,
Difcern him ftruggling in the bowl.

Not yet is hope fo wholly flown,
Nor yet is thought fo tedious grown,
But limpid ftream and fhady tree
Retain, as yet, fome fweets for me.

And

And fee, through yonder filent grove,
See yonder does my Daphne rove:
With pride her foot-fteps I purfue,
And bid your frantic joys adieu.

The fole confufion I admire,
Is that my Daphne's eyes infpire:
I fcorn the madnefs you approve,
And value reafon next to love.

V. Imitated from the FRENCH.

YES, thefe are the fcenes where with Iris I ftray'd;
But fhort was her fway for fo lovely a maid;
In the bloom of her youth to a cloifter fhe run;
In the bloom of her graces, too fair for a nun!
Ill-grounded, no doubt, a devotion muft prove
So fatal to beauty, fo killing to love!

Yes, thefe are the meadows, the fhrubs and the plains;
Once the fcene of my pleafures, the fcene of my pains;
How many foft moments I fpent in this grove!
How fair was my nymph! and how fervent my love!
Be ftill though, my heart! thine emotion give o'er;
Remember, the feafon of love is no more.

1   With

With her how I ftray'd amid fountains and bow'rs,
Or loiter'd behind and collefted the flow'rs!
Then breathlefs with ardor my fair-one purfu'd,
And to think with what kindnefs my garland fhe view'd!
But be ftill, my fond heart! this emotion give o'er;
Fain wouldft thou forget thou muft love her no more.

RURAL INSCRIPTIONS.

By the Same.

I. On a ROOT-HOUSE.

HERE in cool grot, and moffy cell,
We rural fays and faeries dwell:
Though rarely feen by mortal eye,
When the pale moon, afcending high,
Darts through yon' limes her quivering beams,
We frifk it near thefe cryftal ftreams.

Her beams, reflefted from the wave,
Afford the light our revels crave;
The turf, with daifies broider'd o'er,
Exceeds, we wot, the Parian floor;
Nor yet for artful ftrains we call,
But liften to the water's fall.

Would

Would you then tafte our tranquil fcene,
Be fure your bofoms be ferene ;
Devoid of hate, devoid of ftrife,
Devoid of all that poifons life ;
And much it 'vails you, in their place,
To graft the love of human race.

And tread with awe thefe favour'd bow'rs,
Nor wound the fhrubs nor bruife the flow'rs ;
So may your paths with fweets abound !
So may your couch with reft be crown'd !
But harm betide the wayward fwain,
Who dares our hallow'd haunt profane !

OBERON.

II. In a fhady-Valley, near a running Water.

O ! Let me haunt this peaceful fhade ;
 Nor let ambition e'er invade
The tenants of this leafy bow'r,
That fhun her paths, and flight her pow'r.

Hither the plaintive halcyon flies
From focial meads and open fkies ;
Pleas'd, by this rill, her courfe to fteer,
And hide her faphire plumage here.

The

The trout, bedropt with crimfon ftains,
Forfakes the river's proud domains;
Forfakes the fun's unwelcome gleam,
To lurk within this humble ftream.

And fure I heard the Naiad fay,
" Flow, flow, my ftream! this devious way;
" Though lovely foft thy murmurs are,
" Thy waters, lovely cool and fair!

" Flow, gentle ftream! nor let the vain
" Thy fmall unfully'd ftores difdain:
" Nor let the penfive fage repine,
" Whofe latent courfe refembles thine."

III. On a fmall Building in the Gothic Tafte.

O you that bathe in courtly blysse!
   Or toyle in fortune's gibbye spheare!
Doo not too rashlye deeme amysse
   Of him, that bydes contentid here.

Nor yet disdeigne the russet stoale,
   Whyche o'er each carelesse lymbe he flyngs:
Nor yet derbye the beechen bowle,
   In whyche he quaffs the lympid sprynge.

Forgyve hym, if, at eve or dawne,
   Devoyde of worldlye carke he stray:
Or, all besyde some flowerye lawne,
   He waste his inoffensyve day.

So may He pardonne fraud and strife,
  If such in courtlye haunt be see:
For faults there beene in busye lyfe,
  From whyche these peacefull gleanes are free.

A Pastoral **BALLAD,** in Four Parts.
Written 1743.

By the Same.

Arbusta humilesque myricæ.   VIRG.

I. ABSENCE.

I.

YE shepherds so cheerful and gay,
  Whose flocks never carelessly roam;
Should Corydon's happen to stray,
  Oh! call the poor wanderers home.
Allow me to muse and to sigh,
  Nor talk of the change that ye find;
None once was so watchful as I:
  — I have left my dear Phyllis behind.

II.

Now I know what it is, to have strove
  With the torture of doubt and desire;
What it is, to admire and to love,
  And to leave her we love and admire.

Ah

Ah lead forth my flock in the morn,
  And the damps of each ev'ning repell;
Alas! I am faint and forlorn:
  — I have bade my dear Phyllis farewell.

III.

Since Phyllis vouchsaf'd me a look,
  I never once dreamt of my vine;
May I lose both my pipe and my crook,
  If I know of a kid that was mine.
I priz'd every hour that went by,
  Beyond all that had pleas'd me before;
But now they are past, and I sigh;
  And I grieve that I priz'd them no more.

IV.

But why do I languish in vain?
  Why wander thus pensively here?
Oh! why did I come from the plain,
  Where I fed on the smiles of my dear?
They tell me, my favourite maid,
  The pride of that valley, is flown;
Alas! where with her I have stray'd,
  I could wander with pleasure, alone.

V.

When forc'd the fair nymph to forego,
  What anguish I felt at my heart!

Yet.

Yet I thought — but it might not be fo —
  'Twas with pain that fhe faw me depart.
She gaz'd, as I flowly withdrew ;
  My path I could hardly difcern ;
So fweetly fhe bade me adieu,
  I thought that fhe bade me return.

VI.

The pilgrim that journeys all day
  To vifit fome far-diftant fhrine,
If he bear but a relique away,
  Is happy, nor heard to repine.
Thus widely remov'd from the fair,
  Where my vows, my devotion, I owe,
Soft hope is the relique I bear,
  And my folace wherever I go.

II. HOPE.

I.

MY banks they are furnifh'd with bees,
  Whofe murmur invites one to fleep ;
My grottos are fhaded with trees,
  And my hills are white-over with fheep.
I feldom have met with a lofs,
  Such health do my fountains beftow ;
My fountains all border'd with mofs,
  Where the hare-bells and violets grow.

II. Not

II.

Not a pine in my grove is there feen,
  But with tendrils of woodbine is bound:
Not a beech's more beautiful green,
  But a fweet-briar twines it around.
Not my fields, in the prime of the year,
  More charms than my cattle unfold:
Not a brook that is limpid and clear,
  But it glitters with fifhes of gold.

III.

One would think fhe might like to retire
  To the bow'r I have labour'd to rear;
Not a fhrub that I heard her admire,
  But I hafted and planted it there.
O how fudden the jeffamin ftrove
  With the lilac to render it gay!
Already it calls for my love,
  To prune the wild branches away.

IV.

From the plains, from the woodlands and groves,
  What ftrains of wild melody flow?
How the nightingales warble their loves
  From thickets of rofes that blow!

     And

And when her bright form fhall appear,
   Each bird fhall harmonioufly join
In a concert fo foft and fo clear,
   As — fhe may not be fond to refign.

V.

I have found out a gift for my fair;
   I have found where the wood-pigeons breed:
But let me that plunder forbear,
   She will fay 'twas a barbarous deed.
For he ne'er could be true, fhe aver'd,
   Who could rob a poor bird of its young:
And I lov'd her the more, when I heard
   Such tendernefs fall from her tongue.

VI.

I have heard her with fweetnefs unfold
   How that pity was due to — a dove:
That it ever attended the bold,
   And fhe call'd it the fifter of love.
But her words fuch a pleafure convey,
   So much I her accents adore,
Let her fpeak, and whatever fhe fay,
   Methinks I fhould love her the more.

VII. Can

VII.

Can a bofom fo gentle remain
  Unmov'd, when her Corydon fighs?
Will a nymph that is fond of the plain,
  Thefe plains, and this valley defpife?
Dear regions of filence and fhade!
  Soft fcenes of contentment and eafe!
Where I could have pleafingly ftray'd,
  If aught, in her abfence, could pleafe.

VIII.

But where does my Phyllida ftray?
  And where are her grots and her bow'rs?
Are the groves and the valleys as gay,
  And the fhepherds as gentle as ours?
The groves may perhaps be as fair,
  And the face of the valleys as fine;
The fwains may in manners compare,
  But their love is not equal to mine.

III. SOLICITUDE.

I.

WHY will you my paffion reprove?
  Why term it a folly to grieve?
Ere I fhew you the charms of my love,
  She is fairer than you can believe.

With

With her mien fhe enamours the brave;
  With her wit fhe engages the free;
With her modefty pleafes the grave;
  She is every way pleafing to me.

II.

O you that have been of her train,
  Come and join in my amorous lays;
I could lay down my life for the fwain
  That will fing but a fong in her praife.
When he fings, may the nymphs of the town
  Come trooping, and liften the while;
Nay on Him let not Phyllida frown;
  — But I cannot allow her to fmile.

III.

For when Paridel tries in the dance
  Any favour with Phyllis to find,
O how, with one trivial glance,
  Might fhe ruin the peace of my mind!
In ringlets He dreffes his haïr,
  And his crook is be-ftudded around;
And his pipe — oh may Phyllis beware
  Of a magic there is in the found.

IV. 'Tis

IV.

'Tis His with mock paſſion to glow;
  'Tis His in ſmooth tales to unfold,
" How her face is as bright as the ſnow,
  " And her boſom, be ſure, is aſ cold;
" How the nightingales labour the ſtrain,
  " With the notes of his charmer to vie:
" How they vary their accents in vain,
  " Repine at her triumphs, and die."

V.

To the grove or the garden he ſtrays,
  And pillages every ſweet;
Then, ſuiting the wreath to his lays
  He throws it at Phyllis's feet.
" O Phyllis, he whiſpers, more fair,
  " More ſweet than the jeſſamin's flow'r!
" What are pinks, in a morn, to compare?
  " What is eglantine after a ſhow'r?

VI.

" Then the lily no longer is white;
  " Then the roſe is depriv'd of its bloom;
" Then the violets die with deſpight,
  " And the wood-bines give up their perfume."

Thus

Thus glide the foft numbers along,
  And he fancies no fhepherd his peer ;
— Yet I never fhould envy the fong,
  Were not Phyllis to lend it an ear.

VII.

Let his crook be with hyacinths bound,
  So Phyllis the trophy defpife ;
Let his forehead with laurels be crown'd,
  So they fhine not in Phyllis's eyes.
The language that flows from the heart
  Is a ftranger to Paridel's tongue ;
— Yet may fhe beware of his art,
  Or fure I muft envy the fong.

IV. DISAPPOINTMENT.

I.

YE fhepherds give ear to my lay,
  And take no more heed of my fheep ;
They have nothing to do, but to ftray ;
  I have nothing to do, but to weep.
Yet do not my folly reprove ;
  She was fair — and my paffion begun ;
She fmil'd — and I could not but love ;
  She is faithlefs — and I am undone.

II. Perhaps

II.

Perhaps I was void of all thought;
  Perhaps it was plain to forefee,
That a nymph fo compleat would be fought
  By a fwain more engaging than me.
Ah! love every hope can infpire:
  It banifhes wifdom the while;
And the lip of the nymph we admire
  Seems for ever adorn'd with a fmile.

III.

She is faithlefs, and I am undone;
  Ye that witnefs the woes I endure,
Let reafon inftruct you to fhun
  What it cannot inftruct you to cure.
Beware how ye loiter in vain
  Amid nymphs of an higher degree:
It is not for me to explain
  How fair, and how fickle they be.

IV.

Alas! from the day that we met,
  What hope of an end to my woes?
When I cannot endure to forget
  The glance that undid my repofe.

I

Yet

Yet time may diminish the pain:
 The flow'r, and the shrub, and the tree,
Which I rear'd for her pleasure in vain,
 In time may have comfort for me.

V.

The sweets of a dew-sprinkled rose,
 The sound of a murmuring stream,
The peace which from solitude flows,
 Henceforth shall be Corydon's theme.
High transports are shewn to the sight,
 But we are not to find them our own;
Fate never bestow'd such delight,
 As I with my Phyllis had known.

VI.

O ye woods, spread your branches apace;
 To your deepest recesses I fly;
I would hide with the beasts of the chace;
 I would vanish from every eye.
Yet my reed shall resound through the grove
 With the same sad complaint it begun;
How she smil'd, and I could not but love;
 Was faithless, and I am undone!

INDEX

INDEX to the Fourth Volume.

The END of Vol. IV.

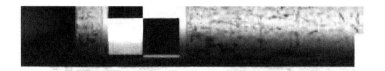